Praise for *Disciplined Entrepreneurship*

"Entrepreneurship is not only a mind-set but a skill set. The 24 Steps present a practical step-by-step process to channel the creative spirit to maximize the chances of success and ultimate impact."

—Mitch Kapor, Founder, Lotus Development Corporation

"While I am not a big fan of business plans, I am a big fan of the business planning process. This book provides an invaluable comprehensive framework for innovation-driven entrepreneurs to execute the business planning process."

—Brad Feld, Managing Director of the Foundry Group, Co-Founder of TechStars, and Creator of the Startup Revolution *book series*

"We have had Bill working with entrepreneurs in Scotland for the past three years using the 24 Steps, and we have been delighted with the results. Not only is the framework an extremely helpful road map, it has also given entrepreneurs the confidence to go on the journey and take their businesses to the next level. This is a very valuable approach that works across borders."

—Alex Paterson, Chief Executive, Highlands and Islands Enterprise Scotland

"This is the book I wish I'd had when I was starting out—concise, great examples, in plain English, combining classic entrepreneurship theory with what's happening in today's startup world. If you're a serious entrepreneur, read it carefully and keep it close at hand for the journey ahead."

—Frederic Kerrest, Co-Founder, Okta, and MIT Patrick J. McGovern, Jr. Entrepreneurship Award recipient

"According to conventional wisdom, entrepreneurship is solely an innate trait. Nothing could be further from the truth. Entrepreneurship is a learned skill which can be honed through crisp execution. This book can help every entrepreneur dramatically increase the likelihood of success by providing step-by-step guidance on how to approach starting a new business. I recommend it to all ambitious entrepreneurs."

—Doug Leone, Managing Partner, Sequoia Capital

"Invaluable. This book superbly summarizes the lessons taught to us at MIT. It is the book I wish I had when we were launching HubSpot six years ago."

—Brian Halligan, Co-Founder and CEO, Hubspot, and author of Inbound Marketing

"Bill and I have had many discussions about entrepreneurship, and I really respect his perspective on the topic. While the spirit of entrepreneurship is often about serendipity, the execution is not. This book takes you through a systematic approach to significantly increase your odds of succeeding in making a world-changing and sustainable company. I loved the content and the simple nature of the book."

—Joi Ito, Director, MIT Media Lab

"Ideas are a dime a dozen but great entrepreneurs are what create value. They have to be passionate and skilled. Maybe passion can't be taught, but execution skills can, and this book does a wonderful job providing a structure and wisdom with each step to help entrepreneurs be more successful. I highly recommend it."

—Paul Maeder, Founding Partner of Highland Capital and 2012 Chair of the National Venture Capital Association

"Bill's concept of a team creating an entrepreneur is intriguing but also validated by research and experience. This list of disciplined steps to creating a venture can not only help entrepreneurs increase their likelihood of success, but also identify the skills and people he/she will need on the team in the crucial early steps in a company's life, and to create a common language the team can share in talking about the tasks before them. I might have suggested that he call his book *The Holistic Entrepreneur.*"

—Thomas A. McDonnell, President and CEO, Ewing Marion Kauffman Foundation

"Social entrepreneurs must develop business models which balance social impact with business sustainability. Soko focuses on building a successful and scalable business model, which will lead to scaled social impact in the communities where we work. The 24 Step process outlined by Bill Aulet is a very useful framework for any type of business to get from an idea to full realization."

—Ella Peinovich and Gwen Floyd, Founders of ShopSoko.com, Africa's first mobile marketplace

"I had the great pleasure to work with Bill and see how his methodical mind breaks down complex problems to their essence and then logically solves them to build a great company. This book will be a great help to entrepreneurs worldwide, which is very important because the world needs more entrepreneurs like Bill."

—Thomas Massie, current member of Congress, and Founder, SensAble Devices and SensAble Technologies

"Entrepreneurship is becoming increasingly scientific each day as the body of knowledge and research grows. This book is a valuable addition in that it provides an end-to-end guide to the product marketing process across multiple industries. It is what you would expect from MIT."

—David Skok, Partner, Matrix Partners

"Training our young engineers to be entrepreneurs is an imperative for the future and this book will help in that regard. It provides a road map for getting the product-market fit as tight as possible. There are many considerations in this process and this book captures them well and provides practical guidance on how to resolve them."

—Tom Byers, Entrepreneurship Professorship Endowed Chair in the Stanford School of Engineering; Faculty Director, Stanford Technology Ventures Program

"This is an excellent practical guide for entrepreneurs so they can see the whole process and not miss critical steps as they bring products to market. Growing out of the actual experience of teaching MIT students, it adds to the growing body of thoughtful literature in the field that bodes well for the consistent development of young entrepreneurs."

—Joe Lassiter, Faculty Chair of the Harvard Innovation Lab, and Heinz Professor of Management Practice at the Harvard Business School

"I am just so excited to see now that entrepreneurs everywhere are going to get what I got at MIT to help hone my entrepreneurial skills. It is years of knowledge and wisdom in a box that every entrepreneur should read, even if you already have a business."

—Sal Lupoli, Founder of Sal's Pizza and Lupoli Companies

"As an intuitive entrepreneur, I prefer less structure. That being said, after having worked through the steps in this book to launch Lark, I realize that some structure is very valuable. This book provides enough guidance to help you succeed but not too much to stifle creativity. It is a must-have for entrepreneurs to read the first time but also as a reference."

—Julia Hu, Founder and CEO of Lark Technologies

"*Disciplined Entrepreneurship* is highly relevant and is on my recommended reading list for entrepreneurship students and entrepreneurs. It moves the reader forward through practical and important steps that they might otherwise miss, in their innovation-driven start-up journey."

—Professor Gregory B. Vit, Director, the Dobson Centre for Entrepreneurial Studies, McGill University

DISCIPLINED ENTREPRENEURSHIP

24 STEPS TO A SUCCESSFUL STARTUP

BILL AULET

Illustrations by
Marius Ursache

WILEY

Cover image: Marius Ursache
Cover design: C. Wallace

This book is printed on acid-free paper. ♾

Published by John Wiley & Sons, Inc., Hoboken, New Jersey.
Published simultaneously in Canada.

For general information about our other products and services, please contact our Customer Care Department within the United States at (800) 762-2974, outside the United States at (317) 572-3993 or fax (317) 572-4002.

Wiley publishes in a variety of print and electronic formats and by print-on-demand. Some material included with standard print versions of this book may not be included in e-books or in print-on-demand. If this book refers to media such as a CD or DVD that is not included in the version you purchased, you may download this material at http://booksupport.wiley.com. For more information about Wiley products, visit www.wiley.com.

ISBN 978-1-118-69228-8 (cloth); ISBN 978-1-118-72081-3 (ebk); ISBN 978-1-118-72088-2 (ebk)

Printed in the United States of America
10 9 8 7 6 5 4 3

THROUGHOUT MY ENTREPRENEURIAL CAREER, MY FAMILY HAS BEEN A ROCK OF GIBRALTAR THAT I COULD ALWAYS COUNT ON WITH UNCONDITIONAL SUPPORT AND LOVE, AND I DEDICATE THIS BOOK TO THEM. FIRST, I HAD THE BEST PARENTS A SON COULD EVER HAVE IN THE NOW-DECEASED BECKY AND HERB AULET. I WAS BLESSED WITH FOUR WONDERFUL SONS, KENNY, TOMMY, KYLE, AND CHRIS, WHO WONDERED WHY THEIR FATHER COULDN'T BE LIKE OTHERS BUT PUT UP WITH IT . . . AND HAVE EXCELLED IN SPITE OF THIS.

MOST OF ALL, I DEDICATE THIS BOOK TO MY WONDERFUL AND PATIENT WIFE OF 30 YEARS, LISA, WHO MARRIED A YOUNG CORPORATE SOLDIER SO MANY YEARS AGO AND ENDED UP WITH A CRAZY OLD ENTREPRENEUR AND STUCK WITH ME THE WHOLE TIME.
THIS BOOK IS FOR YOU.

CONTENTS

PREFACE

THIS BOOK IS DESIGNED as an integrated toolbox for first-time and repeat entrepreneurs so that they can build great enterprises based on new innovative products. Serial entrepreneurs with deep experience in a particular field or industry will also find this 24-step guide useful to more efficiently bring products to market.

As an entrepreneur, I have found many sources to be helpful, from books to mentors, and most of all, my own experiences. However, I have not found a single source that pulls everything together and does it well.

Many of the books I have found are excellent and have great material, including: Geoffrey Moore's *Crossing the Chasm*, W. Chan Kim and Renée Mauborgne's *Blue Ocean Strategy*, Brian Halligan and Dharmesh Shah's *Inbound Marketing*, Steve Blank's *Four Steps to the Epiphany*, Eric Ries's *The Lean Startup*, Ash Maurya's *Running Lean*, and Alex Osterwalder and Yves Pigneur's *Business Model Generation*. These are valuable books and I will reference many of them in this book. However, they are focused in depth on a few key points without providing the more fulsome roadmap that I have felt appropriate when teaching my students at the Massachusetts Institute of Technology (MIT) and in my other workshops. I believe that each is an important tool at the right time during product conception, development, and launch, but what was needed was a toolbox that contained these and more.

Using the analogy of a toolbox, a screwdriver is a great tool for certain situations, but it does not function as well as a hammer in other situations. Likewise, to choose one example, the ideas and techniques in *Inbound Marketing* are extremely valuable, but they are even more helpful as part of a broader context used at the right time.

The goal of this book, then, is to provide guidance in a messy and sometimes confusing process where you, the entrepreneur, are attempting to do something that has never been done before. What a terribly difficult task to take on, but what an incredibly important one. This book comes out of my workshops around the world and MIT courses where I built and refined this approach over years with hundreds of great entrepreneurs.

Certainly, there are other elements to consider when working toward a successful new venture, from culture and team to sales, financing, and leadership. But the foundation of an innovation-driven enterprise is the product that is created, and so that is the focus of this book.

This process will not necessarily be sequential in nature. I tried to make a logical linear process of 24 steps to get you started, but you should realize that when you gain knowledge in one step, you may need to reevaluate previous steps, and refine or even redo your previous work. This iterative process of "spiraling" toward the optimal answer is important because you do not have unlimited time to perfect your work on a particular step. You will need to make first-pass estimates based on research, and they will often need revision.

Each of these steps has rigorously evaluated whether a customer would benefit from your product, regardless of whether an analyst, potential investor, or technology writer standing on the sidelines can see the value. As someone once said to me, "In concept, concept and reality are the same, but in reality, concept and reality are not the same at all."

This book also provides a common language to discuss key aspects of venture creation so that you can more effectively discuss your new venture with advisors, mentors, and fellow entrepreneurs. I have carefully defined each step to refer to a discrete part of the process. I recall my father getting very frustrated when he would ask for a pair of pliers and I would give him a wrench. Now I feel the same way he did when I ask my students what their "business model" is and they talk about their Total Addressable Market or Pricing.

The result of this integrated toolbox with a common language is what we at MIT like to call "disciplined entrepreneurship." Some people tell me that entrepreneurship should not be disciplined, but chaotic and unpredictable—and it is. But that is precisely why a framework to attack problems in a systematic manner is extremely valuable. You already have enough risk with factors that are beyond your control, so the framework provided by disciplined entrepreneurship helps you succeed by reducing your risk in factors that you can have control over. The process can help you succeed, or it can help you fail faster if failure was inevitable for the path you were on. Either way, this process will help you.

This is the book I wish I had 20 years ago when I first became an entrepreneur.

Note on examples in this book: Throughout the book, I include a number of examples from MIT student teams who took the 15.390 New Enterprises course while in their degree programs. These examples are not always fully fleshed out because of the students' time limitations. I provide them in this book as examples that illustrate the basic concepts of the steps. I have altered some of them to better illustrate best practices and pitfalls for various steps, but kept the essence of the situations. The examples are all consistent with my experiences in founding companies. The projects described in the examples might not have turned into full-fledged companies, depending on the decisions the student teams made after completing their coursework, but their examples are educational nonetheless.

ACKNOWLEDGMENTS

A HUGE THANK YOU to my editor-in-chief Chris Snyder and editorial advisor Nancy Nichols, without whom this book would still be in my head and maybe on my computer. A very special thanks to my Romanian entrepreneur and friend Marius Ursache who did the illustrations for this book in such a delightful way that I was always like a kid on Christmas morning when I saw his e-mails come in with new drawings because I was so excited to see them and he never let me down. And thanks to the team at John Wiley & Sons, led by Shannon Vargo, that brought this book to production in record time and with utmost professionalism.

Lauren Abda, Yevgeniy Alexeyev, Greg Backstrom, Christina Birch, Michael Bishop, Adam Blake, Young Joon Cha, Vishal Chaturvedi, Ryan Choi, Kevin Clough, Yazan Damiri, Charles Deguire, Deepak Dugar, Max Faingezicht, Daniel Fisberg, Patrick Flynn, Tim Fu, Pierre Fuller, Megan Glendon, David Gordon, Melinda Hale, Katy Hartman, Kendall Herbst, Nick Holda, Julia Hu, Max Hurd, Ricardo Jasinski, Max Kanter, Freddy Kerrest, Mustafa Khalifeh, Zach LaBry, Jake Levine, Michael Lo, Dulcie Madden, Vasco Mendes de Campos, Aditya Nag, Madeline Ng, Inigo De Pascual Basterra, Ella Peinovich, Giorgi Razmadze, Adam Rein, Izak van Rensburg, Miriam Reyes, Sophia Scipio, Colin Sidoti, Sam Telleen, Jocelyn Trigg, Pedro Valencia, Eduard Viladesau, and Leo Weitzenhoff all need to be acknowledged for their contributions to and/or reviews of sections of this book. Thank you also to 3D Systems and Dollar Shave Club for their permission to include certain images.

This book came about because I have been able to work at MIT for the past six years and interact with the best entrepreneurship faculty in the world. I have been honored to work with them. Of the many who have made enormous intellectual contributions, special acknowledgement must go to Fiona Murray (who co-authored the paper on innovation-driven entrepreneurship that I reference and paraphrase in the introduction and has provided hours of feedback on this book), Ed Roberts, Scott Stern, Charlie Cooney, Matt Marx, Catherine Tucker, Eric von Hippel, Jim Dougherty, Katie

Rae, Reed Sturtevant, Elaine Chen, Peter Levine, and Brian Halligan, and of course my colleague in teaching this material for so many years, the legendary Howard Anderson. Also thanks to David Skok, Thomas Massie, Tom Ellery, Andrew Hally, Bernard Bailey, Marc Dulude, Jim Baum, Bill Warner, Dan Schwinn, Bob Coleman, Ken Morse, Jon Hirshtick, Chuck Kane, Brad Feld, Marty Trust, Sal Lupoli, Joi Ito, Sanjay Sarma, and the many mentors and collaborators I have been so fortunate to have had over the years. They all contributed heavily to the intellectual content of the book, but I take responsibility for the interpretations on how to apply and integrate it for practical implementation, which is the goal herein. Any errors made in this document are mine and no one else's.

The Kauffman Foundation for Entrepreneurship, specifically Wendy Torrance, Lesa Mitchell, and Dane Stangler, have been very helpful in this process and have pushed me to do this book for some time. I finally heard you and got it done. Thank you for your encouragement.

A key enabler of this book as well has been the fabulous team of pirates we have at the Martin Trust Center for MIT Entrepreneurship including Colin Kennedy, Christina Chase, Ben Israelite, Adam Cragg, Vanessa Marcoux, Allison Munichiello, Pat Fuligni, Justin Adelson, and Liz DeWolf. They provided encouragement, perspective, and a sanity check every day I was in the center.

Lastly I want to acknowledge the thousands of students and entrepreneurs who I have had the privilege to work with; you all give us such energy and hope every day. We all want to help you so much, as you are our hope for the future.

INTRODUCTION

NEWS FLASH—ENTREPRENEURSHIP CAN BE TAUGHT!

One of the first questions I often ask when I begin a workshop or a class is, "Do you think entrepreneurship can be taught?" Invariably a silence comes over the group. They wiggle uncomfortably in their seats. Some politely answer in the affirmative, telling me that is why they came to class in the first place. After a polite back-and-forth someone will invariably say what is on the mind of many in the room: "No, either you are an entrepreneur or you are not." That person, once empowered, begins to passionately argue the case.

I have to say that I tend to like this person, in large part because that person would have been me 15 years ago. But now I know that entrepreneurship can be taught. I experience it almost every week in the courses I teach at the Massachusetts Institute of Technology (MIT) and around the world.

When we look at Richard Branson, Steve Jobs, Bill Gates, Larry Ellison, and all the other highly visible entrepreneurs, they seem to be different from us. They seem extraordinary. But each of their successes is a result of great products that made them successful, not some special gene.

To be a successful entrepreneur, you must have great and innovative products. Products can be physical goods, but also services or the delivery of information. All the other factors that influence success are nothing without a product. And the process of making a great product can be taught. This book will teach you how to systematically improve your odds of making a great product.

In this book I present a disciplined step-by-step approach to creating a new venture. This framework is useful both for a classroom setting and for those who want to create a new company that serves a new market. Before we begin, though, we must tackle three common myths about the entrepreneur that often hamper those wishing to start new companies or teach students how to do so.

Three Common Myths That Must Go

There are many misconceptions about what entrepreneurship is and what is required to be an entrepreneur. The first myth is that individuals start companies. While the entrepreneur as a lone hero is a common narrative, a close reading of the research tells a different story. Teams start companies. Importantly, a bigger team actually adds to the odds of success. *More founders = better odds of success.*[1]

[1] Edward B. Roberts, *Entrepreneurs in High Technology: Lessons from MIT and Beyond* (New York: Oxford University Press, 1991), 258.

The second myth is that all entrepreneurs are charismatic and that their charisma is a key factor in success. In fact, while charisma may be effective for a short period, it is difficult to sustain. Instead, research shows that more important than being charismatic, entrepreneurs need to be effective communicators, recruiters, and salespeople.

The third myth is that there is an entrepreneurship gene, that certain people are genetically predisposed for success in starting companies. As the cartoon at the beginning of this chapter suggests, such a physical gene has not and will not be found. Some believe personality traits like flamboyance or boldness are correlated with successful entrepreneurship, but that line of thought is misguided. Instead, there are real skills that increase the odds of success, such as people management, sales skills, and the topic of this book, product conception and delivery. These skills can be taught. They are not genetically gifted to a few lucky souls. People can adapt and learn new behaviors, and entrepreneurship therefore can be broken down into discrete behaviors and processes that can be taught.

For evidence, we need look no further than the one magical square mile that is MIT. Students who attend MIT start companies at an absolutely prolific rate. In fact, as of 2006, over 25,000 existed, and 900 new ones are started each year. These companies employ over 3 million people with aggregate annual revenues of approximately $2 trillion. To put that in perspective, the total annual revenue from MIT alumni–founded companies taken together would make them the eleventh-largest economy in the world.[2]

What Explains MIT's Success in Entrepreneurship?

Why is MIT so successful at turning out entrepreneurs? The first response people often have is that the students at MIT are extremely intelligent. MIT's students are no smarter than those at other top-flight institutions of higher learning throughout the world (Caltech, Harvard, and the like), but none of them, other than Stanford, come close to producing entrepreneurial alumni like MIT. So MIT's success must be attributable to something else.

The second response is that this success comes about because MIT students have access to leading-edge technologies in the laboratories, and thus it is easy for them to start companies. Again, this is a measurable hypothesis. Because of the outstanding Technology Licensing Office (TLO) at

[2] Edward B. Roberts and Charles E. Eesley, "Entrepreneurial Impact: The Role of MIT—An Updated Report," *Foundations and Trends® in Entrepreneurship* 7, nos. 1–2 (2011): 1–149. http://dx.doi.org/10.1561/0300000030.

MIT, there are numbers on how many companies are started each year with technology out of the labs because they have to be licensed through this office. This number is 20 to 30 companies per year, which is very impressive when compared to the stats at other universities. Yet this number seems small when we consider that MIT alumni as a whole start 900 companies per year.[3] While the companies started with MIT-licensed technology have great strategic importance and can be very impactful (e.g., Akamai[4]), they are only a small part of why MIT is so successful at entrepreneurship. Well over 90 percent of the companies started by MIT alumni are started without MIT laboratory–produced technology.

The real reason why MIT is so successful at creating new companies is a combination of spirit and skills. At MIT there is a culture that encourages people to start companies all the time and everywhere, much like in Silicon Valley, Israel, Tech City in London, and Berlin today. Role models are everywhere, and they are not abstract icons, but rather very real people no different from you. An aura of possibility and collaboration so pervades the very air at MIT that students quickly adopt the mindset that "yes, I can start a company too." They become infected with the "entrepreneurial virus," believing in the benefits of launching a new venture.

Students are galvanized by the atmosphere of ambition and collaboration. The work of developing entrepreneurial skills comes from classes, competitions, extracurricular events, and networking programs, and the teachings available both in the classroom and outside are extremely relevant and immediately valuable to the students so that in this environment they attack the subjects with a greater level of interest and commitment. This is also amplified because every student in the class is fully engaged. A class taught in such an engaging environment is far more productive for students and instructors.

A major contributor to this virtuous cycle is the social herding mentality. As the students are learning and working on entrepreneurship, they are also collaborating with fellow students. They talk about their work when they are in social situations, and they naturally start to push one another with subtle or not-so-subtle competitiveness. Not only do they learn from one another, but that learning becomes part of their individual and group identity.

These are the factors that create the environment where entrepreneurship is so successfully "taught" at MIT. It is a positive feedback loop (see Figure I.1).

[3] Edward B. Roberts and Charles E. Eesley, "Entrepreneurial Impact: The Role of MIT—An Updated Report," *Foundations and Trends® in Entrepreneurship* 7, nos. 1–2 (2011): 1–149. http://dx.doi.org/10.1561/0300000030.

[4] "Success Stories," MIT Technology Licensing Office, http://web.mit.edu/tlo/www/about/success_stories.html.

START HERE

Visible successes
and role models
in the community

Spirit of the potential "student" entrepreneur
...belief that "Yes I can & want to be a successful entrepreneur"

Desire to learn
...more about entrepreneurship skills to realize their potential

Application to classes & programs
...with much greater intensity and purpose with other like-minded, fully engaged students

Learn more
...students learn much more & press the instructors

Instructors have to improve
...and they do so with great joy to keep up with driven students

Courses get better
...and better

Students experience success
...and become more a part of the vibrant, well-respected & proud entrepreneurial community

The Positive Feedback Loop at MIT for Spirit & Skills which Creates the Successful Entrepreneurial Ecosystem

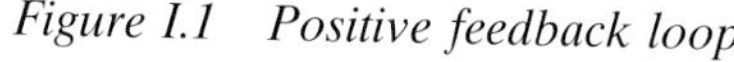

Figure I.1 *Positive feedback loop.*

Distinguishing Two Distinct Types of Entrepreneurship

Entrepreneurship is about creating a new business where one did not exist before. That definition seemed clear until my colleagues Professors Fiona Murray and Scott Stern and I spent a good deal of time talking to various organizations about how to promote entrepreneurship in different regions of the world. We found that when we said "entrepreneurship" to people, it could mean at least two extremely different things—a discrepancy that had important ramifications, because each type of entrepreneurship has dramatically different objectives and needs.[5]

Small and Medium Enterprise (SME) Entrepreneurship The first type of entrepreneurship is small and medium enterprise entrepreneurship (SME). This is the type of business that is likely started by one person to serve a local market and grows to be a small or medium-size business that serves this local market. It is most often closely held, likely a family business, where close control of a small business is important. The business "rewards" for these founders are primarily in the form of personal independence and cash flow from the business.

These businesses generally do not need to raise as much money, so when money is injected into these businesses, the resultant increase in revenue and jobs created is relatively rapid. Such enterprises can be geographically dispersed and the jobs they create are for the most part "non-tradable" in that they cannot be outsourced to someplace else to reduce costs. Frequently these businesses are service businesses or retailers of other companies' products. The key distinguishing factor is their focus on local markets.

Innovation-Driven Enterprise (IDE) Entrepreneurship Innovation-driven enterprise (IDE) entrepreneurship is the more risky and more ambitious of the two. IDE entrepreneurs are aspiring to serve markets that go well beyond the local market. They are looking to sell their offering at a global or at least at a regional level.

These entrepreneurs usually work in teams where they build their business off some technology, process, business model, or other innovation that will give them a significant competitive advantage as compared to existing companies. They are interested in creating wealth more than they are interested in control, and they often have to sell equity in their company to support their ambitious growth plans.

While they are often slower to start, IDE entrepreneurs tend to have more impressive exponential growth when they do get customer traction (See Table I.1). Growth is what they seek, at the

[5] Bill Aulet and Fiona Murray, "A Tale of Two Entrepreneurs: Understanding Differences in the Types of Entrepreneurship in the Economy," Ewing Marion Kauffman Foundation, May 2013, www.kauffman.org/uploadedfiles/downloadableresources/a-tale-of-two-entrepreneurs.pdf.

Table I.1 SME vs. IDE Entrepreneurship Table

SME Entrepreneurship	IDE Entrepreneurship
Focus on addressing local and regional markets only.	Focus on global/regional markets.
Innovation is not necessary to SME establishment and growth, nor is competitive advantage.	The company is based on some sort of innovation (tech, business process, model) and potential competitive advantage.
"Non-tradable jobs"—jobs generally performed locally (e.g., restaurants, dry cleaners, and service industry).	"Tradable jobs"—jobs that do not have to be performed locally.
Most often family businesses or businesses with very little external capital.	More diverse ownership base including a wide array of external capital providers.
The company typically grows at a linear rate. When you put money into the company, the system (revenue, cash flow, jobs, etc.) will respond quickly in a positive manner.	The company starts by losing money, but if successful will have exponential growth. Requires investment. When you put money into the company, the revenue/cash flow/jobs numbers do not respond quickly.

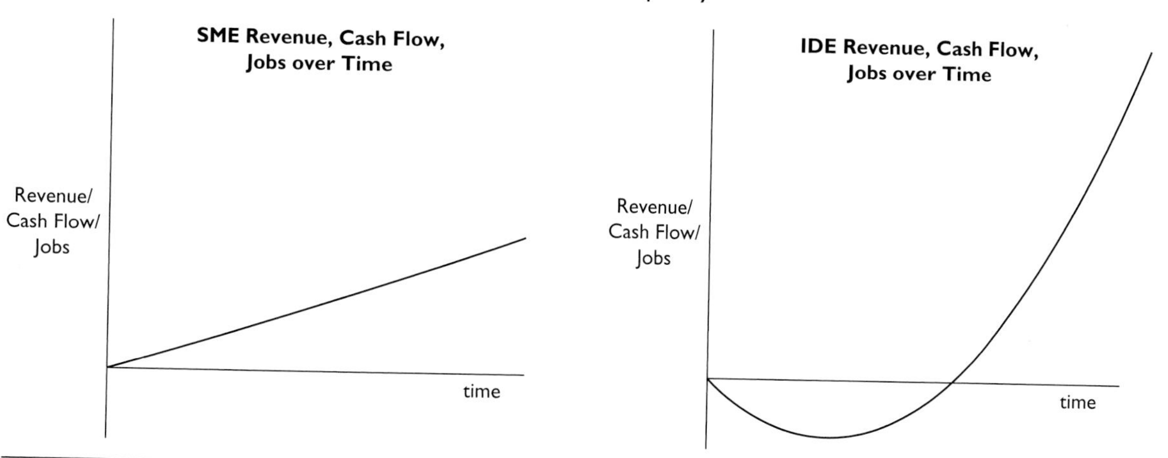

Source: Bill Aulet and Fiona Murray, "A Tale of Two Entrepreneurs: Understanding Differences in the Types of Entrepreneurship in the Economy," Ewing Marion Kauffman Foundation, May 2013, www.kauffman.org/uploadedfiles/downloadableresources/a-tale-of-two-entrepreneurs.pdf.

risk of losing control of their company and having multiple owners. While SME companies tend to grow up and stay relatively small (but not always), IDE companies are more interested in "going big or going home." To achieve their ambitions, they have to become big and fast-growing to serve global markets.

IDE entrepreneurship creates companies that have "tradable" jobs that may well be outsourced if it makes the overall business more competitive. These companies are much less likely to be geographically diverse and instead are concentrated around clusters of innovation. It is also generally the case that any injection of investment or money requires a much longer time to show results in terms of new revenues or jobs.

In the short run, the SME model will be more responsive; but with patience, the IDE ventures have the capacity to produce profound results as we have seen with companies like Apple, Google, Hewlett-Packard, and other publicly traded companies.

Our Focus Is Innovation-Driven Enterprise

A healthy economy consists of both types of entrepreneurship and both have their strengths and weaknesses. Neither is better than the other. But they are substantively different enough that they require different mindsets and different sets of skills to be successful. Therefore, in this book, rather than teach "entrepreneurship," I will teach IDE entrepreneurship, because this is what I know best, having co-founded two companies (Cambridge Decision Dynamics and SensAble Technologies) based on an innovation.

What Is Innovation?

Innovation has become an increasingly clichéd term, but it has a simple definition, which I have adapted from MIT professor Ed Roberts[6]:

$$\text{Innovation} = \text{Invention} * \text{Commercialization}$$

I modify Roberts's definition, which involved addition, because innovation is not a sum of invention and commercialization, but a product. If there is commercialization but no invention (invention = 0), or invention but no commercialization (commercialization = 0), then there is no innovation.

[6] Edward B. Roberts, "Managing Invention and Innovation," *Research Technology Management* 31, no. 1 (January/February 1988): 13, ABI/INFORM Complete.

The invention (an idea, a technology, or some sort of intellectual property) is important, but the entrepreneur does not need to create the invention. In fact, the inventions that lead to innovation-driven companies often come from elsewhere. Such was the case with Steve Jobs, who identified others' inventions (the computer mouse created by Xerox PARC is the most famous example) and commercialized them effectively through Apple. Likewise at Google, which has made most of its money through AdWords, the text-based, keyword-driven advertisements on their search results pages. A different company, Overture, had invented such advertisements, but Google was successful through its commercialization of Overture's invention.

These examples show that the capability to commercialize an invention is necessary for real innovation. An entrepreneur, then, serves primarily as the commercialization agent.

I very consciously do not use the term "technology-driven" entrepreneurship because innovation is not limited to technology. Innovation can come in many varieties including technology, process, business model, positioning, and more.

Some of the most exciting innovations of our time, such as Google, iTunes, Salesforce.com, Netflix, Zipcar, and many more are, at their core, business model innovations. They are enabled by technology, yes—Zipcar would find it difficult to maintain its large network of cars without keyless-entry technology for its members. But at its core, Zipcar's innovation is treating a rental car as a substitute for owning a car, rather than as temporary transportation for car owners and business travelers visiting far-flung areas. Zipcar doesn't have to understand the intricacies of its technology to be successful, but it has to understand what it means for its customers to "collaboratively consume."

As technology becomes more and more commoditized, you will see more business model innovations that leverage technology. There will still be many opportunities for technology-driven innovation in areas like energy storage, power electronics, wireless communications, and much more, but this is not the sole definition of innovation.

Six Themes of the 24 Steps

The 24 Steps are discrete and can be grouped into six themes. Each step should be done in numerical order with the understanding that in each step, you will learn things that will prompt you to revise the work you have done in earlier steps. These themes present a general outline of how the 24 Steps will help you create a sustainable, innovation-based business.

START HERE
1 market segmentation
2 beachhead market
3 end user profile
4 beachhead TAM size
5 persona
6 life cycle use case
7 high-level specs
8 quantify value proposition
9 next 10 customers
10 define core
11 chart competitive position
12 determine DMU
13 map customer acquisition process
14 follow-on TAM
15 design business model
16 pricing framework
17 LTV
18 map sales process
19 COCA
20 identify key assumptions
21 test key assumptions
22 define MVBP
23 show dogs will eat the dog food
24 develop product plan
MVBP

WHO IS YOUR CUSTOMER?

1. Market Segmentation
2. Select a Beachhead Market
3. Build an End User Profile
4. Calculate the TAM Size for the Beachhead Market
5. Profile the Persona for the Beachhead Market
9. Identify Your Next 10 Customers

WHAT CAN YOU DO FOR YOUR CUSTOMER?

6. Full Life Cycle Use Case
7. High-Level Product Specification
8. Quantify the Value Proposition
10. Define Your Core
11. Chart Your Competitive Position

HOW DOES YOUR CUSTOMER ACQUIRE YOUR PRODUCT?

12. Determine the Customer's Decision-Making Unit (DMU)
13. Map The Process to Acquire a Paying Customer
18. Map the Sales Process to Acquire a Customer

HOW DO YOU MAKE MONEY OFF YOUR PRODUCT?

15. Design a Business Model
16. Set Your Pricing Framework
17. Calculate the Lifetime Value (LTV) of an Acquired Customer
19. Calculate the Cost of Customer Acquisition (COCA)

HOW DO YOU DESIGN & BUILD YOUR PRODUCT?

20. Identify Key Assumptions
21. Test Key Assumptions
22. Define the Minimum Viable Business Product (MVBP)
23. Show That "The Dogs Will Eat the Dog Food"

HOW DO YOU SCALE YOUR BUSINESS?

14. Calculate the TAM Size for Follow-on Markets
24. Develop a Product Plan

STEP 0

Getting Started

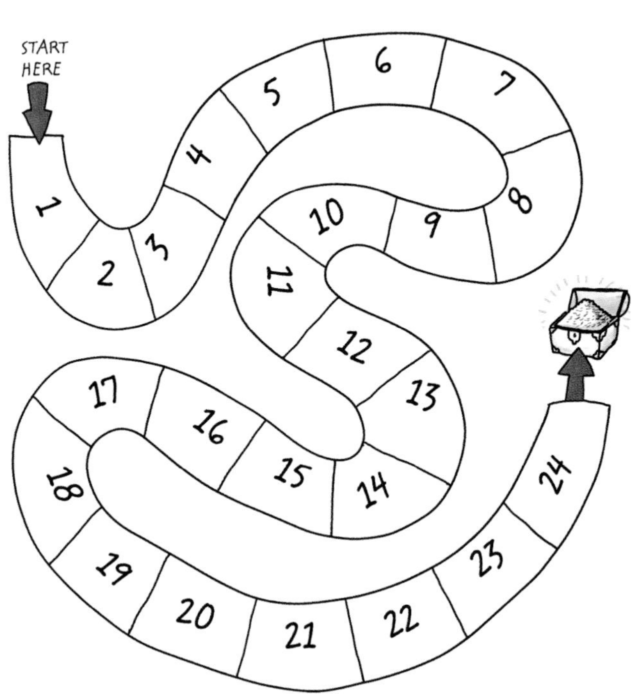

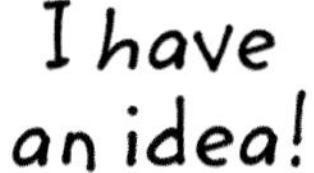

Three ways to start a new venture

THREE WAYS TO START A NEW VENTURE

When I listen to my students, I hear a diverse range of reasons as to why they are interested in entrepreneurship. Some students have worked in one industry for years and want a change. Some want to push their skills to the maximum and have the biggest impact on the world. Some want to be their own boss. Some hold patents and are interested in the different ways they can commercialize them. Some have an idea about how their own life could be improved and they wonder if that idea is interesting to others.

All of these reasons can be synthesized into three distinct categories (see Table 0.1):

1. **Have an Idea:** You have thought of something new that can change the world—or some small part of it—in a positive way, or something that can improve an existing process you're familiar with and you want to implement it.
2. **Have a Technology:** You have come up with a technological breakthrough and want to capitalize on it, or simply expedite its deployment to have a positive effect on society. Or, you have learned about a technological breakthrough and you see great potential for a business.
3. **Have a Passion:** You are confident and you are comfortable pushing yourself to develop your skills in the most comprehensive way possible. You also might believe that being an entrepreneur is the way to have the biggest impact on the world. You simply might know that you want to work for yourself and control your own destiny, but you don't have an idea or technology yet, so you'd like to learn about entrepreneurship while looking for a good idea, technology, and/or partner. (Read on to learn how to find a good idea or technology based on your passion.)

I am frequently told that an entrepreneur cannot start without knowing a "customer pain"—a problem that bothers someone enough that they would be willing to pay to alleviate the problem. But that approach can be discouraging to someone who is unfamiliar with entrepreneurship. Furthermore, it discounts the importance of starting a company in line with the entrepreneur's values, interests, and expertise. In time, they will find a customer with a pain, or opportunity, where the customer is willing to pay for a solution.

No matter how you have become interested in entrepreneurship, you need to start by first answering the following question: *What can I do well that I would love to do for an extended period of time?*

Table 0.1 Idea versus Technology versus Interest

What does it sound like to have an idea versus a technology versus a passion? You should be able to sum up your idea, technology, or interest in one succinct sentence.		
Idea:	**Technology:**	**Passion:**
"I want to start a company in Africa that will create a sustainable business model to improve life for the people there and empower them with jobs." Here, the idea is that a sustainable business model will reduce poverty in Africa more effectively than charitable contributions to the poor. This sentence is enough to move on to the next step of Market Segmentation, though as you will see, you will have to be much more specific before you can turn the idea into a business.	*"I have a robot that allows you to feel objects rendered by a computer."* This statement radiates with potential. How could someone benefit from being able to have a three-dimensional object on their computer screen and still be able to feel it, in some way, in physical space? I co-founded a company, SensAble Technologies, around this very technology, and throughout the book, I share SensAble's story.	*"I have a master's in mechanical engineering and I can quickly prototype most any technological gadget you want . . . now I want to put my skills to use in the most impactful way possible, and be my own boss."* This person has identified a personal comparative advantage, the ability to prototype gadgets quickly, which can help a business go through product iterations faster. The person may want to consider a hardware-based business, as it would line up well with the comparative advantage.

Once you have answered this question, you will have taken the first step toward discovering a customer pain—a pain that you are interested in alleviating because it is in line with what you are interested in and have expertise in.

HOW TO GO FROM "I HAVE A PASSION" TO "I HAVE AN IDEA OR TECHNOLOGY"

Many of my students who are interested in entrepreneurship do not yet have an idea or a technology, so if this is you, you are not alone. By first taking stock of your personal interests, strengths, and skills, you can more readily identify good opportunities. You can do this exercise either alone or with a group of potential co-founders.

Consider the following:

- *Knowledge:* What was the focus of your education or career?
- *Capability:* What are you most proficient at?
- *Connections:* Who do you know that has expertise in different industries? Do you know other entrepreneurs?
- *Financial assets:* Do you have access to significant financial capital, or will you be relying on a meager savings account to start out?
- *Name recognition:* What are you or your partners well-known for? Skills in engineering? Understanding fiber optics?
- *Past work experience:* In previous jobs you've held, what inefficiencies or "pain points" existed?
- *Passion for a particular market:* Does the idea of improving healthcare excite you? How about education? Energy? Transportation?
- *Commitment:* Do you have the time and effort to devote to this endeavor? Are you ready to make a new venture your primary (or only) focus?

If you or your founding group have strong coding and project management skills, you may be more inclined to develop a web app. If you are a pro at rapid prototyping, you may want to consider creating a physical product of some sort. Or if your past work experience is in education or medicine, you may want to consider what you can create that would improve those areas.

Often, you will find an idea or technology that improves something for you personally, then realize that idea or technology has the potential to help many others. This phenomenon is called "user entrepreneurship"; the Kauffman Foundation has found that nearly half of all innovation-based startups that are at least five years old were founded by user entrepreneurs.[1]

FINDING A FOUNDING TEAM: ENTREPRENEURSHIP IS NOT A SOLO SPORT

In 15.390 New Enterprises, the foundational entrepreneurship class I teach with other faculty at MIT, students who go through the 24 Steps must form teams within two weeks, due to the time constraints

[1] Ewing Marion Kauffman Foundation "Nearly Half of Innovative U.S. Startups Are Founded by 'User Entrepreneurs,' According to Kauffman Foundation Study," March 7, 2012, www.kauffman.org/newsroom/nearly-half-of-innovative-startups-are-founded-by-user-entrepreneurs.aspx.

of the academic semester. This process is not an optimal way to form teams, but it is enough for the student teams to gain experience in team formation and for teams to implement (in an accelerated manner) the 24 Steps over the course of a semester. From the ideas in the class that turn into businesses, some teams stay intact, but far more often teams undergo a healthy reconfiguration of their membership at the end of the semester to create a stronger, more unified team that is better suited to capture an opportunity on a longer-term basis. This is an important evolutionary process.

Your choice of co-founders is extremely important. The research at MIT suggests that businesses with multiple founders are more successful than those founded by an individual.[2]

There are many resources that go into more depth about finding good co-founders. Probably the single best and most rigorous book on this topic is Harvard Professor Noam Wasserman's book, *The Founder's Dilemmas*. For other valuable perspectives, here are a few articles that may be helpful:

Paul Graham, "What We Look for in Founders," *PaulGraham.com*, October 2010, www.paulgraham.com/founders.html.

Margaret Heffernan, "Want to Start a Business? First, Find a Partner," *Inc.*, May 9, 2012, www.inc.com/margaret-heffernan/you-need-a-partner-to-start-a-business.html.

Pejman Pour-Moezzi, "How to Find That Special Someone: Your Co-Founder," *GeekWire*, April 8, 2012, www.geekwire.com/2012/find-special-cofounder.

Helge Seetzen, "5 Rules for Cofounder Heaven," *The Tech Entrepreneurship Blog*, March 27, 2012, www.techentrepreneurship.com/2012/03/27/5-rules-for-cofounder-heaven.

WHERE YOU GO FROM HERE

Once you have identified an idea or technology as the basis for your innovation-driven business, you must rigorously test and flesh out your proposal through the 24 Steps. Your first goal is to assess the needs of potential customers, focusing on a target customer with the goal of achieving product–market fit—a product that matches what customers in a specific market are interested in buying. Focus is very important because entrepreneurs have very limited time and resources and so must be hyper-efficient. Focus is so crucial to determining your target customer that I refer to the first five steps of the 24 Steps—from Market Segmentation to profiling your Persona—as "The Search for the Holy Grail of Specificity" (see Figure 0.1).

[2] Edward B. Roberts, *Entrepreneurs in High Technology: Lessons from MIT and Beyond* (New York: Oxford University Press, 1991), 258.

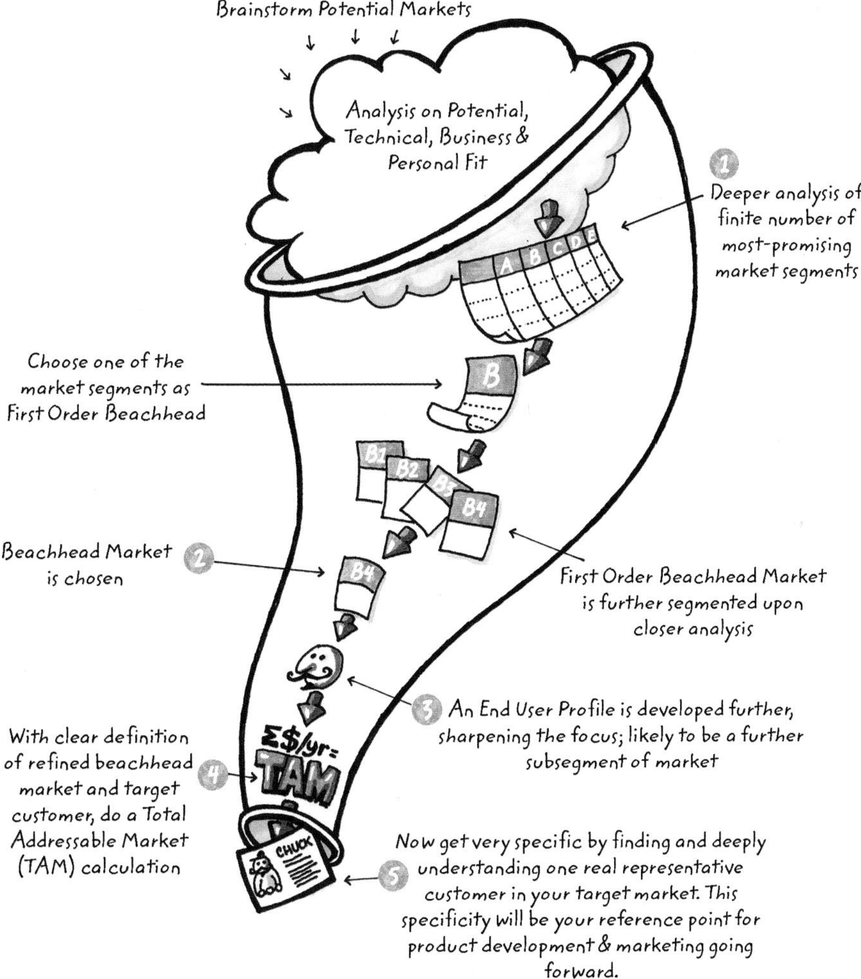

Figure 0.1 The Holy Grail of Specificity.

STEP 1

Market Segmentation

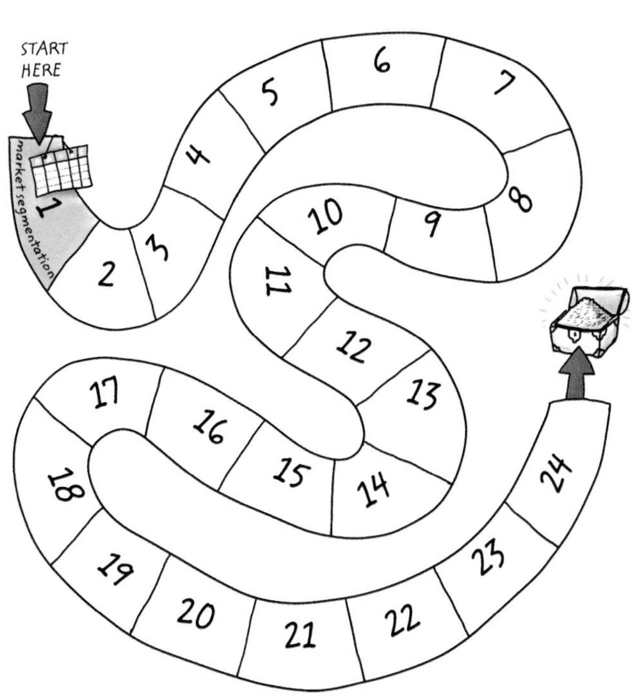

IN THIS STEP, YOU WILL:

- Brainstorm a wide array of potential customers and markets for your business.
- Narrow your list down to your top 6–12 markets.
- Gather primary market research on your top 6–12 markets.

vs.

For success in entrepreneurship, there are some glasses that are better than others to view the situation.

Once you have completed Step 0, Getting Started, you should have an idea or technology that answers the question, "Is this something the world could benefit from, and is it something I do well and would love to do for an extended period?" You should also have a team of co-founders. (Throughout the 24 Steps, I will use "you" to refer collectively to your team.)

Now you will begin the 24 Steps by taking that idea or technology and brainstorming a wide array of potential customers who might be interested in some application of it. Then you will choose 6–12 top opportunities and do in-depth primary market research, where you directly interview potential customers to learn more about them.

THE SINGLE NECESSARY AND SUFFICIENT CONDITION FOR A BUSINESS

Regardless of your business, you must ask yourself, "What is the single necessary and sufficient condition for a business?" It is not a product, a technology, a customer need, a business plan, a vision, a strong team, a CEO, money, investors, competitive advantage, or company values. While all those are great things for a business to have, none of them is the right answer.

The single necessary and sufficient condition for a business is **a paying customer**.

The day someone pays you money for your product or service, you have a business, and not a day before. This simple truth will keep you focused on what is important. You cannot define a business as a product, because if nobody buys your product, you simply do not have a business. The marketplace is the final arbiter of success.

Now, just because you have a paying customer does not mean you have a *good* business. In order to have a good, sustainable business, you will need to gain enough customers paying enough money within a relatively short period of time so you do not run out of capital, but instead, become profitable. And as a startup, you have few resources, so every action you take must be hyper-efficient.

Therefore, you will not start by building a product or hiring developers or recruiting salespeople. Instead, you will take a customer-driven approach by finding an unmet need and building your business around it.

CREATE A NEW MARKET THAT YOU WILL DOMINATE

Creating an innovative product where no market currently exists is essential to the success of a startup. By creating a new market, you will have a very high, if not dominant, market share that you can use as a basis for future expansion. Being a "me-too" company in an existing market is a more difficult proposition given your limited resources.

To create this company in a newly defined market space, you will focus on a target customer. A target customer is a group of potential customers who share many characteristics and who would all have similar reasons to buy a particular product. Focus is the most important skill for an entrepreneur, and as you will find throughout these steps, it is difficult to focus too much. You must work hard to identify and understand customers through primary market research, because relying on "educated assumptions" or third-party analysis is guesswork when you are creating new markets.

Once you have established a foothold within that target group, meaning that you've provided that group with a substantially superior product and they are paying you for it, you will have enough resources to expand to an adjacent market. In an adjacent market, some customer characteristics will be the same as your primary market, but there will be enough differences to require tailoring your strategy appropriately. That process is covered in Steps 14 and 24.

WHEN "PAYING CUSTOMERS" LEAD YOU ASTRAY

While paying customers ultimately determine whether your product is successful, there are two common pitfalls you may encounter if you do not focus on creating a new market.

The first is "selling to everyone," which is the idea that you, as a fledgling startup with little to no resources, can make products that fit the needs of anyone you run across.

Let's say you have invented a new polymer that waterproofs fabric better than anything on the market. You first hear from your friend Sally, who read in the newspaper that camping equipment is a lucrative market, so she suggests you sell tents. Your cousin Joe chimes in; he wants waterproof underwear. A neighbor thinks that easy-to-clean stuffed animals for children would be just lovely.

To design and execute any of these products will take time and resources. If you start production on one product, and find there aren't enough customers to make your venture profitable, you almost certainly will not have the resources to keep making products until you find a profitable market.

The second common pitfall is "The China Syndrome," also known to my students as "fun with spreadsheets." Rather than create a new market, the thinking goes, one could choose a huge existing market, get a fraction of the market share, and reap the rewards. After all, if you could get even a tenth of a percent of the toothbrush market in China (population 1.3 billion), wouldn't you make a lot of money?

The logic would go something like this: "The Internet says China has over 1.3 billion people. If they all have teeth, the market size is 1.3 billion customers. I'll build a toothbrush for the Chinese market, and maybe we'll get 0.1 percent market share in the first year. If each person buys three toothbrushes a year, we could sell 3.9 million toothbrushes per year, and if we sell them for $1 each, we have $3.9 million in sales the first year, with lots of room to grow."

I call such a high-level market analysis "fun with spreadsheets," because you have not demonstrated in a compelling manner why people would buy your product or why your market share would increase over time. You also have not validated any of your assumptions by learning directly from customers—you probably haven't even been to China. After all, if entrepreneurship were this easy, wouldn't everyone sell toothbrushes to China?

Big companies with lots of resources can afford to work hard to gain incremental market share, but entrepreneurs don't have the luxury of resources. Don't get ensnared by "The China Syndrome."

Take your resources and apply them to a narrow, carefully defined new market that you can dominate.

COMPLEX PAYING CUSTOMERS: PRIMARY VERSUS SECONDARY CUSTOMERS AND TWO-SIDED MARKETS

Thus far, I have used "customer" to refer to the entity—such as a household, organization, or individual—who pays for, acquires, and uses your product. Within the broad definition of a customer, there is the end user, who ultimately uses your product, and the economic buyer, who makes the final decision about whether to acquire the product. The end user and economic buyer can be the same person, depending on the situation. (I describe the various roles of a customer in more detail in Step 12, Determine the Customer's Decision-Making Unit [DMU].)

But there are two cases in which this definition gets more complicated. The first is when your business model calls for both primary customers (end users) and secondary customers (economic buyers) in order to make money. Often, these businesses are structured where the primary customer is charged at below cost, or gets a product for free, and a third party pays for access to the primary customer and/or the primary customer's information. For instance, Google's search engine is free to use, but Google sells advertisements on search results pages to make money. Google's ability to provide advertisers with keyword-targeted ad placement and demographic information about search users further enhances Google's value proposition to advertisers.

You likely will not have a primary/secondary customer delineation until you have completed Step 15, Design a Business Model, so for now, focus on your primary customer as you complete the first several steps.

The second case is called a two-sided or multi-sided market, where you need multiple target customers for your business to exist. eBay is a good example, because it needs both sellers and buyers (supply and demand) to participate in its auctions to be successful.

If you have a multi-sided market, you will complete each step once for each side of the market. But you will likely find through your primary market research that one side of the market is more critical to win for your business to succeed; so you will want to focus there. For instance, two of my former students, Kim Gordon and Shambhavi Kadam, started Mediuum, an iTunes-like platform for digital artwork. As they investigated this concept, they realized that getting the demand side of customers to sign up to put digital art on their mobile phones, tablets, PC, and TVs was not the challenge. The hard work was going to be signing up the digital artists who create the art and having them agree to make it available. Thus, while both supply and demand were needed for the new venture to succeed, their primary focus would be the digital artists.

HOW TO DO A MARKET SEGMENTATION

Step 1A: Brainstorm

Start by brainstorming a wide array of market opportunities. Include even the "crazy ideas" that you think are longshots, because they are helpful in expanding the boundaries of possibilities to where some of the most interesting opportunities might exist.

Even at this early stage, talking about your idea or technology with potential customers will give you clear and accurate feedback for your market segmentation. You will find them at trade shows, through connections with fellow students and professors (perhaps some of them would have been potential customers at their previous jobs), or, if others have heard about your idea or technology, perhaps they will be contacting you, suggesting potential uses. The best scenario is when you are the potential customer yourself and have a deep understanding of the problem you are trying to solve.

If you have an idea, you may think you already have a specific market and a specific application in mind. However, as a first-time entrepreneur, you will want to carefully determine whether your perceptions are correct. Likely, your defined market is not specific enough, but you may also find that the market you have in mind is not a good match for your idea, or that other markets are better for starting a business. Be open-minded and creative.

For instance, if you are expressing your idea as "I want to create an online social network for high school teachers and parents to communicate about their children's progress in school," you may lock yourself into a path that does not produce a sustainable business. Start instead with "I want to improve education with technology." Then ask yourself why you are passionate about that idea. If technology is your primary passion, you probably want to consider a wider range of industries than just education. If your passion is education, you can simply segment the education industry, but be open to other solutions besides one involving a high degree of technology.

If you have a new technology, you probably can think of a large number of industries that could benefit from your product. While you may have domain expertise in a certain field, that field may not have any good applications for your technology, so be open to different industries. Later on, you will filter your ideas to take your passions into account.

Start by identifying potential industries for your idea. Then, list who might benefit in each industry from your idea. Focus on end users, not customers, because you will need a committed group of end users to have a sustainable business. A school doesn't use a textbook, or a chalkboard, or a lesson plan, but teachers do.

For instance, if your idea is to improve education with technology, who would be your end user? Teachers, administrators, parents, and students are all potential end users. Each category can be further subdivided. Are you focusing on end users in universities or in grade school? What different types of schools are these end users associated with? Which countries and regions do the end users work and live in?

To elaborate on one example, in the grade school category for teachers, there are public school, private school, parochial school, and homeschool teachers. Within public school teachers, there are various levels of schooling, depending on their country and region. Within each category, there are urban, suburban, and rural schools. In most middle and high schools, teachers specialize in a specific subject. Even within a subject, such as social studies, there are subcategories such as history and geography. In most schools, there are art, music, and physical education teachers, as well as paraprofessionals and special education teachers. See Figure 1.1 for a visual example.

Next, identify the different tasks your end user performs. For a high school science teacher in a suburban area, these tasks may include teaching, grading, preparing lessons, training, discipline, dealing with parents, ordering chemicals, and more. An elementary school teacher in a major city may not need to order chemicals, but may need to buy classroom supplies, sometimes out of pocket. Also, an elementary school teacher likely teaches multiple subjects, so you would subdivide "teaching" by the different subjects.

You may find enough similarities between certain subcategories that you can group them, depending on what your idea is, but you will find that out during your primary market research. Do not start combining categories without knowing more about your customer.

Sometimes, my students have an easy time segmenting end users when starting with an employee like a teacher, but have a much harder time when the end user is a consumer, purchasing for personal or household use. A useful question to ask is why the consumer would purchase a product in a particular industry segment. For the education segmentation above, why would a parent purchase a product that improves education?

Or, consider a technology such as a long-lasting battery. If you are looking at the transportation industry, and have segmented down to consumers buying a vehicle for personal transportation, why would a consumer use such a product? Some possibilities include environmental conscientiousness,

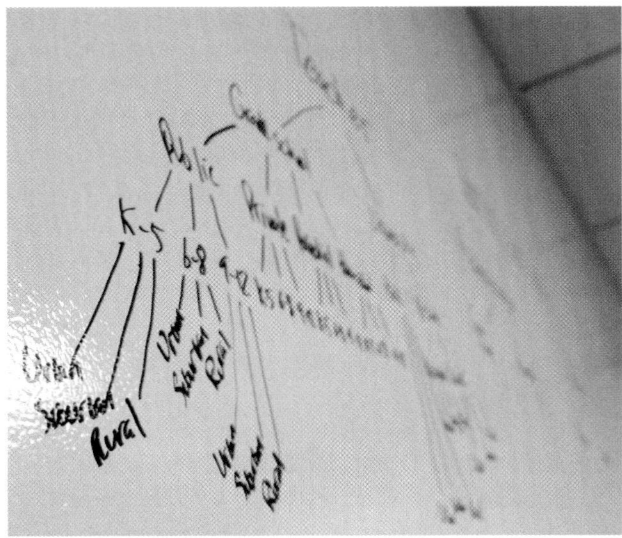

Figure 1.1 When you segment out your market, you will find there are a lot of segments, and that seemingly broad categories have a lot of important differences. Segment first, and then determine whether any categories are common enough to merge.

high performance, luxury, convenience, and value. Even within high performance, you can subdivide between consumers looking for a low-cost but high-performance vehicle, and price-insensitive consumers whose primary objective is high performance.

Be broad and expansive when segmenting end users for your new product. You are brainstorming now; later, you will narrow the list as you start to analyze each segment.

Step 1B: Narrow

You have by now identified numerous potential end users and applications for your idea or technology. Your next task is to list the top 6–12 particularly interesting market opportunities, where a market opportunity consists of a specific end user and one or a handful of applications. As you do primary market research, the specific application you have in mind may not be one the end user is looking for, so it is better to focus on end users for now.

In *Inside the Tornado*, Geoffrey Moore identifies five criteria that the company Documentum used to narrow down its list of 80 potential markets. I have expanded this number to seven by splitting the first criterion into two parts, and adding one of my own to incorporate the passions of your founding team into the discussion.

1. **Is the target customer well-funded?** If the customer does not have money, the market is not attractive because it will not be sustainable and provide positive cash flow for the new venture to grow.
2. **Is the target customer readily accessible to your sales force?** You want to deal directly with customers when starting out, rather than rely on third parties to market and sell your product, because your product will go through iterations of improvement very rapidly, and direct customer feedback is an essential part of that process. Also, since your product is substantially new and never seen before (and potentially disruptive), third parties may not know how to be effective at creating demand for your product.
3. **Does the target customer have a compelling reason to buy?** Would the customer buy your product instead of another similar solution? Or, is the customer content with whatever solution is already being used? Remember that on many occasions, your primary competition will be the customer doing nothing.
4. **Can you today, with the help of partners, deliver a whole product?** The example here that I often use in class is that no one wants to buy a new alternator and install it in their car, even if the alternator is much better than what they currently have. They want to buy a car. That is, they want to buy a whole functional solution, not assemble one themselves. You will likely need to work with other vendors to deliver a solution that incorporates your product, which means that you will need to convince other manufacturers and distributors that your product is worth integrating into their workflows.
5. **Is there entrenched competition that could block you?** Rare is the case where no other competitors are vying to convince a customer to spend their budget on some product to meet the identified need. How strong are those competitors, from the customer's viewpoint (not your viewpoint or from a technical standpoint)? Can the competition block you from starting a business relationship with a customer? And how do you stand out from what your customer perceives as alternatives?
6. **If you win this segment, can you leverage it to enter additional segments?** If you dominate this market opportunity, are there adjacent opportunities where you can sell your product with only slight modifications to your product or your sales strategy? Or will you have to radically revise your product or sales strategy in order to take advantage of additional market opportunities? While you want to stay focused on your beachhead market, you do not want to choose a starting market from which you will have a hard time scaling your business. Geoffrey Moore uses the metaphor of a bowling alley, where the beachhead market is the lead pin, and dominating the beachhead market knocks down the lead pin, which crashes into other pins

that represent either adjacent market opportunities or different applications to sell to the customer in your beachhead market.

7. **Is the market consistent with the values, passions, and goals of the founding team?** You want to make sure that the founders' personal goals do not take a back seat to the other criteria presented here. In the case of a company I co-founded, SensAble Technologies, we wanted to "get liquid" (go public or get bought) within four to five years, a relatively short time horizon for the type of technology we created, because co-founders Thomas and Rhonda Massie wanted to move back to Kentucky, where they were from. Therefore, an important factor for us was whether we could show results in an acceptable time frame in whichever market we chose.

Start by asking these questions at an industry level. Then, consider what the answers would be for the end user of your product. Within an industry, if you have segmented your potential end users by branching out into many categories, like in the education example above, ask the questions at each branching level. For instance, consider the example from earlier of teachers vs. parents vs. administrators vs. students, then higher education vs. grade school, then country, then public vs. private, etc.

Your limiting factor is time—you will research each of these markets in depth, and you do not have time to consider an unlimited number of options. Six to twelve market opportunities is more than sufficient—with a realistic number being much closer to six than twelve.

Step 1C: Primary Market Research

Now that you have narrowed your market opportunities, it is time for primary market research, talking directly with customers and observing customers will help you get a better sense of which market opportunity is best.

Because you are identifying a new market opportunity for a product that does not yet exist, you will not be able to rely on Google searches or on research reports from research firms. *If there is already a market research report out there with all the information you need, it is probably too late for your new venture.* You have missed the window of opportunity—someone else has beaten you to the market.

Instead, you will gather the vast majority of your information from direct interaction with real potential customers about their situations, pain points, opportunities, and market information. Unfortunately, there are few shortcuts in this process. While you should find out what you can about customers and markets before you talk to potential customers, it is impossible to overstate the importance of doing direct customer research, as any other sources of information and knowledge are frequently superficial and likely of minimal value.

How to Talk with Potential Customers When you talk with potential customers, encourage the flow of ideas; don't restrain them or try to gain a commitment. If the potential customer senses you are trying to sell them something, they will change their behavior; they will either say little or say things that are related to the market opportunity you seem to be presenting them, rather than providing you with new, innovative ideas for markets. As a result, you will get less market data, and what you do get will be biased.

Likewise, you should not count on your customer to design your product or tell you the answer to their problems. The goal of this research is to understand their pain points, and later design a solution that will be of great value to them. To do so, you will need to thoroughly understand the underlying issues and sources of opportunity, whether by speaking with them or, even better, watching them as they work ("primary observational research"). Actions are more important than words, because people sometimes say things that are contrary to how they actually do things.

You will want to talk with as many end users as possible, but individuals who are not end users may also give you valuable advice or may point you in the right direction. You may even find that you misidentified the end user in your segmentation.

There are a few key factors that are integral to collecting accurate information:

- You must have a high level of intellectual curiosity.
- You must be fearless about getting on the phone, in the car, or on a plane to pursue this information.
- You must have an ability to listen and get people to talk.
- You must be open-minded and unbiased, and never presuppose a solution (inquiry, not advocacy).
- You must have the ability to explain what the essence of your proposed offering might look like while also being flexible.
- You must have time and patience to devote to this important step.

There are three important caveats when conducting your primary market research:

1. You do not have "the answer" for your potential customers and their needs.
2. Your potential customers do not have "the answer" for you.
3. Talk with potential customers in "inquiry" mode, not "advocacy/sales" mode. Listen to what they have to say, and don't try to get them to buy anything.

Organize Your Research The main categories you are trying to obtain information on for each market are:

1. **End User:** Who specifically would be using your product? The end user is often your "champion," who you need on board so that your product is successfully adopted. You have narrowed down your end user some already, but as you do primary market research you may find the category can be even further segmented. (The end user is not necessarily the person who decides to purchase the product, as we discuss later in Step 12, Determine the Customer's Decision-Making Unit [DMU]. If you are making a children's video game, the kid who plays it is your champion, because he tries to get his parents, the economic buyer, to purchase it.)
2. **Application:** What would the end user be using your product for? What is the task that would be dramatically improved by your new venture?
3. **Benefits:** What is the actual value that the end user would gain from the use of your new product? Not feature or functions, but specifically what the end user gains from the product. Is it a time savings? A cost savings? Additional profit?
4. **Lead Customers:** Who are the most influential customers that others look to for thought leadership and adoption of new technology? These are sometimes referred to as "lighthouse customers" because they are so respected that when they buy, others look to them and follow their lead, gaining you instant credibility. Some people call these customers "early adopters," but lead customers are not technological enthusiasts. They must be respected by others as innovative and successful customers who purchase because the product provides them with real value and not simply bragging rights.
5. **Market Characteristics:** What about this market would help or hinder the adoption of new technology?
6. **Partners/Players:** Which companies will you need to work with to provide a solution that integrates into the customer's workflow? Sometimes, this category will tie into the "Complementary Assets Required" category below.
7. **Size of the Market:** Roughly, how many potential customers exist if you achieve 100 percent market penetration?
8. **Competition:** Who, if anyone, is making similar products—real or perceived? Remember, this is from the customer's perspective and not just yours.

9. **Complementary Assets Required:** What else does your customer need in order to get the "full solution," that is, to get full functionality from your product? You will likely need to bundle your product with products from other manufacturers so that customers can easily buy your product and have full functionality. At the very least, you will need to identify which other products your customer will need to buy to use your product. For instance, if you are developing a game for the Sega Dreamcast video-game console, your customers will need to be able to purchase the console as well. Since the console is not sold anymore, this need will limit your customer's ability to purchase your product.

It is easiest to organize this information in a matrix, where each potential market opportunity is a column header, and each category of information is a row. The SensAble example further on shows how such a matrix could be organized.

There may be other categories that are relevant to your situation. Also, some of the rows in the example matrix may be unnecessary for your situation; but this general format can be a good starting point for you to customize as appropriate. This matrix has proven to be helpful for hundreds of companies; also some have added or removed categories of information to make the matrix more valuable to their specific context.

HOW LONG SHOULD I SPEND ON MARKET SEGMENTATION?

Give your full attention to this research for at least a few weeks (and maybe much longer if your situation permits). Also, make sure you are talking to customers in the target market to get good data. The amount of time you spend will depend largely on how effective your team is at getting primary market research. You should spend enough time so that you can fill out the matrix for all your top segments with some accuracy. Don't just search the Internet and debate this in your office.

It is likely you will not find a perfect market opportunity, but there rarely is one that is "perfect." Do not let yourself fall into "analysis paralysis."

Do not let the market segmentation be a never-ending process. The objective is just to get an accurate assessment of the market opportunities so you can move to the next step. After all, this is Step 1—you have 23 more steps to go! You will likely revisit this step as you get more information from the future steps. While the steps are presented in a sequential manner for the sake of simplicity, they are often iterative in nature, as the overview illustration shows at the beginning of the book (Six Themes of the 24 Steps).

EXAMPLE

SensAble Technologies

SensAble Technologies started its life as a powerful but raw technology that enables people to feel three-dimensional (3D) objects rendered by a computer. Based in the MIT Artificial Intelligence Laboratory and specifically in the Robotics Laboratory supervised by the legendary Professor Rodney Brooks, then-MIT undergraduate Thomas Massie created, working with his Professor Ken Salisbury, a new device that would give its user the sense of touching virtual objects using a stylus-like interface. The device, named the PHANToM, would simulate shapes, motion, weight, and many other physical properties by increasing or decreasing the resistance or force felt by a user when moving a finger or stylus as shown in Figure 1.2.

As others heard about this breakthrough idea and subsequent technological implementation, Massie received queries from all over the world about potential uses for the technology. He started to sell versions of the lab product. However, his "early adopters" consisted mainly of universities and research labs—"technological enthusiasts" who will buy almost any innovative product. (Geoffrey Moore's book *Crossing the Chasm* goes into greater detail about technological enthusiasts, and says that these customers can be a first bridge to the ultimately most desirable broader market called the "early majority.")

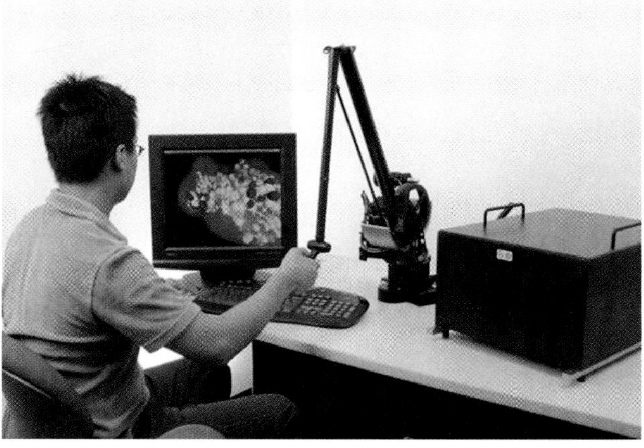

Figure 1.2 The SensAble PHANToM.

When I first met Thomas, he was selling these devices to researchers under the company name SensAble Devices. He was interested in building a much more commercially oriented business that could have a bigger impact on the world, so we joined forces to create SensAble Technologies.

We worked hard to find a scalable market opportunity that would allow our business to reach the goals we had set out to achieve: being a company worth tens of millions of dollars in the relatively short time horizon of five years or less. I worked with our business development manager, John Ranta, who had experience in previous startups identifying such market opportunities and doing the hard work of primary market research with customers to discover their real needs. We spent weeks building out a list of potential markets, using our current customers, trade show feedback, incoming product inquiries, and our own imaginations as sources of ideas.

No idea was too crazy at this point: a boxing channel, fixing space stations, computer mice that vibrated, helping to perform medical surgery, pornography, new computer games, educational opportunities, data analysis, flight simulators, virtual worlds, museums, sports training, computers for the blind. We did not prejudge any idea; rather, we wanted to open the aperture as wide as possible.

We discussed ideas weekly, sometimes nightly, and we discussed our core values and personal passions, which made certain markets unattractive (e.g., pornography). Another outcome of our brainstorming was that we saw where our product's real value was—applications that used 3D data, not those using two-dimensional (2D) data.

Once we had a comprehensive list of possibilities, we then systematically narrowed the field down to eight industries, made the outline for a market segmentation chart (see Table 1.1), and then spent weeks doing the primary market research to fill out the matrix. Somewhere around 90 percent of the data in the chart came from direct interaction and talking with real potential customers in these industries about their situations, pain points, opportunities, and market characteristics. Very little data came from research reports by well-known research firms or by finding data on the Internet.

Each of these market segments were legitimate candidates for our initial market, and each was distinctive with different sets of customers, end users, and applications. For example, "Entertainment" was chosen as a potential market because of the strong interest we received from computer animators making 3D movies like *Toy Story*. Our tool would make it easier for them to design on the computer without their design intent being compromised. They could also do it in a much more productive manner than was available at that time.

Similar to what we learned in the digital entertainment industry from an application standpoint, the "Industrial Design" industry was selected based on feedback that product designers wanted to create 3D shapes on the computer in a way that was as easy as working with physical clay.

Likewise in each group—Medical Visualization (of 3D data), Surgical Simulation (and training), Micro Surgery (robotic-controlled operating room procedures), Geophysical Visualization (analysis of 3D seismic data), Non Visual C.H.I. (Computer Human Interface for the blind to use computers),

Table 1.1 The SensAble Market Segmentation Chart

Industry	Entertainment	Industrial Design	Medical Visualization	Surgical Simulation	Micro Surgery	Geophysical Visualization	Non Visual C.H.I.	Prototyping
End User	• Animator	• Stylist • Designer	• Radiologist • Surgeon	• Med Student • Surgeon	• Surgeon	• Geophysicist	• Blind Person	• Engineer
Application	• Sculpt • Animation • Paint	• Sculpt • Paint • Modeling	• Segmentation • Navigation • Surgical planning • Diagnosis	• Training • Surgical planning	• Opthalm. Surgery • Neurosurgery	• View enhancement • Drill plan	• H.U.I.	• Design review • Model evaluation
Benefits	• Ease of use • Reduce cycle	• Reduce cycle • Increase accuracy	• Ease of use • Increase accuracy	• Increase use of new tech. • Increase accuracy	• Reduce cycle • Increase accuracy	• Reduce errors • Increase yields	• Increase access, "mainstream"	• Reduce cycle • Improve designs
Lead Customers	• Disney • ILM • Dreamworks	• Toyota • Ford • Rollerblade	• Brigham & Women's • German Cancer Rsrch	• U. of Colorado • Penn • BDI	• Dr. Ohgami • Ottawa Eye	• BHP • WMC / CSIRO	• Certec • U. of Delaware	• Volkswagen • Stratasys • Toyota
Market Characteristics	• Early adopt. • High-priced talent • High growth	• Dislike CAD & computers • High-priced talent	• Mainstream • High-priced talent • HMO	• Mainstream • High-priced talent • HMO	• Early adopt • High-priced talent • HMO • Not computer automated	• Late main. • Oligopoly	• Late main. • No money • Gov't sponsor	• Mainstream • Pressure to reduce prod. cycle
Partners/ Players	• Alias • Soft Image • Discrete Logic	• PTC • Alias • Imageware	• GE • Siemens • Picker	• Smith & Neph • Heartport • Ethicon • US Surgical	• Toshiba • Hitachi	• Landmark • Fractal Graphics	• IBM • Apple • SUN • HP • Microsoft	• PTC • Solid Works
Size of Market	40,000	X00,000	X0,000	X0,000	X,000	X,000	X,000,000	X00,000
Competition	Watcom	None yet	None yet	Immersion	None yet	None yet		None yet
Platform	• SGI • Windows	• SGI • SUN	• SGI • SUN	?	None	• SGI • SUN	• Windows	• SUN, HF
Complementary Assets Required	• NURBS • Stylus • Dynamics	• NURBS • Stylus	• Voxels • Stylus • VRML	• 6 DOF • Custom devices	• 3 Finger scaling	• Voxels • Stylus	• Windows I/F • P300	• NURBS • VRML • Dynamics

and Prototyping (virtual prototyping of CAD/CAM files to see how they worked together; for example, to check to see assembly feasibility)—we had enough evidence to know that the market satisfied well the seven key questions presented earlier in this step.

For each of these segments, we then had to do primary market research to fill out the matrix.

We had the luxury of already selling to technological enthusiasts, which gave us enough of a revenue stream that we could spend over three months on the market segmentation analysis. You will want to spend at least a few weeks, but you are unlikely to have the good fortune to be able to spend several months.

Our matrix included a line for "platform," which referred to the computer operating system and hardware that our technology would require for it to be adopted by that particular market segment. This may or may not be relevant to you but it was to us at the time because there was a big difference from running on dedicated graphics computers (Silicon Graphics Incorporated—SGI—at the time) versus much lower-cost personal computers.

Our row labled "Complementary Assets Required" depended on which industry we would target. For us, the row labeled "Complementary Assets Required" varied quite a bit depending on the industry we would target. For the animator in the entertainment market segment, we included a NURBS (which stands for Non-Uniform Rational B-Splines) geometry engine so it could output the data files to the Alias Wavefront visual rendering animation suite. This software program was used by animators worldwide to create three-dimensional animated images rendered in color to make the captivating scenes you see in animated movies today. The device would also have to include a stylus because the animators loved to sketch in 2D and were very accustomed to this. The last piece that we needed to include was a dynamics engine so that the figure could move in a realistic manner. All three of these items were generally available through other vendors so they were not critical parts. However, it was important to have a very specific understanding of what our end users were using, to know what else was needed to make our system complement existing systems, and to have access to this information or technology through other vendors.

For our partners and customers, NURBS was a very specific requirement that we needed to fulfill because it was the required data format to fit with the significant investments already made. In other words, we needed to understand what data was upstream of our solution, how we would receive it, what was downstream from our solution, and how we had to output files.

SUMMARY

The market segmentation process identifies multiple potential market opportunities. Once you have a list of potential markets, direct market research-based analysis on a finite number of market segments will help you determine which markets are best for your idea or technology. The goal of the research is not to provide a perfect solution, but to present a wide spectrum of market opportunities as you start to think about where you will focus your business. Primary market research, which involves talking directly with customers and observing them, is by far the best way to identify good market opportunities. This research will help you select a beachhead market in the next step.

STEP 2

Select a Beachhead Market

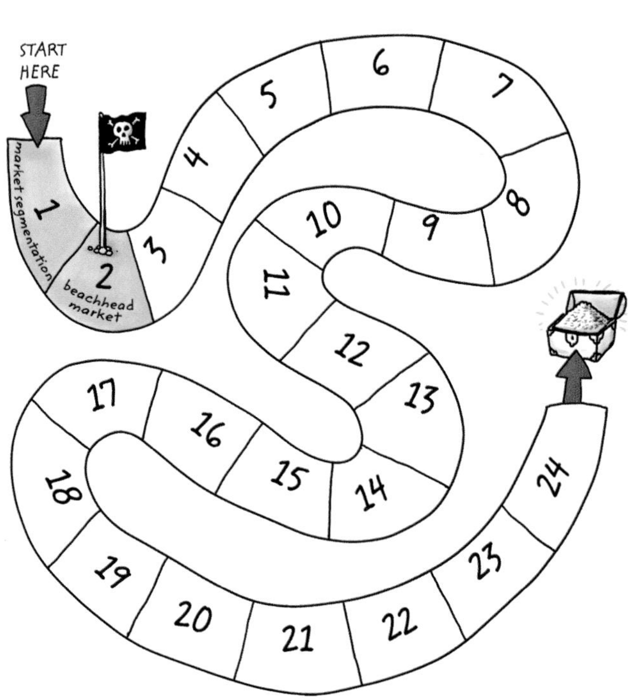

IN THIS STEP, YOU WILL:

- Analyze your top 6–12 market opportunities and choose *one* to pursue.
- Further segment that market to determine your beachhead market.

Selecting a beachhead market is part of the critical process of narrowing your focus and attention to one critical area of attack.

In the previous step on market segmentation, you built a matrix based on your primary market research on your top 6–12 markets. Now, select just one market opportunity from the matrix to pursue as your beachhead market; ignore the other markets.

Almost all first-time entrepreneurs find that ignoring market opportunities is difficult and even painful. They doggedly hold on to the idea that more markets increases their odds of success and that they are best off hedging their bets until one market takes off.

In fact, such thinking will decrease your odds of success, because you and your new enterprise will lack the necessary focus required to succeed. A key determinant of success for entrepreneurs their ability both to select a market and to stay disciplined by deselecting the other markets.

Focus can be difficult, especially for entrepreneurs. People keep options open even when it is not in their best interest, according to former MIT professor Dan Ariely, who discusses the topic in his 2008 book, *Predictably Irrational*. According to his research, when people are given what appear to be multiple paths to success, they will try to retain all the paths as options, even though selecting one specific path would have guaranteed them the most success.

By choosing a single market to excel in, your startup can more easily establish a strong market position, and hopefully a state of positive cash flow, before it runs out of resources. By focusing in this way, you will position yourself to most quickly achieve the all-important positive word of mouth (WOM) that can be the source of success or failure for entrepreneurs.

HOW TO CHOOSE YOUR BEACHHEAD MARKET

In military operations, if an army wants to invade enemy territory with water access, the army may employ a beachhead strategy, where the army lands a force on a beach in enemy territory, controlling that area as their base to land more troops and supplies, and to attack other enemy areas. The 1944 invasion of Nazi-controlled Europe by the Allied forces is one of the most famous examples of a beachhead strategy. The Allied forces established beachheads on the shores of Normandy, which allowed them to gradually capture all Nazi-controlled territory on the European mainland. Without conquering the beachheads, they would have had no starting point for their invasion.

Likewise, your beachhead market is where, once you gain a dominant market share, you will have the strength to attack adjacent markets with different offerings, building a larger company with each new following.

In many cases, there are multiple paths to success, so it is not imperative to choose the absolute best market. (SensAble is a good example of a technology that could have been successful in any number of market segments.) Therefore, get started doing, rather than getting stuck in "analysis paralysis." Your goal is to start a company, not become a professional market analyst. Action will produce real data that will tell you quickly if the market will or will not be viable. If the one you have selected is a viable market, great. If not, you will still hopefully have time and resources because you acted quickly and efficiently, to allow you to return to your matrix and attempt a second market.

The seven criteria I mentioned in Step 1 for narrowing your market opportunities are also useful in choosing your beachhead market:

1. Is the target customer well-funded?
2. Is the target customer readily accessible to your sales force?
3. Does the target customer have a compelling reason to buy?
4. Can you today, with the help of partners, deliver a whole product?
5. Is there entrenched competition that could block you?
6. If you win this segment, can you leverage it to enter additional segments?
7. Is the market consistent with the values, passions, and goals of the founding team?

It is better to avoid selecting the largest or very large markets, even if they seem like the "best" segments. The first market you attack will be a significant learning experience for you, so you are better off learning in a smaller market where you can quickly get high exposure among the base of potential customers. This principle is similar to learning a sport—you will learn a lot from playing against someone slightly better than you. If you start by playing against a top professional, you will learn only that the professional is very good at the sport—you might as well be watching from the sidelines. Choose a smaller beachhead market—for example, if you live in a small geographic region, start there before trying to launch in a larger region. Large companies do the same thing; they test-market new products in lower-exposure countries and regions before rolling them out worldwide.

YOUR BEACHHEAD MARKET STILL NEEDS TO BE SEGMENTED FURTHER

As you begin to focus on your beachhead market, you will quickly recognize that it almost surely can be segmented into smaller markets. This is standard good practice. You should not worry about being focused on too small a market (we will check the Total Addressable Market size in a later step) as I have yet to see an entrepreneur focus too much—it is always the other way around, where the entrepreneur doesn't focus enough. You want to start in a market where you have great ability to dominate in a relatively short time period; a narrow, focused market is the best way to do so.

How do you tell if your market is targeted enough? You want to continue segmenting until your market opportunity matches the three conditions that define a market. This definition expands on one that Geoffrey Moore presents in *Inside the Tornado.*

Three Conditions That Define a Market

1. The customers within the market all buy similar products.
2. The customers within the market have a similar sales cycle and expect products to provide value in similar ways. Your salespeople can shift from selling to one customer to selling to a different customer and still be very effective with little or no loss of productivity.
3. There is "word of mouth" between customers in the market, meaning they can serve as compelling and high-value references for each other in making purchases. For example, they may belong to the same professional organizations or operate in the same region. If you find a potential market opportunity where the customers do not talk to each other, you will find it difficult for your startup to gain traction.

These three criteria for defining a market mean that you will get efficiencies of scale in the market and you have a good chance to do that magical thing that all startups want, "to go viral."

EXAMPLE

SensAble Technologies

After much deliberation, we chose the industrial design industry as our beachhead market based on the seven criteria above, but we had not segmented the market any further, so after choosing the market, we discovered that industrial designers could and should have for our situation be divided into three distinct groups. One group handles rectangular shapes with sharp edges, incorporating a lot of simple geometry. A second group handles highly stylized shapes with smooth surfaces, best represented by mathematical equations. A third group works with highly organic and sculpted forms, often designing with clay.

Our product was most appropriately suited for free-form designing, so the third group was the optimum market for us to focus on. The customers in this group were primarily toy and footwear companies with extensive clay studios and many sculptors among their designers (Figure 2.1).

Much to our surprise, we were able to group toy and footwear companies as one market, because industrial designers in the toy and footwear industries acted so similarly that they completely met the

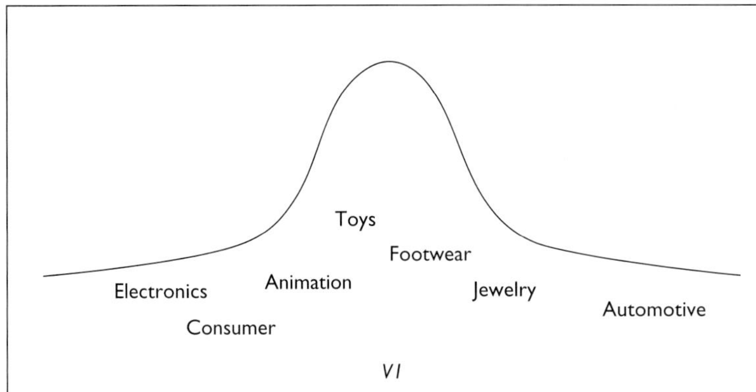

Figure 2.1 The toy and footwear markets were our primary focus. The next adjacent markets were likely animation and jewelry, but we would need to do more research when we prepared to scale.

three conditions of a market presented earlier in this step. They both used lots of clay to sculpt highly organic, 3D art shapes that were shipped to China on a very tight schedule. They would buy the same design products and use them in the same way. The pressures they faced were the same. The sales processes and value propositions were identical. Further, in a very telling sign, the designers frequently moved between toy and shoe companies to advance their careers; they even belonged to the same subgroup in the Industrial Design Society of America.

Smart Skin Care

In one of my classes, a PhD student entered with a promising new technology out of the laboratory of MIT professor Bob Langer. The student, Pedro Valencia, figured out how to synthesize more quickly nanoparticles for medical uses. One particular application was a nano-scale polymer coating that binds to skin and can slowly release medication over a 24-hour period.

Pedro and his team spent weeks researching different applications for this polymer, including medical applications in hospitals and outpatient services, including treating cancer. Another market segment they considered was sunscreen, using the time-release feature to slowly release sun-blocking chemicals over a long period of time. After deliberating, they found that a consumer market such as sunscreen required less time and money than medical markets, which need a thorough FDA review. The consumer market would allow the team to work closely with real customers and get a feedback loop going so they could more efficiently develop the technology into a product.

However, the sunscreen market proved to be too large and too diverse for the team, which continued to subsegment the market through primary customer research. Eventually, they settled on one of the subsegments, extreme athletes in their thirties who do triathlons. These athletes are extremely competitive with a lot of disposable income that they spend on their fitness. When the team approached a number of these athletes with their idea, they were extremely positive toward the concept (or potential product). The team also realized that if these extreme athletes bought the product, other markets would be easier to enter. The extreme athlete proved an appropriate choice for a beachhead market.

SUMMARY

Choose a single market to pursue; then, keep segmenting until you have a well-defined and homogenous market opportunity that meets the three conditions of a market. Focus is your ally.

STEP 3

Build an End User Profile

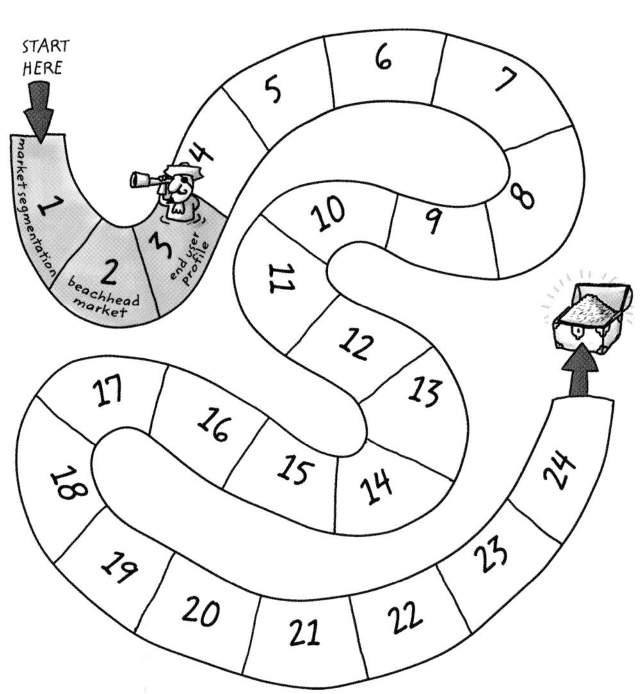

IN THIS STEP, YOU WILL:

- Use primary market research to flesh out a detailed description of the typical end user within your market segment.

Start by beginning to define your customer with a target customer profile.

Now that you have identified a specific beachhead market, you will need to learn about your target customer. It is critically important that you recognize that to be successful, you must build your business based on the customer you are serving, rather than pushing onto the market the product or service you want to sell.

Each customer actually consists of an *end user* and a *decision-making unit*. The end user very likely is an integral part of the decision-making unit but may or may not be the most important person within it. More specifically:

- **End User:** The individual (a real person!) who will use your product. The end user is usually a member of the household or organization that purchases your product.
- **Decision-Making Unit:** The individual(s) who decide whether the customer will buy your product, consisting of:
  - ***Champion:*** The person who wants the customer to purchase the product; often the end user.
  - ***Primary Economic Buyer:*** The person with the authority to spend money to purchase the product. Sometimes this is the end user.
  - ***Influencers, Veto Power, Purchasing Department, and so on:*** People who have sway or direct control over the decisions of the Primary Economic Buyer.

In this step, you will build a profile of the end user that is specific enough for calculating the Total Addressable Market size of your beachhead market. Later, you will add much more specificity by identifying one end user who fits the End User Profile to serve as your Persona. Your focus will be on the end user, because if the end user does not want your product, you will be unable to reach your customer.

You may think that after choosing a beachhead market, the End User Profile will be easy. However, it typically requires a lot of time, thought, and further research. You will find that even in your narrow beachhead, the end users are not all alike. You will first need to further focus by choosing a specific demographic of end users.

WHY TARGET A SPECIFIC DEMOGRAPHIC?

Even though your beachhead market is narrow, you will find much variety among the end target users. They may be young or old, they may work and/or live in urban, suburban, or rural settings, or they may be worldly or may have stayed in the same town their whole lives. Most important, they may have different goals, aspirations, or fears. As a startup, you will have to exclude many potential customers in order to stay focused on a key group of relatively homogenous end users, who will provide the much-needed initial cash flow.

As I will note throughout this book, you must continually talk, observe, and interact with your target customer to obtain this information and reconfirm it. Primary market research is fundamental to your success. This is the only way you will collect the invaluable information that is not available anywhere else and you will understand what is behind the information. Once you have done this primary market research, it may well be the most valuable information you will have. Good, direct customer research is paramount to this process; you will not be able to simply think through the profile on your own.

Your goal is to create a description of a narrowly defined subset of end users with similar characteristics and with similar needs. Look for a subset the same way you looked for a beachhead market. Trying to sell a product to a wide variety of end users is as unfocused as trying to sell to multiple markets. Your sales strategy may not be equally effective for both 25-year-olds and 50-year-olds; your feature sets may differ depending on the priorities of the end user. Therefore, you will not try to describe every end user. You do not want to spend your time and resources trying to be everything to everybody.

POTENTIAL CHARACTERISTICS TO INCLUDE IN YOUR END USER PROFILE

- What is their gender?
- What is their age range?
- What is their income range?
- What is their geographic location?
- What motivates them?
- What do they fear most?
- Who is their hero?
- Where do they go for vacation? For dinner? Before work?
- What newspapers do they read? Websites? What TV shows do they watch?
- What is the general reason they are buying this product? Savings? Image? Peer pressure?
- What makes them special and identifiable?
- What is their story?

You may not yet be able to answer many of the above questions; they also may not be relevant to your situation—or so you might think at this point. You will revisit many of these questions and more with greater specificity in Step 5 when you build the Persona.

DOES YOUR FOUNDING TEAM INCLUDE SOMEONE IN THE END USER PROFILE?

It is a huge advantage if someone who fits the End User Profile is on your team from the beginning, as this depth of understanding you will then have about your customer will be a critical factor in your success. Because an end user is on your team, you will not have to rely on assumptions, which are often inaccurate about who your end user is and what they want. If you don't have someone from the demographic already on your founding team, you should hire a target end user for your executive team.

EXAMPLES

SensAble Technologies

In the End User Profile for SensAble in Table 3.1, we are starting to understand our target customer in a much more specific way. Yes, there is a demographic cohort to help us build a market size in the next step (which is important), but there is also the rich context that will be so important as we move forward to make this real and will probably be the defining factor in your success.

Ride-Sharing Company, Russia

This student team wanted to create a new ride-sharing service for a group of customers in Moscow who did not have such a service. They focused on younger tech-savvy drivers who they thought would be more likely to use the service, and they were interested in using the new infrastructure of mobile phones and social media to do this in a capital-efficient way that had not been possible before.

When they presented their End User Profile, they were not nearly specific enough in their demographics. The company was trying to be inclusive with its profile, but the result was lost focus.

For the end user's gender and age, they specified both male and female, with an age range of 17–40 years old. This demographic is far too general. Do all males and females ages 17–40 have the same goals, aspirations, and fears?

For the end user's occupation, they listed students, young professionals, migrants to Moscow from rural areas of Russia, and middle management. Likely, the beachhead market was not segmented enough. They should have tried using the question, "Why would the end user want to use my product?" to further segment their beachhead.

They also listed a vague category called "social level" and said their end users were "medium or high" within that category. What does "social level" mean, and how can you be more specific in describing the social level of your end users?

Table 3.1 SensAble End User Profile

Industrial Designer in Toy and Footwear Companies	
Gender	Male (90%), Female (10%)
Age	24–35, estimating that the average is close to 31
Level at Company	Individual contributor and not a manager
Income	\$50K–\$60K per year, depending on the region
Education	Rhode Island School of Design, Pasadena School of the Arts, or other high-end arts school
History	This is not their first job in the industry so they have some experience. However, this is not their end job either. This is something they will do as long as it is interesting and fulfilling. The industry is tough and they realize they can be laid off if things don't go well. This also leads to a lack of strong attachment to their job, so if another job comes up, they will move on without reservation.
Context	The designers see themselves as artists, not businesspeople. While they might want to be doing great art outside of the commercial world, they have realized that they need a paycheck to survive and have made that compromise. They may do some art on the side but they also are serious about wanting to create products that show off their artistic skills, and they are frustrated with products that don't properly convey their very specific design intent. Hence they have not given up using clay studios, which convey design intent much better than the new digital tools that are being forced on them. The new tools are engineering tools that have been modified for designers but make it very difficult to convey design intent. While the designers are tech-competent and even savvy when it comes to creative tools, that is not at their core. It is a means to an end. They might have an Apple computer at home and one in their department, but at the office, they are primarily working on their Windows-based PC.
Personality	The designers like to socialize but would never be confused with fraternity boys. They do not have much money and are careful to not waste it. They drink carefully and/or do light recreational drugs when they go out. They like to sit around and listen to technopop music (like Thomas Dolby) and talk about the arts. They generally wear all black and a good number of them have body piercings and maybe even artfully done tattoos. While they do like to socialize, they can also be quiet and introverted much of the time.

There were some specific factors, such as the end users had smartphones, though they did not specify the type of smartphone, which can be important as there may be significant differences between groups that use different brands of smartphones or providers of service. They also said their users are technologically advanced, early adopters of new tech products, and active users of social networks. All of these can be further specified (which social networks?) as well.

This team really needed to go back and do more primary market research and be much more specific about their End User Profile. Narrowing categories like gender, age, and occupation will give them clarity regarding the specific priorities of that demographic, how they position the product, what features to develop, what their messaging should look like, and how to accelerate word of mouth.

Baseball Buffet

This team was looking to make a one-stop site for sports fans (starting with baseball fans) where they could get information about their favorite team and interact with other like-minded fans. It would be a case of an uncensored ESPN meets Sports Talk Radio, but much more interactive and multidimensional than either. The site could also integrate the then-exploding interest of participating in fantasy sports leagues.

The team decided to focus its product on one very specific part of the sports fan base—young online males between the ages of 18 and 34. This segment was a very attractive group to capture, because liquor, automotive, and electronics companies were anxious to advertise to this demographic as they started to earn significant incomes and form buying habits that might last a lifetime. The team did its primary market research and found there was receptivity. They also used some secondary research to learn more about their demographic.

Figure 3.1 shows a key component of their End User Profile.

The charts presented in the figure indicate that they were able to use certain metrics to narrow their focus to 25-to-34-year-old males making over $75K per year. Implicit in this choice is the team will be deselecting the other demographics and pursuing only one demographic to start. The criteria of "target audience interests" is a good example of needing to confront the brutally honest facts about your demographic, rather than looking at the end user through rose-colored glasses. From the secondary research presented here, the two top website choices for the broader 18–34 age demographic are sites to look at girls (we hope nice sites—but we will have to find out the reality to truly understand the end user) and sports sites.

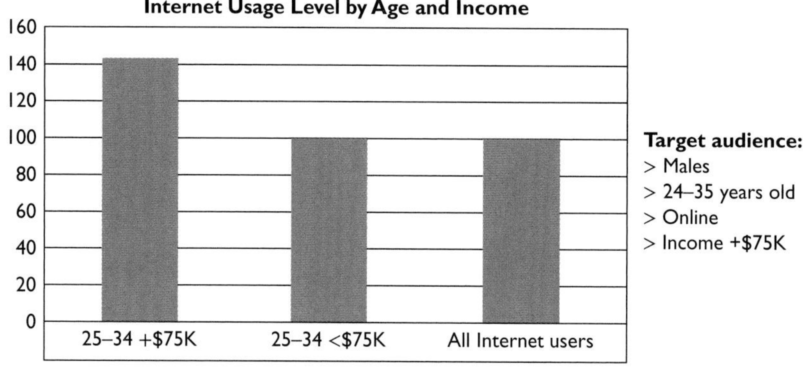

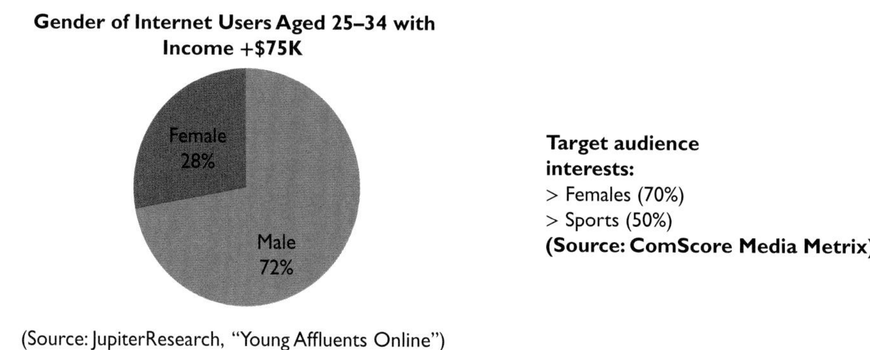

Figure 3.1 Baseball buffet end user profile.

SUMMARY

Your analysis of your target customer is nowhere near complete, but the End User Profile points you in the right direction for future steps. The journey is only beginning, but you are starting off with the right focus—a well-defined target customer. This is a critical step in your search for specificity and starting to make your customer concrete and very real. It is also a critical part of the process to help ingrain the mentality that you should build the company around the customer's needs, not based on *your* interests and capabilities. The latter does matter, but it is secondary to how you should think about your business.

STEP 4

Calculate the Total Addressable Market (TAM) Size for the Beachhead Market

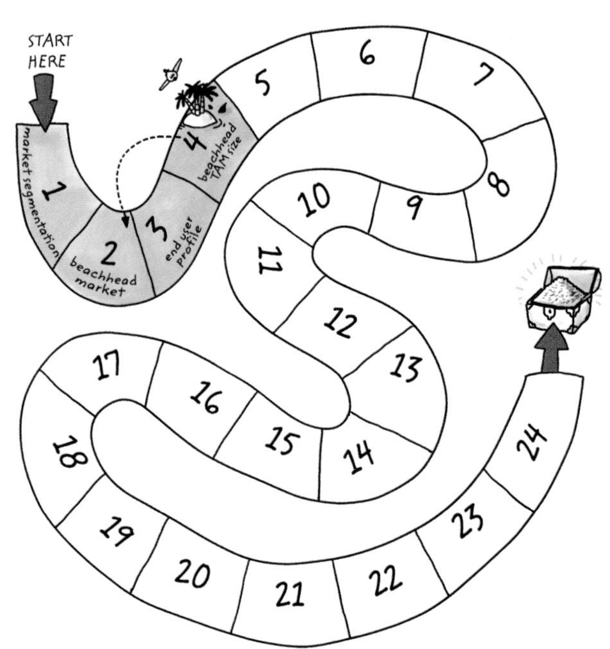

IN THIS STEP, YOU WILL:

- Use the demographics from the End User Profile to determine quantitatively how large your beachhead market is.
- Use this market size number to determine whether you need to further segment the market to have a more appropriately sized beachhead market.

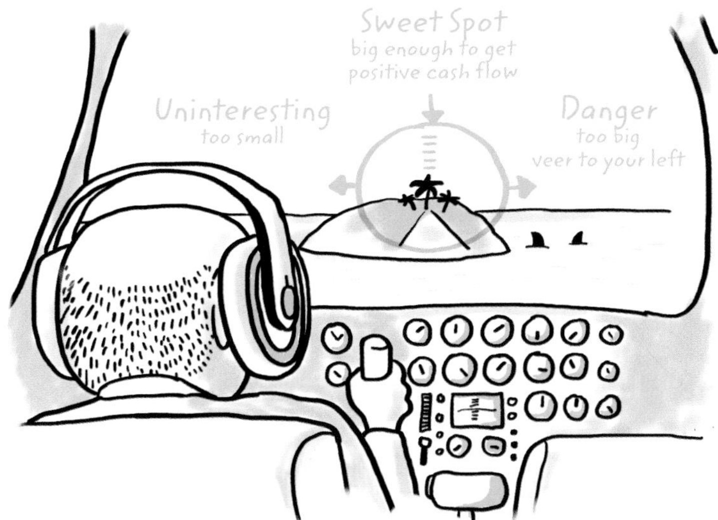

Beachhead TAM calculation is your sanity check that you are headed in the right direction

It is important to start to understand the size of the market you are targeting early; you will modify this as time goes on, but it is wise to be thinking about this point early on and develop at least a rough market size to know you are heading in the right general direction.

Defining your beachhead market and End User Profile provides you with enough specificity to make a first-pass calculation of the Total Addressable Market (TAM) size for the beachhead market. The TAM for your beachhead market is the amount of annual revenue, expressed in dollars per year, your business would earn if you achieved 100 percent market share in that market.

To calculate the TAM, first determine how many end users exist that fit your End User Profile using a bottom-up analysis based on primary market research. Then, complement this with a top-down analysis to confirm your findings. Then determine how much revenue each end user is worth per year. Multiplying the two numbers results in the TAM.

You are looking for a market that is big enough for you to get to critical mass, develop key capabilities, and get to cash-flow positive in the market. However, if the market is too big, you will likely not have sufficient resources to compete, and as a result you may get overwhelmed and either not succeed or have to raise money without much of a track record for potential investors to evaluate.

Entrepreneurs often tend to inflate the TAM with excessive optimism, but a big number is not necessarily better. The goal of this exercise is not to impress others, but to develop a conservative, defensible TAM number that you have faith in.

BOTTOM-UP ANALYSIS

The best way to calculate the number of end users that fit your End User Profile is a bottom-up analysis, often termed "counting noses." Customer lists, trade associations, and other sources of customer information can help you identify how many customers there are, as well as how many end users each customer has. Sometimes this is called "counting noses" because you are getting very specific and you know where each potential customer is.

TOP-DOWN ANALYSIS

A top-down analysis starts by using secondary market research, such as market analysis reports, to determine how many end users meet different characteristics. This data is usually expressed with an inverted pyramid that has several horizontal levels, where the bottom-most level is the smallest and contains all end users who meet your End User Profile. A top-down analysis should be complementary to your bottom-up analysis for two reasons. First, in top-down analysis, you will often overestimate the number of end users in the market because you are not being as specific in your analysis. Second, too much top-down analysis will lead you to focus on spreadsheets, not customers; I have never seen a real live customer hiding in a cell on a spreadsheet.

FROM "HOW MANY END USERS?" TO "SHOW ME THE MONEY"

Once you have counted the number of end users who fit your End User Profile, you will determine how much annual revenue an individual end user is worth. Multiplying the revenue per end user by the number of end users will give you the TAM as dollars per year.

You will have to make some assumptions about how much a customer is willing to pay per end user. As much as possible, base the number on the budgets of the potential customers you have identified. How much are they spending today to accomplish what your product does? How much have they paid in the past for other new products? How much value does your product create for them?

WHAT SHOULD MY TAM BE?

If, at this point, the estimated value of your TAM is less than $5 million per year, it is possible that your new venture has not identified a big enough beachhead market, especially because entrepreneurs often inflate the size of their market and their expected market share. Usually, the market will be even smaller than you think, and you will not be able to achieve the level of market share that you think you will. Your advisors, partners, and investors know these things, so if your TAM is very low to start, they will assume it is actually even lower. In such a small market, it will likely be very difficult to get to cash-flow positive and achieve critical mass.

Generally, a TAM that is between $20 million per year to $100 million per year is a good target. Anything over $1 billion certainly raises flags. It is possible that an initial TAM of $5 million per year could be a successful business, if you can capture the market quickly and convincingly, especially if the gross margins on your product would be very high (e.g., 90 percent as it would be for software, mobile apps, information-based business models) and you do not need a lot of employees to do it. This could create positive cash flow from the market, which would be a significant accomplishment and a good beachhead market.

As you learn more in the later steps, you will likely come back and revisit this calculation and modify it to make it more credible. Determining the TAM is a fundamental part of creating a successful product or service. You will also need to have a clear understanding of your market when presenting your idea or technology to others, such as advisors and investors, because they will expect you to present a TAM figure and explain your logic behind it. However, do not spend an inordinate amount of time on the TAM calculation, because there will be other factors that influence your success as well, such as gross margin, speed, potential for dominant and sustainable market share, and strategic value. As you get more sophisticated, you will also be very interested in the growth rate of the TAM. You would measure that using something called the Compound Annual Growth Rate (CAGR).

EXAMPLES

SensAble Technologies

Our very clear focus allowed us to do a bottom-up analysis in a reasonable amount of time, counting real customers. We had already talked with a few toy companies, such as Hasbro, and we were able to easily determine how many other major toy companies there were from generally available free data at the library. We also befriended a staffer at the Industrial Design Society of America who helped us refine this list.

TOY INDUSTRY LIST OF CUSTOMERS

- Hasbro (United States, Asia, Europe)
- Mattel (United States, Asia, Europe)
- Fisher-Price (United States)
- FP Brands (United States)
- Creata (United States, Asia)
- Equity Marketing (United States, Asia)
- Marketing Store (United States)
- Gemmy (United States)
- Gentle Giant (United States)
- Whitestone (United States)
- Bandai (Asia)
- Tomy (Asia)
- Unitec (Asia)
- Hermon Industries (Asia)
- Luen Shing (Asia)

- Synapse (Europe)
- Schleich (Europe)
- Playmobil (Europe)
- Disneyland (Europe)

One early realization was that toy companies existed in three different geographic regions—the United States, Asia, and Europe. We had not adequately segmented the market, and would need to choose one of these geographic regions.[1] A better way to display the customers, then, was a three-column chart, as shown in Table 4.1.

Then we calculated how many industrial designers were at each company. Since we had a lot of dialogue with the user base and built up trust and confidence, we were able to easily determine how many industrial designers were at one customer, Hasbro. We then spoke to our friends at Mattel and Fisher-Price and determined with high confidence the number of industrial designers at each.

As we determined the exact number of designers at a number of companies, we were able to start calculating a number that we called "designer density," which gave us the number of designers per

Table 4.1 SensAble List of Customers for Toy Industry

Europe	United States	Asia
• Synapse	• Hasbro	• Bandai
• Hasbro	• Mattel	• Tomy
• Schleich	• Fisher-Price	• Unitec
• Playmobil	• FP Brands	• Creata
• Mattel	• Creata	• Hermon Industries
• Disneyland	• Equity Marketing	• Luen Shing
	• Marketing Store	• Mattel
	• Gemmy	• Hasbro
	• Gentle Giant	• Equity Marketing
	• Whitestone	

[1] We actually sold to all three markets when we started out because we did not yet understand the value of defining markets with specificity.

thousand employees and the number of designers per million dollars of revenue. The calculation helped us make educated guesses about other companies where we did not have sufficient time or connections to "count noses."

We did the same process for the footwear industry. This list, likewise, needed to be segmented by region.

FOOTWEAR INDUSTRY LIST OF CUSTOMERS

- Adidas (United States, Europe, Asia)
- Nike (United States, Asia)
- New Balance (United States)
- Reebok (United States, Europe, Asia)
- Fila (United States, Europe)
- Ecco Design (United States, Europe)
- Stride Rite (United States)
- Spalding (United States)
- Rockport (United States)
- Timberland (United States)
- Wolverine (United States)
- Doc Martens (Europe)
- Alsa (Europe)
- Gabor (Europe)
- Kurt John (Europe)
- Clark (Europe)
- Regra Design (Europe)
- Pou Chen (Asia)
- Feng Tay (Asia)
- ASICS (Asia)

The number of industrial designers was a key input to the TAM. We then had to determine how much budget per designer existed for each customer, which required additional data as well as some assumptions and calculations. We started by looking at how much customers were spending today for a similar but inferior digital product, or what they were spending to simply get the job done without a digital product. While there are other costs the customer may presently incur, such as shipping and scanning of physical products, elongated product cycles, and additional iterations, we focused on how much the customer spends per designer; this was an easier data point to tabulate and seemed to best represent our market potential.

Each customer budgeted for a clay workbench for each designer, which when fully equipped, cost approximately $20,000 per bench in the United States and Europe, with a five-year replacement cycle. Each customer also budgeted for a digital workstation and software for each designer that costs about $15,000 in the United States and Europe and had a three-year replacement cycle. Both of these costs would be displaced by SensAble's product. (We found that these two items often cost less for companies buying for designers based in Asia, as Table 4.2 shows.)

We also included an estimated annual growth rate, based on our primary market research. While it did not directly affect the TAM calculation, it was a useful data point for future steps that we could easily collect during this round of research. Also, a positive growth number is a good indicator of a healthy market opportunity.

OnDemandKorea

A group of MIT students noticed a very simple market opportunity. Quite a number of their classmates and friends who were born in Korea and living in the United States were particularly interested in staying current with news and shows in their homeland. One of the major ways to do this was to watch Korean soap operas. The students noticed that many of them visited websites where they could watch bootlegged, low-quality versions of these shows. With their background, technical skills, and connections, the students were confident they could build a site that would display much higher-quality video and do it legally. The analogy would be iTunes as compared to Kazaa or the original version of Napster.

So the team dutifully built their End User Profile as you can see in Figure 4.1. They researched the number of Koreans in the United States. The first number they found was a census number of 1.7 million people; but this was a low number, as it is for many immigrant census numbers. These numbers do not include the international students and others who do not register in the census. Further digging and research online unearthed articles suggesting the number was 2.5 million, which was what businesses serving this community used as the more accurate number. While this number was good to know and valuable for the long term, the question that was more relevant to the team was how "How many of these Koreans actually go to the websites that they had seen their Korean friends use?"

To solve this problem, the team worked to identify the 89 websites (including Joonmedia, Bada, and Dabdate) that illegally showed Korean dramas in the United States. Then they used the Internet service Compete to determine the amount of traffic each website received. The total traffic for these websites was 1.2 million unique users. They were validating that there was a market here already. But they were far from done!

Next, the team ran tests to see how much of the user base was female, as opposed to male, as their End User Profile was female, aged 20–35. After they had run many tests, they started to become confident that the ratio was 60:40 (percent of female to male users of these services). That narrowed the base down to 720,000 potential end users. Further tests found that about 55 percent of the user base were in the 20–35 age range. This resulted in 400,000 end users who fit the team's End User Profile.

Table 4.2 SensAble Technologies Beachhead Market TAM Calculation

	United States	Europe	Asia
Industrial Designers/Sculptors (Toys)	1,500	1,000	1,000
Industrial Designers/Sculptors (Footwear)	750	500	500
Estimated Annual Growth Rate	8%	8%	8%
Primary Market Research:			
Price per clay workbench	$20,000	$20,000	$15,000
Price per digital workstation	$15,000	$15,000	$10,000
Life of physical clay workbenches	5 years	5 years	5 years
Life of digital workstations	3 years	3 years	3 years
Annual expenditure per designer (based on assumption that each designer would otherwise have both a clay workbench and a digital workbench, and we can replace them both with our offering)	$9,000	$9,000	$6,333
TAM Calculation:			
Industrial Designers/Sculptors (Toys)	$13,500,000	$9,000,000	$6,333,333
Industrial Designers/Sculptors (Footwear)	$6,750,000	$4,500,000	$3,166,667
Total TAM for Beachhead ($/year)	**$20,250,000**	**$13,500,000**	**$9,500,000**

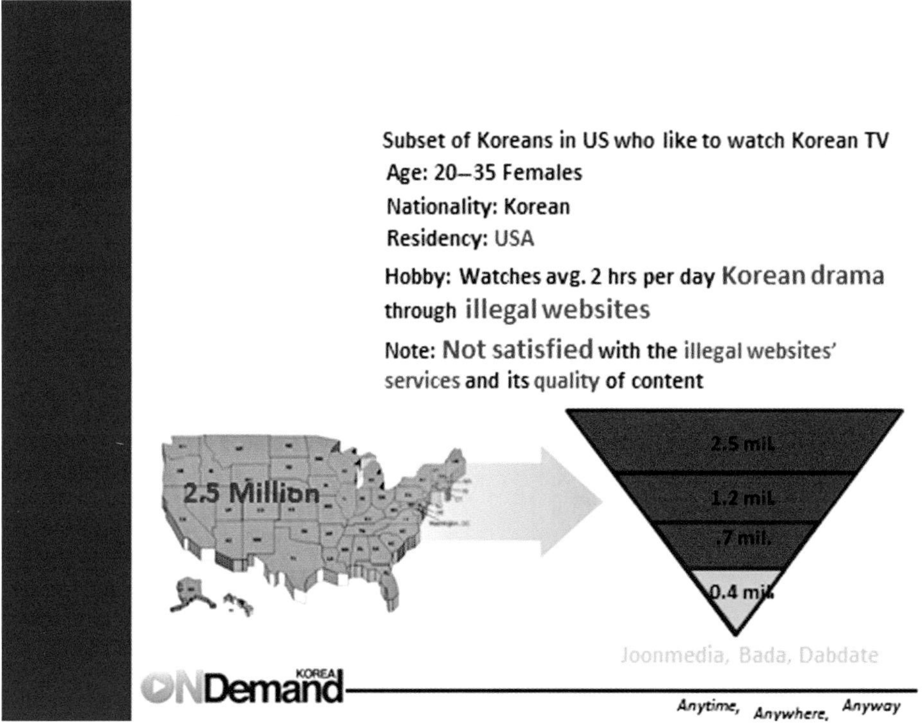

Figure 4.1 TAM sizing example: OnDemandKorea.

While this was an excellent start to calculating the TAM, it did not end here. The TAM is not a number of customers, but rather dollars per year. So to complete the TAM calculation, the team needed to determine how much the 400,000 potential customers would pay in a year.

Toward this end, they assumed they would use an advertising model. This was such a well-defined and attractive customer base that when OnDemandKorea did the job they knew they could, the company would have a very loyal following, spending at least an hour per day on their site. With this information, they researched potential advertising rates and used $1.25 per month, per user as a reasonable target. They assumed no other revenues so they could be on the conservative side. This translates to $15 per year per user. When this is multiplied by the 400,000 primary customers, they arrived at a beachhead TAM of $6 million per year.

While this might not seem a very exciting market for some, especially large companies, because of the company's low costs and high margins, this was a sufficient beachhead market to get them to cash-flow positive. It was also a way to build critical capabilities and critical mass in the company to get started. They were confident that once they won this market, they could expand and increase the revenue per customer with new offerings, or simply expand their market dramatically by adding subtitles in Chinese at very little cost. Once they had the Chinese subtitles, they had become confident from their research that the Chinese living in the U.S. would readily adopt Korean soap operas as well. Once they had their beachhead, there were many ways to grow it, but the beachhead had to be big enough to get them to cash-flow positive and achieve critical mass.

This is a good example of how to do a good TAM calculation for a B2C new venture.

SUMMARY

The TAM is how much annual revenue you would accumulate if you achieved 100 percent market share. This is used only for your first beachhead market. A bottom-up analysis, where you can show how many potential customers you have identified from your primary market research and extrapolated to the broader market, will give a more accurate picture of your market. Complementary to this, but much less compelling on its own, is a top-down analysis where you are working with market analysis reports and extrapolating without direct interaction and validation. Often, very important subtleties are missed in top-down analyses, so you need both.

STEP 5

Profile the Persona for the Beachhead Market

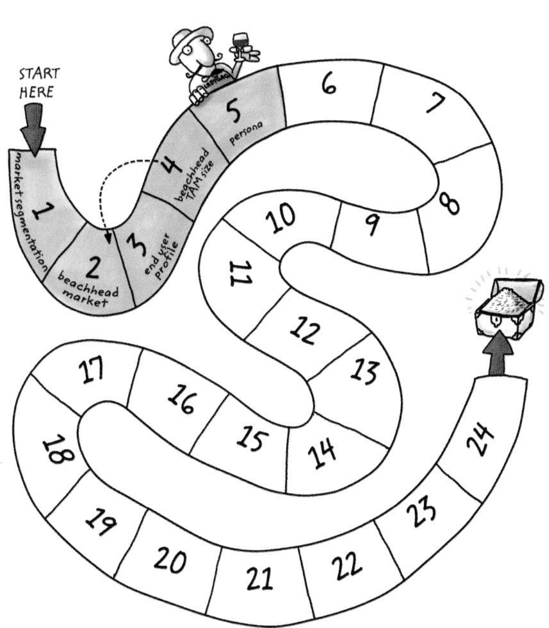

IN THIS STEP, YOU WILL:

- Choose one end user from one potential customer to be your Persona.
- Build a detailed description of that real person.
- Make the Persona visible to all in the new venture so that it gets referenced on an ongoing basis.

The Persona ensures that everyone is unambiguously focused on the same target.

One of the most fun and unifying steps of the 24 Steps process is developing the Persona. Unlike the End User Profile in Step 3, which is a composite of a person that represents your target customer, the Persona is a person who best represents the primary customer for the beachhead market. The Persona you are creating is of one end user from one potential customer who best exemplifies your End User Profile. The process of defining a Persona for your beachhead market makes your target customer tangible so that all members of the founding team, and all employees, have absolute clarity and focus on the same goal of making your target customer successful and happy. Rather than guessing or arguing about what your potential customers might want, the Persona answers these questions definitively.

Those with a marketing background are likely familiar with the concept of a Persona, using a generic name like Mary Marketing or Ollie Owner as a composite of what the marketing team thinks the typical customer is like. This is what they do at HubSpot, which has been extremely helpful for them. But while even a generic Persona can be helpful, it is best to push the process even further. The Persona should be a real person, not a composite.

By choosing an actual end user as your Persona, your Persona becomes concrete, leaving no room for second-guessing. Is your target customer happy with their region's education system? Would your target customer be interested in a puppy? Does your target customer prefer a closed software ecosystem like the one the Apple iPhone provides, or an open ecosystem like the Android mobile operating system? Or does your target customer simply want to check e-mail reliably on the go? You can debate these questions internally, but if your Persona is a real person, there is only one right answer.

No one end user represents 100 percent of the characteristics of every end user in your End User Profile. But as you work toward defining the Persona, you will be able to find someone who matches the profile quite well. You will then focus your product development around this individual, rather than on the more-general End User Profile.

HOW TO CHOOSE AND PROFILE YOUR PERSONA

The process of creating a Persona is important, so you should involve all the key members of your team, regardless of their role in the group. Team members who are involved in the process, even if they do not think they have a lot to contribute, will end up enjoying, embracing, and getting a lot of value out of the process of creating the Persona. They will feel ownership and understand the nuances of the Persona that might not get written down, and gain appreciation for the other members of the team and their perspectives.

If you already have sales, an analysis of the most successful customers to date would be very valuable data and a good starting point. If you have not sold any product yet, then look at the primary market research you have already done, and analyze some of the customers who showed the most interest in your potential offering. Make sure they would actually pay for it and are not "just interested." There is a big difference.

You are looking to answer the question, "If I had only one end user to represent our End User Profile, who would it be?" From your End User Profile, you have a good start. The Persona should conform very well with this profile while also providing more specific details.

You and your team should take the primary market research you have on some of these customers, as well as the End User Profile, and discuss the pros and cons of making each customer the Persona. After this analysis, you will choose one to be the Persona, knowing that you might change it later as you get more information. Don't spend too much time worrying whether you have the perfect Persona; just make your best guess and get the process started.

Then, prepare a fact sheet about the Persona, based on the information you already have. Include a drawing or photograph of the individual. You will typically want to include information about the person's life (born, raised, education, family, age, etc.) as well as the person's job (what company, how many years, training, managers, salary, performance metrics if a B2B case, etc.). All of this information should be specific—not just that they make a five-figure salary or live in the northeastern part of the country, but that they earn $65,000 a year and live in a specific town. By preparing a fact sheet, your team will also identify key facts specific to your business that you will want to include in order for the Persona to be useful to you.

In your fact sheet, you will use the end user's real name. It might seem a bit creepy to use a real name, so if you feel uncomfortable, you can use an alias instead. Typically, once people understand the purpose and role of the Persona, they are okay with using a real name, at least for internal use within the company.

Most importantly, you want to list the Persona's Purchasing Criteria in Prioritized Order, as these priorities will dictate what purchasing decisions the Persona makes. The top priority is the concern that keeps the Persona awake at night. It is the thing that she either fears the most or gets most excited about. It is what will get her fired or promoted and often the most visible thing that could go right or wrong. It is crucial to understand how your customer prioritizes their needs and wants. You will build off of this list throughout the 24 Steps. A list provided by the end user will get you started, but when interviewing your end users, you cannot necessarily believe everything the end user tells you; you should validate what they say. Often the end user actually believes what they are saying, but will in reality take very different actions.

Now that you have identified what facts you have and don't have, interview the end user who is your Persona (you presumably have already met the individual at least once in the course of your primary market research) again and fill in the gaps in what you know. Allow the conversation to be open-ended, because you will likely learn additional facts that are relevant to your Persona. Add this information to the fact sheet in another team meeting to make sure everyone is on the same page and that no crucial details have been omitted or overlooked. Also, go beyond what your Persona says and carefully notice all the details about her as well. Is her desk organized? Does she have pictures in her office? What kind of clothes does she wear? Are there particularly odd characteristics, such as in our Persona of Chuck Karroll (see Table 5.1), where he still has a beeper? These details are often the most telling of all.

Once you have finalized your fact sheet, summarize a few key areas on a sheet of butcher paper or other large sheet of paper, and post it on the wall so that your team does not forget who they are in business for (see Figure 5.1). Some companies make a cardboard cutout of the Persona and keep it

Figure 5.1 Making the Persona visual means everyone on your team will be more engaged in the process and will keep the Persona in the front of their minds.

Table 5.1 Chuck Karroll Persona

Facilities Manager, IBM NE Data Center, in Littleton, MA	
Environment	• Now has just over 20K Blade servers today growing at 15 percent per quarter for the past two years and for the foreseeable future.
Personal Information	• He is second-generation American (parents from Ireland). • Born in Medford, Massachusetts. • Medford High to Middlesex Community College. • Moved to Winchester. • Family with 2 kids (12, 15). • Just turned 40 this year.
Career Context	• Mid-career, 18 years at IBM and not looking to leave. • He is technical in the technician sense, not the engineering development sense. • He is maintenance-focused and his vocational degree is relevant. • Has been in current job for five years and has had three different managers already but hopes to keep this job for next five years at least. • Promotion path forward is to manage more facilities. • Makes $65K per year and has the potential for a 5 percent bonus at the end of the year, based on the unit's overall performance and his contribution as determined by his boss, the data center manager. • Eligible for salary increase each year, based on his appraisal (can be between 0 and 12 percent). • He has been consistently ranked a 1 or 2 (on a scale of 1–5 where 1 is the best) in his yearly performance review, with reliability and supporting the business unit's growth as two key metrics upon which he is rated.
Information Sources	• He prefers people to websites when he looks for information and answers to questions. • Belongs to AFCOM (association for data center management professionals) and gets a lot of information from them, and especially likes to go to the Data Center World conference in early October each year in Las Vegas. • Second-biggest influence is the Uptime Institute. • Has started to look at Green Grid but not impressed.

Table 5.1 *Continued*

Facilities Manager, IBM NE Data Center, in Littleton, MA	
	• Also starting to get forwarded e-mail about a blog (Hamilton and Manos) that other influential facilities managers are starting to read, and he has recently bookmarked it himself
Purchasing Criteria in Prioritized Order	1. Reliability (highest priority) 2. Growth (high priority) 3. Costs (medium priority) 4. "Greenness" (low priority—extra credit)
Other Noteworthy Items	• Drives a Ford F-150 pickup truck and always buys American • He wears a beeper that is always on • Listens to country music • He used to be a volunteer fireman and is proud of it. He makes level-headed decisions when there is a crisis, calling in his training to act fast and put out fires

in the office. Other leading-edge companies pull up an electronic version of the Persona when making important decisions in order to discuss what the Persona's perspective would be on the subject.

THE PERSONA IS MORE THAN JUST AN EXERCISE

The value of the Persona persists well beyond the completion of this step. The Persona should become a touch point as you think about decisions going forward. What features should you prioritize? Drop? How should you allocate resources? Who should you hire to sell the product? What should your message be? Who should you partner with? Where do you go to meet your customers? Who is influencing your customer's mindset on your product?

The process of answering these questions starts to bring alignment among the team and resolves misunderstandings that are bound to occur from imprecise communications. Once the Persona is done, it is also useful to maintain this alignment going forward. If done effectively, it will help guide all kinds of decisions and create a consistent vision throughout the company.

You may find that you made errors while developing your Persona fact sheet, or that your Persona does not adequately represent the End User Profile, so you may need to go back and revise your Persona in an iterative fashion in later steps. This is not only okay, but highly recommended and a productive exercise.

The point is that the Persona build is not a one-time event but rather should be visible or at least accessible to all members of the team as you move forward with your business. It should be your North Star.

SHOULD I CREATE MULTIPLE PERSONAS? IF SO, WHEN?

As we discussed in Step 1 when talking about how we define "customers," companies similar in nature to eBay and Google should actually start out with two Personas. This is not due to a lack of focus, but rather to the fact that their core businesses are two-sided markets; so they needed one Persona for each market. For example, when eBay first started its auction site, it would have had one Persona for a buyer and a completely different Persona for a seller. Likewise, Google, at the beginning, should have had one Persona for its target search user and another Persona for its target buyer of advertisements.

Google and eBay are so large today that they have many personas to match the many areas of their business, and entrepreneurs sometimes like to point to the two companies as reasons why startups too can have multiple personas. However, large companies have the resources to cover multiple markets and use multiple personas. You do not have this luxury, so don't be led astray by what large companies do with personas. Focus on your one Persona; or, if you have a multi-sided market, one Persona for each side of the market.

THE PERSONA HELPS YOU FOCUS ON WHAT TO DO—AND WHAT NOT TO DO

The Persona exercise can even be extended to make personas who you explicitly decide not to serve. Such an exercise can help you to focus and not distract your precious resources. You can even talk about how you handle these customers and efficiently redirect them. It is very hard and takes practice for entrepreneurs to turn away business, but it is exactly that type of focus that will allow you to build a scalable and profitable business. Often in entrepreneurship, your success is determined as much by what you do not do as by what you do.

EXAMPLES

Mechanical Water Filtration Systems Persona (B2B)

The team working on this project had an idea for a water filtration system that they thought could be best deployed in a beachhead market of cooling data centers, specifically those at large companies or real estate entities that manage large data centers shared by multiple clients. The TAM was calculated to be $50 million per year, with a compound annual growth rate of 20 percent. Therefore, it was an attractive and properly sized market, but one that would rapidly attract competitors as well. As such, the team needed to be focused and conquer this market quickly.

The team initially thought the end user would be the data center manager; but, their primary market research found that the actual end user was the facilities manager, who reports to the data center manager. The facilities manager also controlled the budget that would purchase a water filtration system. After a half-dozen interviews with facilities managers at these data centers, the team started to get a clear picture of the end user.

The team eventually decided that one of the potential end users, Chuck Karroll, best represented the facilities manager they were trying to sell to. *(I have changed his name and some of the details to protect his identity.)* The team chose him because they had talked to many customers and they felt he very well represented the customer base. He was also someone that the team had ready access to for ongoing questions. After talking to many customers, it just seemed like an organic and easy process because a pattern had emerged and Chuck fit very well into the recurring theme. (See Table 5.1.)

Notice how you can very much visualize Chuck from these details.

Chuck's background helps the team understand the social pressures and incentives he faces. (There was, in fact, a great deal more the team knew about Chuck, which provided a much deeper understanding of him and his psyche, but I summarized the key points here for the sake of brevity.) His career information helps them understand his performance incentives—promotions, wages, and recognition—and how established he is at the company. They also understand where he gets his information from, which is important because Chuck will be vetting everything that the team tells him against these sources.

These are not generalizations or assumptions based on stereotypes. These observations are based on talking directly with Chuck and other end users who have validated these observations for the beachhead market. Not every volunteer firefighter will identify with Chuck, but many data center facilities managers in this beachhead market will have a similar mentality, even if they don't have a beeper or aren't members of the volunteer fire department (although a surprising number of them do and are).

Chuck's priorities in making purchasing decisions are especially important to the team. When the team first started, they believed their unique selling proposition was being environmentally friendly, but their primary market research showed that Chuck cared much, much more about reliability than reducing his carbon footprint. Sure, there was a lot of talk about "green data centers," but that was a nice-to-have, not a need-to-have. Chuck's main priority is preventing data center downtime, because his customers (higher-ups in his own company) and his customers' customers (the actual paying end customers) expected the data center to be as reliable as an electric utility. If the system went down, Chuck's phone would immediately ring and it would not be pleasant. In fact, it could be the CEO of his business unit, who was generally nice, but irate when the system was down. This was Chuck's biggest fear in life and he would do whatever was necessary to make sure that there were no outages.

After preventing data center downtime, meeting the business unit's growth objectives was priority two since the general manager of the business unit was a very influential person who wanted to make his numbers and keep getting promoted. This could only be done if the data center continued to grow. If Chuck did not meet these growth goals, the pressure would come down from the business unit manager to Chuck's manager (the data center manager); then Chuck would be in jeopardy of being replaced.

Chuck's third priority was to not exceed his budget, which would impact his performance review. He was much more likely to get fired for substandard reliability or not meeting growth objectives, but staying within budget was important as well. In fact, if he did a great job with the first two priorities, he was given a bit of a pass on priority three.

Environmental issues ranked only fourth in his priorities. He had to be conversant in green issues, and would put together an annual e-mail to his manager and the center's new "green guru" about environmentally friendly steps he was taking, but doing well on environmental issues was considered the way a student considers an extra-credit problem on a test—nice to have, but not the main thing.

SensAble Technologies

At SensAble, we had a Persona, though it did not fit perfectly with our End User Profile. Let's call our Persona Ed Champ (that was not his real name) who was actually the manager of the designers. He was 40 years old, approximately 10 years older than the target profile, but he understood and empathized with the designers. He was young in spirit for his age, but he also had enough perspective to give us meaningful answers when we asked questions. As in the previous example, he not only had deep domain expertise, but he understood the rational, the emotional, and the social considerations of our end user, because he was from that group and still resided deeply in that territory. It was key, too, that we had a terrific relationship with him. When we had questions about product development (e.g., the priority and value of specific features) or sales and marketing (e.g., pricing, messaging, decision-making process), and we could not figure out the answers based on the description of our Persona, we would simply call and ask him.

The profile of Ed Champ is shown in Table 5.2.

It is interesting that after all these years, I can still see this person and his white flowing hair and stocky build. In fact, when writing this book, I was able to write the description below off the top of my head, because he seemingly was part of our family.

Table 5.2 Ed Champ Persona

Name	Ed Champ
Title	Sculpting Manager, Boys' Toys R&D, Hasbro, Pawtucket, Rhode Island
Age	40 (he is about 10 years older than the developers he hangs out with; but he fits in well with the group and is thought to be one of the guys—they are almost all guys—even though he is their supervisor)
Income	$73.5K (he is the highest paid in the group, by a good margin, due to his seniority; he has been at Hasbro in this location for 14 years and has been a top performer and promoted through the ranks)
Schooling	Missouri State University—Bachelors of Fine Arts & Science: Sculpture and Anatomy (he secretly admires Rhode Island School of Design—RISD—graduates but that is not how he got here)
Personal	Has a girlfriend, but no talk of marriage; he seems to be married to his job. He has a child from a previous relationship, but the child does not live with him; many of his friends are gay.
Career Promotion	It is very unlikely he will get further promoted as he does not like management and it is not his forte. He hopes to make more money to keep up with inflation, but mostly he just loves his job and living in Rhode Island with creative types—and at his age, the job security is good.
Industry Associations	A very strong and active member of IDSA (Industrial Design Society of America) above all else. There are local meetings which he looks forward to. These can be epic, in part because of the relevant content, but even more so because he gets

(Continued)

Table 5.2 *Continued*

	to hang out with people from RISD, Pasadena Arts Center College of Design, and the like, and talk into the night about the latest in art and design. There are national meetings as well, and he sometimes he goes to the big SIGGRAPH conference (often held in Los Angeles) where there are some great parties.
Music	His group listens to technopop artists like Thomas Dolby; while he is not wild about it, he likes it.
Socializing	His social life often revolves around his work. He likes to hang out with designers; but they don't have much money so when they go to bars, they drink wine (but not beer) and sip whatever drink they get so that it lasts. They have little disposable income so they have to be very careful to not blow money. Interestingly, they are more likely to do designer drugs (e.g., ecstasy) than to lose control by getting drunk. At the bars they go to in Providence, he and his friends often wear all black. It is also common for them to have body piercings, wear jewelry, and have discreet tattoos. But always, their life revolves around art and talking about art.
Heroes	Milton Glaser, John Lasseter (Disney & Pixar), Steve Jobs
What Gets Him Motivated	Making great products and seeing them get to market with his design intent.
What He Fears Most	1. Having to leave Hasbro because it is bought or something worse. This is not true for the other designers, but unique to him. 2. Putting out a product that he feels is crap because he ran out of time to get it done right. 3. Having his design intent ruined by the engineers after he sends it on to them.
Priorities	1. Time to market. 2. Being able to express his design intent. 3. Being assured his design intent is not lost when engineers get ahold of it.

SUMMARY

The process of developing a Persona provides specific details about the primary customer within your beachhead market. You are now selling not to some "end user profile," but to a specific individual. Your whole team should be involved in this process to ensure everyone is on the same page and truly understands the Persona, so they can maintain a customer-based focus. An important detail to understand about the Persona is his or her Purchasing Criteria in Prioritized Order. You should really understand your customer and what makes them tick, not just at a rational level, but at an emotional and social level as well. The better you understand your Persona's needs, behaviors, and motivations, the more successful you will be at making a product and a new venture to serve them. Once you have made a picture or visual of your Persona and fleshed out the fact sheet, make it all visible within your business so that everyone works toward the same common goal.

STEP 6

Full Life Cycle Use Case

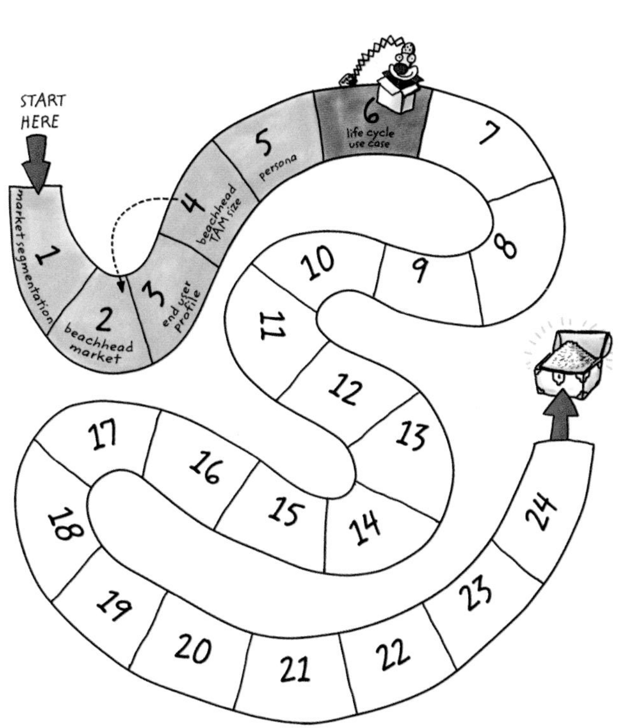

IN THIS STEP, YOU WILL:

- Describe in detail how your Persona finds out about your product, acquires it, uses it, gets value from it, pays for it, and buys more and/or tells others about it.
- Understand why this expanded use case is important to identify and resolve problems in the most timely and cost-effective manner.
- Gain additional clarity and alignment throughout your team by detailing the various aspects of the Full Life Cycle Use Case.

Building a Full Life Cycle Use Case further focuses the discussion on what specifically your product will do for your customer . . . and what your customer will do with it.

Now that you have assembled great specificity about your end user and are focused on your target customer, you have to collect equally specific details about how this person will use the product. You will construct a use case, but your use case will be more expansive than the traditional definition.

You must determine how your product fits into your Persona's value chain. What are the key interface points? Why exactly would customers want to acquire the product? What barriers to adoption might arise? The Full Life Cycle Use Case should include not just how the customer would use the product, but also the acquisition (including the payment for the product) and post-installation support processes. To fully complete the analysis, it would be extremely valuable to understand if and when the user would purchase your product again.

Rather than simply describing how your Persona will use your product, you should also detail how the end user determines they have a need for your product. Then determine how they acquire your product and ultimately how you will get paid for your product. You will start by mapping out the process from beginning to end for your Persona and then check to see if it is consistent with other potential customers as well. The easiest way to start is by mapping out how your Persona uses the product once it is acquired. From there, map out the acquisition and post-acquisition support cases.

Once again, you will be using primary market research. It is imperative in this process that you see your product through the eyes of the customer and not through your eyes. When entrepreneurs see the Full Life Cycle Use Case through their own eyes, they tend to overestimate many things. First of all, they overestimate the enthusiasm the customer has for their product. Also, they are often overconfident regarding what the customer will gain from using their product and how easy it will be to use. This type of Full Life Cycle Use Case is often fictional and misses the fact that the user has many competing priorities and may not be particularly interested in taking on risk by integrating a new product from a new company into their value chain. Without doing a complete Full Life Cycle Use Case, you will not notice any problems until your order volume decreases and you are scrambling to gain first-time and repeat customers.

WHAT TO INCLUDE IN A FULL LIFE CYCLE USE CASE

The Full Life Cycle Use Case should first explain how the Persona determines that their existing needs are not being met by existing products, and how the Persona would find out about your product. Since you have been doing extensive primary market research, your Persona likely found out about the product through the course of your research, so you should instead detail how your Persona would have heard about the product if they had been a completely new prospect.

It is helpful to outline the customer's current workflow, because by knowing the customer's current process, it is easier to integrate your product into their operation. Customers who are generally satisfied with their workflow will rarely want to radically overhaul their process even if your product provides benefits over their current system.

The following factors are all essential parts of the Full Life Cycle Use Case:

1. How end users will determine they have a need and/or opportunity to do something different.
2. How they will find out about your product.
3. How they will analyze your product.
4. How they will acquire your product.
5. How they will install your product.
6. How they will use your product (in detail; see the Satisfier example further on).
7. How they will determine the value gained from your product.
8. How they will pay for your product.
9. How they will receive support for your product.
10. How they will buy more product and/or spread awareness (hopefully positive) about your product.

The Full Life Cycle Use Case should be visual, using diagrams, flowcharts, or other methods that show sequence.

EXAMPLES

The "How Will They Use Your Product" Section of a Use Case: Satisfier

The hospitality industry lives and dies by the quality of their customer service. From hotels to restaurants to entertainment venues, the sales and profit of a location fall quickly if customers are not happy when they leave. Regional managers with many locations to oversee have their issues compounded because they need to guarantee the satisfaction of a large number of customers. Regional managers are constantly looking for tools to more accurately and rapidly measure customer satisfaction for their specific environments.

Toward this end, one student team had an idea to take advantage of the increasingly ubiquitous nature of smartphones to provide real-time survey feedback for businesses. After their primary market research, they determined that the quickest and most capital-efficient way to get their company off the ground would be targeting a specific group of food service companies that served universities. The team's idea was to create posters with a picture of the food offerings available on that day and put it at the exit of the eating establishment. Under each picture were two QR (Quick Response) codes that allowed the consumer to easily register either their approval or disapproval of a food option. In such a scenario, the food service companies could get instant feedback on their menu. The student team prepared a mini-use case (Figure 6.1), detailing how the customer would use their product.

1) Management creates one or more surveys on Satisfier's website

2) Banner/flyer is placed on a key location

3) Customers rate their experience using smartphones

4) Results are immediately available on Satisfier's website

Figure 6.1 Satisfier use case.

This is an easily understood segment of the Full Life Cycle Use Case that can be presented to potential end customers for feedback. The team has thought through how its product would be used by the customer to create value. The example forced them to be specific about many things that can otherwise be glossed over. They incorporated not just what their product was (from Step 7) and who the Persona was (from Step 5), but now they could detail how everything interacted and how the entire story would play out. They learned about key people and roles they needed to consider. It generated common understanding and alignment throughout the team regarding the problem being solved and how their product solved it.

Such a use case might seem obvious, but it is much harder than teams anticipate and it is always a valuable touch point as you go forward. This use case, while helpful, is incomplete in that it leaves out many of the early elements (How did your customer find out about your product and then decide to bring it in for a test?) and the later elements (How does the customer pay for your product, get service for it, and ultimately help generate a following for your business by buying more products and/or generating word of mouth for your company?). However this is where most companies begin and then build out the front and back ends.

A More Robust Use Case: FillBee

Another student team was looking to revolutionize the furniture shopping experience by making it possible to see what any combination of furniture in your home would look like before you buy it. Through a sophisticated 3D rendering platform that took in the dimensions of your house or apartment, a 3D world would be created where the user could use a computer to try out different pieces of furniture before purchase. Conceptually it sounded great, but what often works conceptually does not work in reality.

Fillbee started its use case development by mapping the Persona's perspective on how they currently shop for furniture.

A primary pain point in the furniture acquisition process—that the furniture sometimes does not fit in the user's home and has to be returned—is shown clearly in Figure 6.2. To arrive at this point, they went through many visual iterations with a multidisciplinary team. Working backward, FillBee identified "research + plan" as the step where improvements can be made regarding measuring rooms and furniture. FillBee's product also condenses certain steps, such as condensing "research + plan," "browse," and "buy" into one online process rather than a combination in-person/online process.

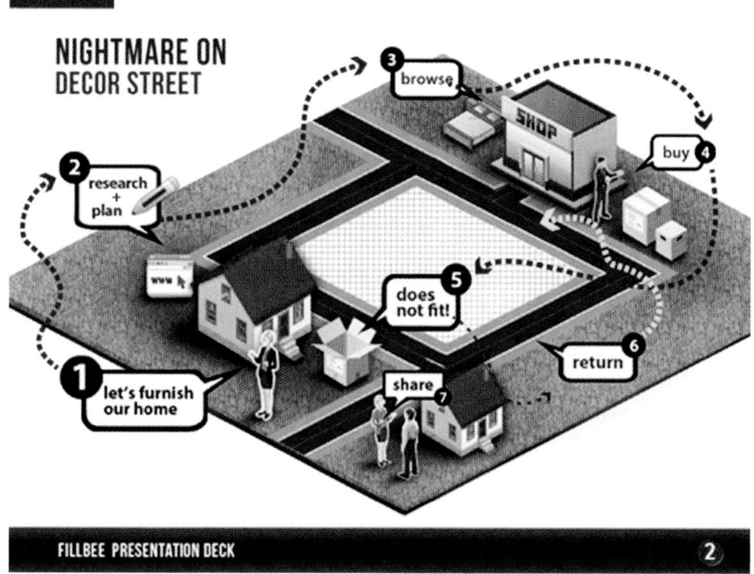

Figure 6.2 FillBee's nightmare on Decor Street (example of Full Life Cycle Use Case before new solution is implemented).

FillBee is also a good example of a product that has a two-sided market, where furniture buyers and furniture sellers are both FillBee customers. Therefore, the team created a Full Life Cycle Use Case for each side of the market. The team demonstrated, in its "how they will use your product" step for the buyer Persona, how to tie in the Persona to each step of the process, using lots of detail to fully flesh out how their buyer Persona, Amanda Phillips, would use the product. The more detail provided, the easier it will be for you to find weaknesses or flaws in your plan, based on your knowledge of the Persona. The deeper your knowledge of the Persona, the better it will be for your analysis. This analysis should increase your confidence level and will be much more cost-effective than trying to fix the problems later on.

As you can see in Figure 6.3, FillBee's use case is rich in details. It is clear they have spent a good deal of time with their Persona. When Amanda says she would like to use the system and is willing to pay for it, she is not speaking in conceptual terms, but rather understands the specifics of what she is agreeing to sign up for.

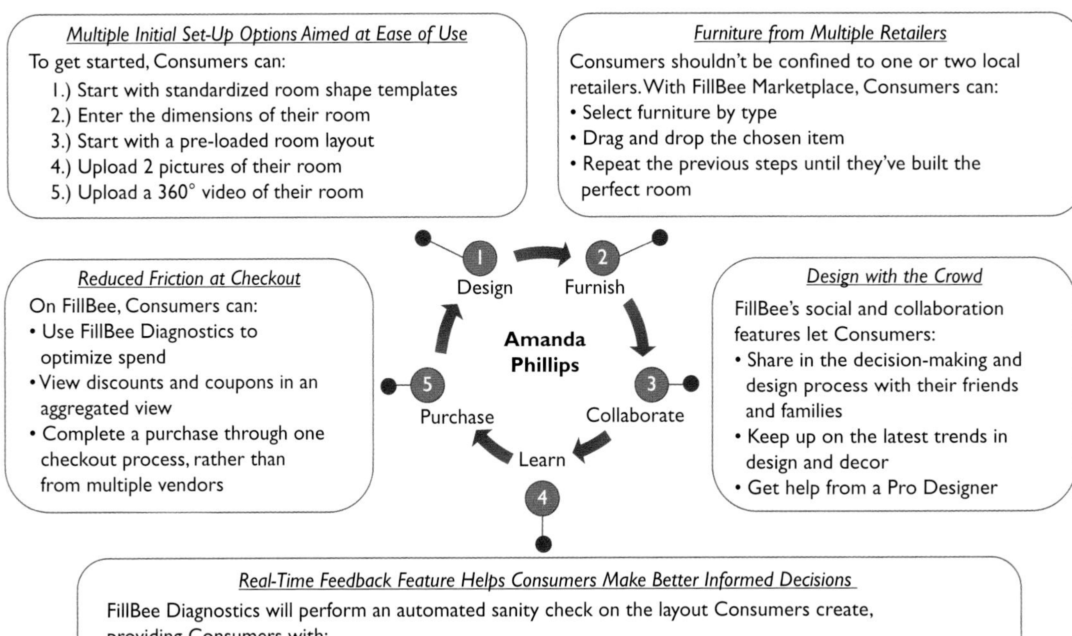

Figure 6.3 FillBee's Amanda Phillips Use Case; good but still missing some upfront and backend elements.

SUMMARY

Creating a visual representation of the full life cycle of your product enables you to see how the product will fit into the customer's value chain and what barriers to adoption might arise. Just showing how the customer uses the product (the typical definition of "use case") will not provide an accurate enough picture to fully understand what obstacles will come up when trying to sell your product to your target customer.

STEP 7

High-Level Product Specification

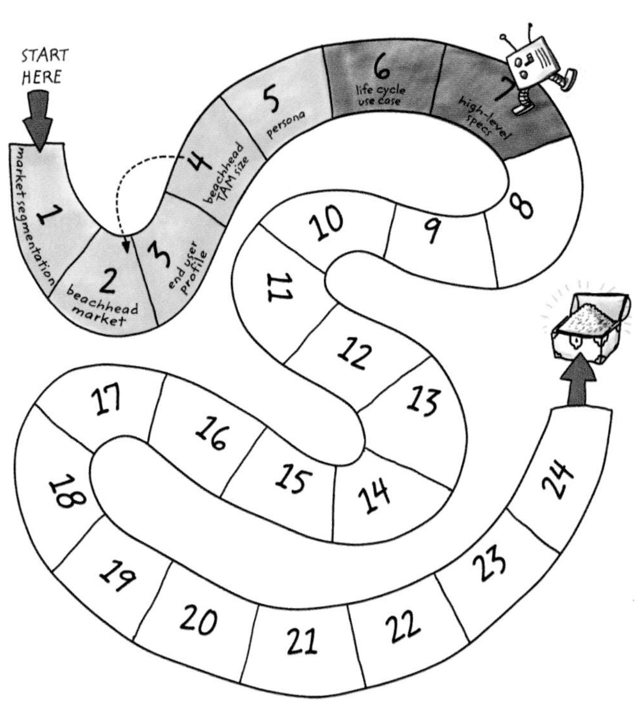

IN THIS STEP, YOU WILL:

- Create a visual representation of your product.
- Focus on the benefits of your product created by the features and not just the features.

Defining the High-Level Product Specification at this time ensures that it is more focused on your target customer and also that everyone agrees on what "it" is.

We are already at Step 7 and only now beginning to outline what your product will look like. So far, you have tightly defined your customer, what they need, and how they will use what you want to sell them, even though the actual details of the product are still rather fuzzy. That all starts to change now. You will start by creating a general definition of the product. You will continue to learn more and to refine this product definition over the remaining 24 Steps.

Traditionalists would argue that this step is coming too late in the process, but if you start by defining the product rather than learning about your customer, your product will likely not connect with customer needs. Even if you believe you know what the product should be, always start with the customer needs and work your way back. This way, you are tailoring your product to the specific beachhead market where you will be able to gain market share, rather than trying to force a product on a market and watching your product get lost in the sea of a large, general market.

CREATING A HIGH-LEVEL PRODUCT SPECIFICATION

A High-Level Product Specification is, at its core, a drawing. It is a visual representation of what your product will be when it is finally developed based on what you know at this point of the process. It is something you draw without understanding all the underlying details, but which gains consensus within your team on where you are going.

It is amazing how much this exercise of drawing a picture of what your product will be forces convergence on a team and removes misunderstandings. It sounds like it should be easy to do, but more often than not entrepreneurs find it harder to do than they initially thought as issues and disagreements arise within the team. Now is the time to resolve any issues, because if you run into them after you have built out your new venture and there is not full alignment on the ultimate deliverable, the cost will be much higher and much time will be lost to inefficiencies.

If the product is software or a website, storyboards should be made showing the user's logical flow from one screen to another. If it is hardware, then diagrams are useful. The key here is that you have something concrete and specific enough that your team understands thoroughly. As you refine the product (with lots of iterations with the target customer), you will all have a common understanding of what the product is.

At this stage, the product does not have to be built and almost surely should not, because this will incur unnecessary costs and create something that your team is too attached to. Keep it high level and don't get distracted at this point. It will not only cost you more if you build at this stage but it will immediately get you distracted, and the team will start to focus on the wrong things, like the particulars of the technology.

This simple visual representation of your product can now also be shared with potential customers, immediately generating an unambiguous understanding of your product. You are not selling the product, but are merely iterating with customers so that you more thoroughly understand the strengths and weaknesses of your product spec. This is very important. There is still a lot left to learn before you are sure you have the right product and know how you will make it, price it, and distribute it.

This product specification will change over time and be refined, like many of the other steps in this book.

THEN, MAKE A PRODUCT BROCHURE

The process of identifying and outlining your High-Level Product Specification is further strengthened by describing the various features of your product, explaining how these features translate into function, and most importantly, describing the benefits your customer gains from each. Always be specific about what you are offering, and how each component of the offering benefits the customer. Why does your target customer need your product?

Some have suggested creating a short, one-page press release about your product at this point. While that can have similar benefits, I prefer the approach of making a brochure for your product. Target the brochure at your Persona, and draw on the work you have done in the Persona and Full Life Cycle Use Case steps (Steps 5 and 6) as well as the visual representation of the product that you have already created.

Building a brochure helps you to see your product from the customer's point of view and provides you with a concrete "straw man" to test with your customer (Figure 7.1). It forces you to see your new venture from your customer's vantage point, in their words. It also allows you to validate your ideas and learn if you are on the right track. Often, when entrepreneurs begin to write down features, they become too inwardly focused. Creating a brochure helps to avoid that pitfall.

EXAMPLES

Altaeros Energies

The students behind Altaeros started with the idea of building a wind turbine in the sky, high enough to get consistent wind, and anchored to a platform in the ocean. Conceptually, it sounded simple, but when the team tried to explain it to other people in the class, the instructors and potential customers,

Spiraling Innovation

Figure 7.1 The spiraling process of innovation with a product can be significantly accelerated by making a brochure—but not getting too attached to it. It is a tool to focus the knowledge capture process.

they encountered a lot of questions regarding what exactly this meant in terms of implementation. It was hard to have a meaningful conversation. Finally, the team built an image of what the product would be, and found that even within the team they had some disagreement on what the product would look like. Ultimately, they came up with the image you see in Figure 7.2. By the end of the process, the team had a common understanding of the product, and could easily use the product spec as a basis for more in-depth customer research.

Baseball Buffet

I first described this baseball-themed website in Step 3, based on the idea that young males aged 25–34 making over $75K were a very attractive demographic that could be captured for hours a day if they had a website focused on one of their primary passions—fantasy sports. The concept was a sound one

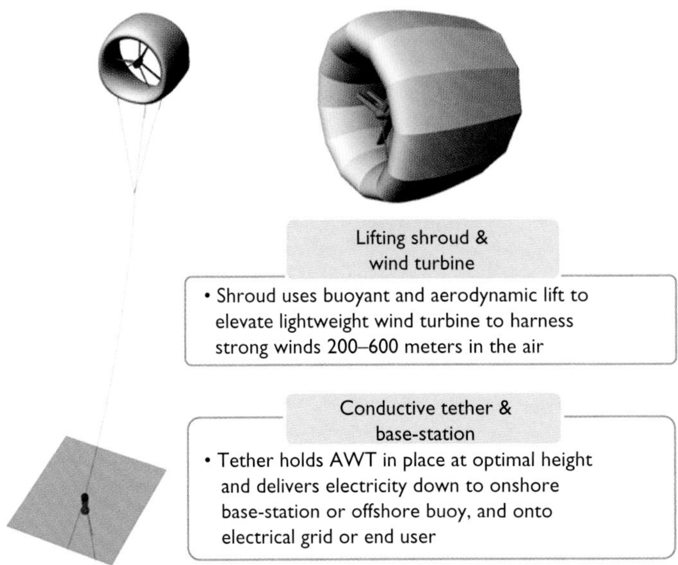

Figure 7.2 High-level product spec: Altaeros.

and attractive on many levels as a potential business. The team developed a clear Persona but had a weaker Full Life Cycle Use Case, so they created the High-Level Product Specification in part to provide clarity to the use case.

A screenshot from this team's website is shown in Figure 7.3. The team aimed to create a single source for all baseball news of interest to a specific user. The "national plate," as you can see, is just one of three tabs displayed on the homepage, which also has a "local plate" and a "personal plate." The team developed renderings of the local plate and personal plate, and then used them to walk through their idea with potential customers, getting some very specific feedback on what the customers liked and did not like.

There was no underlying code at the time for these screens because this was not necessary to achieve their goal of clarifying their product offering. If they had spent the time and money to code a website, the coding would have been money spent unwisely, because the team did not yet have a clear definition of the product and had to be flexible to customer feedback. To put it in technical terms, there were still too many oscillations in the system and it had not yet reached a steady state where efficient development could take place.

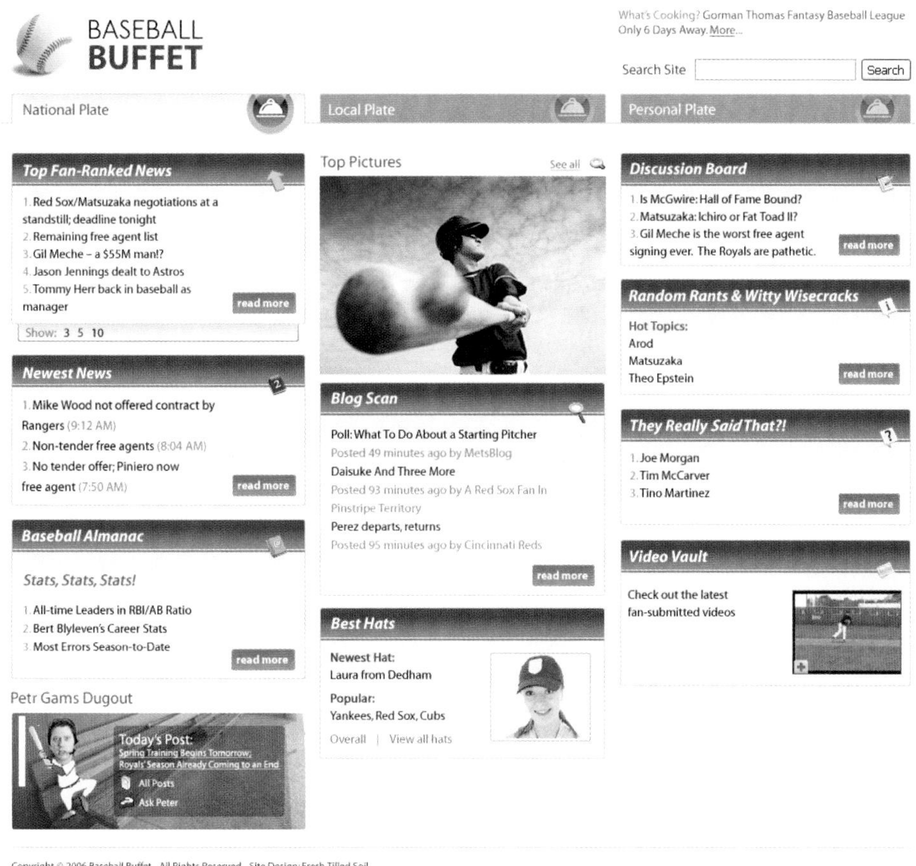

Figure 7.3 Baseball buffet national plate.

My colleague, MIT lecturer Elaine Chen, would argue that the website's design had too much detail, and that people would get distracted by the actual pictures or colors, rather than focusing on the features, functions, and benefits of the product. Elaine would recommend using a wireframing tool like Balsamiq® Mockups in order to focus on the workflow, staying at the functional level rather than delving into minute details like this team did, because this can be distracting and counterproductive.

SensAble Technologies

Our "digital clay" solution, which we called FreeForm, included both hardware (the physical PHANToM) and software. In the new digital clay molding bench, the hardware was not the critical item as we could imagine the hardware getting smaller and more stylish. We even felt that we could contract out production of this component if we wanted to. That was the relatively easy part. The hard part was going to be designing the software, so that is what we focused on.

As such, the goal was to produce a product that would have the ease of use of clay, but also the benefits of having digital files so that designs could be saved, modified, and sent electronically around the world, and upgrades and enhancements could be provided to users as well.

We started to develop the High-Level Product Specification as a set of PowerPoint slides in a less-precise way than the previous Baseball Buffet example. We showed the tools that designers used at the time and then we showed how that tool set would not only be replicated, but expanded with our digital clay molding bench (Figure 7.4).

There would also be drop-down menus that would allow the user to digitally select the materials, the tool, the end effector, and whether a template was to be used (Figure 7.5). This made it much easier for us to focus and test the viability of some concrete ideas with ourselves as well as potential customers.

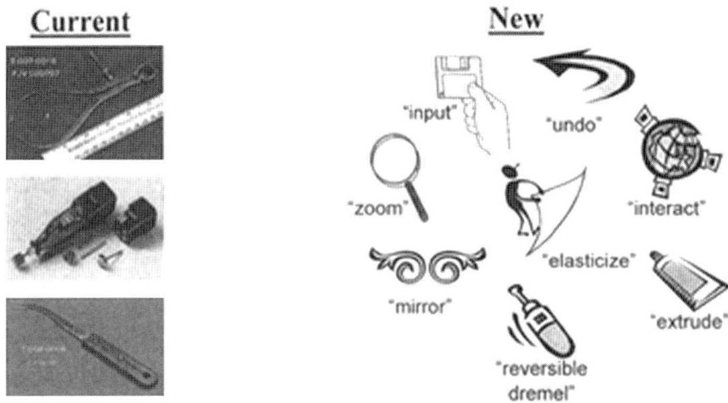

Figure 7.4 SensAble replaces and expands current tool set.

User Selections

Materials:	Tools:	End Effector:
☐ Soft Clay	☐ Sculpt	Point
☐ Medium Clay	☐ Hot Sword	● Ball
☐ Hard Clay	☐ Push/Pull	♦ Triangle
☐ Blue Foam	☐ Extrusion	■ Square
☐ Ren	☐ Dremel	Half Elipse
☐ Metal	☐ Scribe	Hook
☐ Other	☐ Other	Other
		Template:
		☐ Yes
		☐ No

Figure 7.5 SensAble user selections.

Another screenshot showed a clay studio, with a hunk of clay in the center, and with drop-down menus above, to show designers the interface they would be using to mold their digital clay.

Our High-Level Product Specification allowed us to get good feedback on our product from our customers. Our final product looked much different, but the spec was still successful because we needed a starting point to test and iterate on. This easy-to-construct product description of the key parts of our solution did not take a lot of time, was a great exercise to construct, and was a wonderful communications tool when done.

Example of a Brochure: Lifetime Supply

In this example, there were two entrepreneurial programmers, Max Kanter and Colin Sidoti, who were developing a plan for a new venture called "Lifetime Supply," whereby its customers could get a lifetime supply of any of the products that they offer. The original idea was that a well-to-do young male, Ivan the Investment Banker, would not want to go shopping but knew he would need white athletic socks for the rest of his life and this product would not change. As such, the new venture would take a payment and provide Ivan this service in perpetuity.

Once they started to research this idea, it quickly became clear that making this a subscription business was a much better idea, where both sides had the option to renew annually and where the pricing could be adjusted. With some clever pricing and logistics expertise, this could be a real business. They were confident that they could build such a website and mobile app. It was important to be accessible from the mobile phone, because in their primary market research, they found that convenience was a major attraction of this service. If customers could just reorder with one touch on their mobile phone, this concept would become much more valuable. So building a site and app was the easy part. What exactly to build and getting people to buy into their service was harder.

After some analysis and talking to many potential customers, they chose parents of college students as their beachhead market as they had both the financial means to buy the subscription and a strong interest in supporting and staying in touch with their children, especially when it came to areas like personal hygiene. They set out to describe their product to these key constituencies in as easy and efficient a manner with a brochure, which is shown in Figures 7.6 and 7.7.

Figure 7.6 shows the outside of brochure they produced.

Figure 7.7 shows the inside of the brochure, which is a tri-fold design.

You can see that the exercise of building this brochure forced the team to clarify many questions. What are the benefits to the student? What are the benefits to the parents? What are the products that Lifetime Supply will offer? How should we start to think about the pricing? By choosing to include pricing, though, the team has created a detail with the potential to distract both itself and potential customers. If customers disagree with the prices presented, they may be less likely to give feedback on the venture's main idea, which is providing supplies to college students on an all-you-can-use basis.

As you will notice, there are no pictures of the actual Lifetime Supply website or app. They had already created screenshots and storyboards for how people use the product, but details about each

Figure 7.6 Lifetime Supply brochure, outside.

Figure 7.7 Lifetime Supply brochure, inside. The original brochure also included logos for popular brands within each of the seven supply categories.

web page the user would see were not important in this brochure. In fact, the brochure may have been more helpful than the storyboards in determining exactly what the product would be. The final product offering for Lifetime Supply likely looks very different than what this brochure shows, because this brochure started a healthy process of iteration so that the team would arrive at the best product offering.

SUMMARY

Visually laying out your product will allow your team and your potential customers to converge around an understanding of what the product is and how it benefits customers. Staying at a high level, without too many details or a physical prototype, allows for rapid revision without investing too much time and resources this early in the process of creating your new venture. Building a visual representation of the product will likely be harder than you think, but will get everyone on the same page, which will prove extremely valuable going forward. A brochure with features, function, and benefits to the customer further clarifies your product offering and is a great complement to the pictures you create.

STEP 8

Quantify the Value Proposition

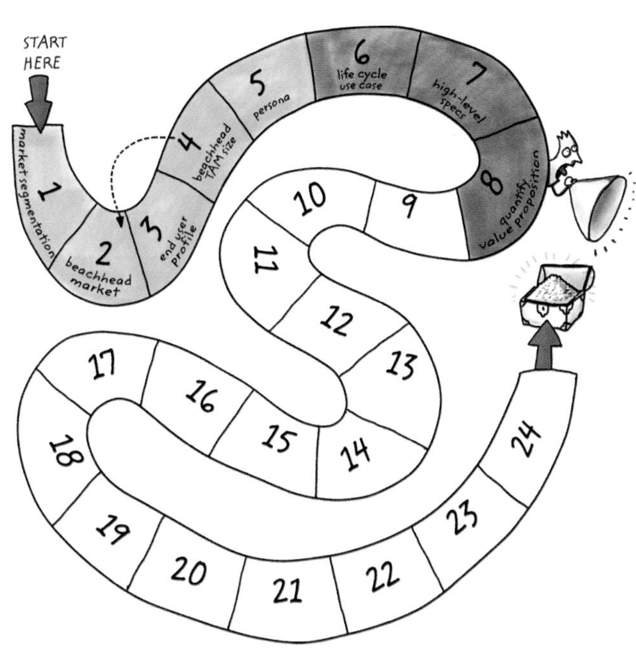

IN THIS STEP, YOU WILL:

- Determine how the benefits of your product turn into value that the customer gets out of your product.
- Calculate quantitative metrics (in most cases) to show this value to the customer.

The relentless march for specificity continues. The Quantified Value Proposition gives you a concrete understanding of the measureable benefits your product will bring to your target customers.

"When you can measure what you are speaking about, and express it in numbers, you know something about it; but when you cannot measure it . . . your knowledge is of a meager and unsatisfactory kind."

—*Lord Kelvin*

Your Quantified Value Proposition converts the benefits your Persona gets from your product into a tangible metric that aligns with the Persona's top priority, or in some cases priorities.

Products often have a large number of benefits. For instance, your product may help a customer simplify a process or reduce their environmental impact, or help a business gain additional sales for their own products. In a simple view of the world, benefits fall into three categories: "better," "faster," and "cheaper." The goal of the Quantified Value Proposition is to clearly and concisely state how your product's benefits line up with what your customer most wants to improve.

The Quantified Value Proposition focuses on what potential customers want to gain rather than going into detail on technology, features, and functions. When a customer purchases a product, they are asking themselves, "What value do I get out of this product?" Customers must justify the investment required to acquire your product by offsetting this against how much money your product will make for them, or how you will improve their life in a way that really matters to them.

ALIGNING YOUR VALUE PROPOSITION WITH THE PERSONA'S PRIORITIES

You've already identified the top priorities of the Persona. You have charted your Full Life Cycle Use Case, so you understand how your customer will use your product.

You will now create a value proposition focused on the criteria you identified as your Persona's top priority. If their top priority is time to market for producing goods, and your product's value is that it will lower the cost of production, your value proposition—"Our product saves $XX per month"—will not persuade your target customer to buy your product. Your value proposition is not aligned with their highest priority, so purchasing your product will not be a high priority for the target customer, and will get lost in their pile of less-than-urgent things to do. If your product also lowers the time to market, you should focus your Quantified Value Proposition on that.

KEEP IT SIMPLE: THE "AS-IS" STATE VERSUS THE "POSSIBLE" STATE WITH YOUR PRODUCT

Once you know the priority of your Persona, simply focus all your efforts on this factor. Set up a simple comparison of the "as-is" state that does not involve use of your product and then compare this to the "possible" state that you are confident will exist when the customer is using your solution. In both cases, you make it as quantifiable as possible. The difference in value between them is your Quantified Value Proposition. It is that simple. Don't make it too complicated.

Once you are able to state your Quantified Value Proposition in one sentence, create a supporting diagram showing the "as-is" state as compared to the "possible" state that visually illustrates the value your product has to the customer. Also, be sure to use the words of the customer in your diagram so they can understand that it is customized to them—or at least to their industry.

Define the "as-is" and "possible" states so clearly that any target customer will easily be able to understand, agree or disagree, and then comment on the assessment. It will also really help you understand in depth the key area where your new product will add value, and give you credibility with the customer.

Be sure to make the numbers in the "possible" state ones that you are highly confident your product can attain. You do not want to be too aggressive and fall short of what you set as an expectation. Often, entrepreneurs are much too aggressive in claiming how beneficial their product is to customers. As a result, they fall short of expectations and lose credibility. Even if they do something impressive, that value is offset by a loss of credibility for the new venture. Following the mantra of "underpromise, overdeliver" is very wise, especially for new B2B ventures trying to build up credibility, because the B2B environment depends on stable, consistent vendors.

EXAMPLES

SensAble Technologies

The SensAble Persona we selected was an industrial designer in the toy industry. The Persona could be applied to the footwear industry as well because the two industries are similar. The top priority for the Persona (particularly because it was a priority for the Persona's management, a critical part of the decision-making process for purchasing new products) was time to market for new toys. For new toys based on currently hot movie or video game characters, less time to market means less turnaround time before being able to sell toys around that temporary window of opportunity. For new toys based on a movie, less time to market means the company can gather more information about how successful a movie might be before manufacturing toys for it. (Shoe designers also prioritize time to market, as it allows them to put out more designs in a year.)

As such, we first determined the average time to market for a new toy using the current software available. We were careful to see the development process the way the customer does—in this case the toy manufacturer—using the customer's own words to describe the process. We iterated with one toy manufacturer until they believed we had it right; we then went to another toy manufacturer to see if their process was similar. After a while, we believed we had defined a very good "as-is" state for the process that captured the essence without getting into insignificant details. We also validated the process with footwear companies and found that the process was identical between the two industries.

Then, we mapped how long each stage of the process would take using our product (see Figure 8.1), based on our Full Life Cycle Use Case.

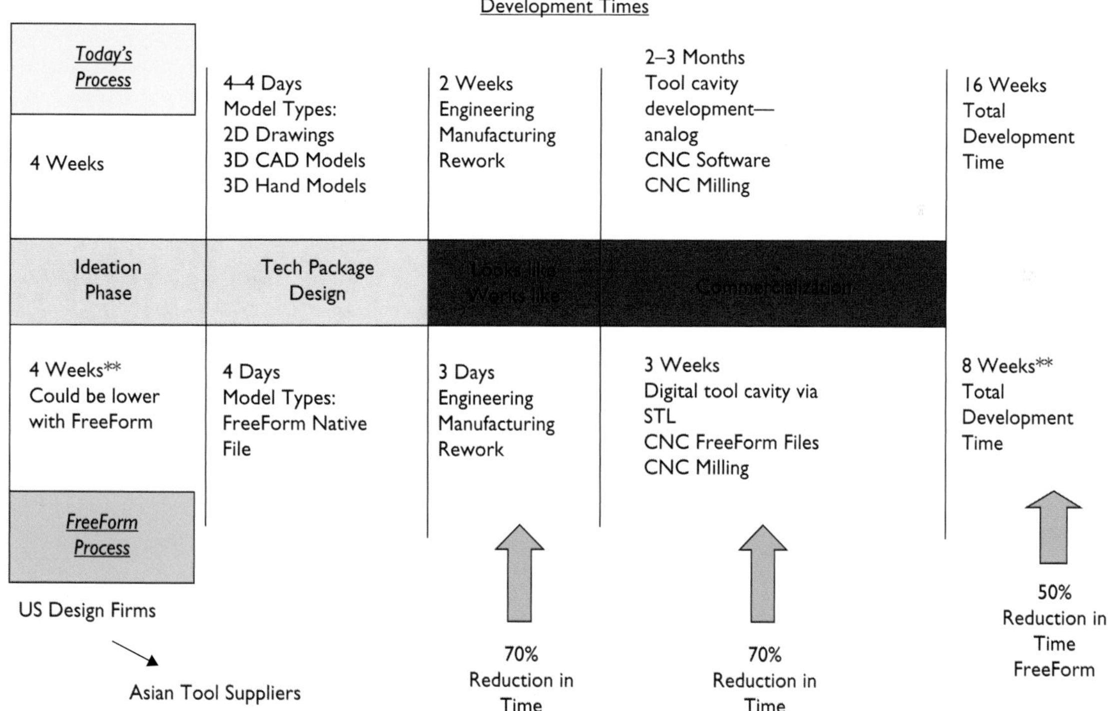

Figure 8.1 SensAble quantified value proposition.

The 50 percent reduction in time to market our offered product could mean both increased profits of hundreds of thousands to millions of dollars per toy or shoe line. We did not have to express our value proposition in dollars because the actual dollar amount would vary widely. Also, manufacturers were fluent enough in their process to know what a 50 percent reduction in time meant for them. The manufacturers could take that number to anyone in the company and they would understand that value. This worked extremely well and is an excellent example of a Quantified Value Proposition.

InTouch

Not every value proposition is a clear-cut number. One example is InTouch, a hardware/software product for first-time mothers-to-be who wanted a higher level of intimacy with their unborn child. The system would be a patch or belt the pregnant mother wears, with sensors near the fetus that would read the heartbeat and other vital signs of the unborn baby. The system would then take all of the data it had collected and put it through their proprietary algorithm and indicate whether the baby was healthy, stimulated, and happy. For instance, the mother could read to the unborn baby and then see if this made the fetus more or less "happy." Or, it could be simply to check the baby's heartbeat and general health.

You might consider this an unconventional idea (and you are in the majority), but that does not matter as long as there is a large enough target market that finds this concept attractive and compelling and, most of all, is excited enough about it to motivate them to pay for such a product.

The team knew the Persona's top priorities were to have reassurance that the fetus was okay and to establish intimacy with the unborn child. The team determined the "as-is" state to include expensive and cumbersome heart-rate monitors, imprecise and unpredictable intuition, costly and inconvenient professional ultrasounds, and the haphazard and uncomfortable consultation with "Dr. Google" online (Figure 8.2).

The "possible" state was using the inTouch product—which only existed as a High-Level Product Specification at this point—and gaining deep intimacy rapidly. They did not have to quantify the intimacy gain because their visual representation of the "as-is" versus "possible" states resonated with the first-time mothers, who validated it for them.

Meater

This team started with biosensor technology that was significantly better than what was currently available in the market at the time in terms of size, efficiency, and pricing. They went through the

Figure 8.2 inTouch value proposition example.

process to determine an appropriate beachhead market and settled on the cattle ranching industry. The proposed solution was a biosensor that could be affixed to a cow's ear, much like how cows are currently tagged, to detect disease earlier. Sick cows identified earlier can be separated from the herd, reducing infection rates, and allowing more effective treatment of diseases due to earlier detection than current methods.

The Persona, a rancher, was primarily driven by money. The Persona had no personal attachment to the cattle; making as much money as possible was by far the rancher's top priority.

First, the team determined the current economics for a typical herd of cattle (the "as-is" state), verifying it with numerous ranchers and refining it until it was clearly valid and credible. The team then determined the "possible" state from using their product, making some conservative assumptions they could support with compelling validity evidence, and then showing how much money a

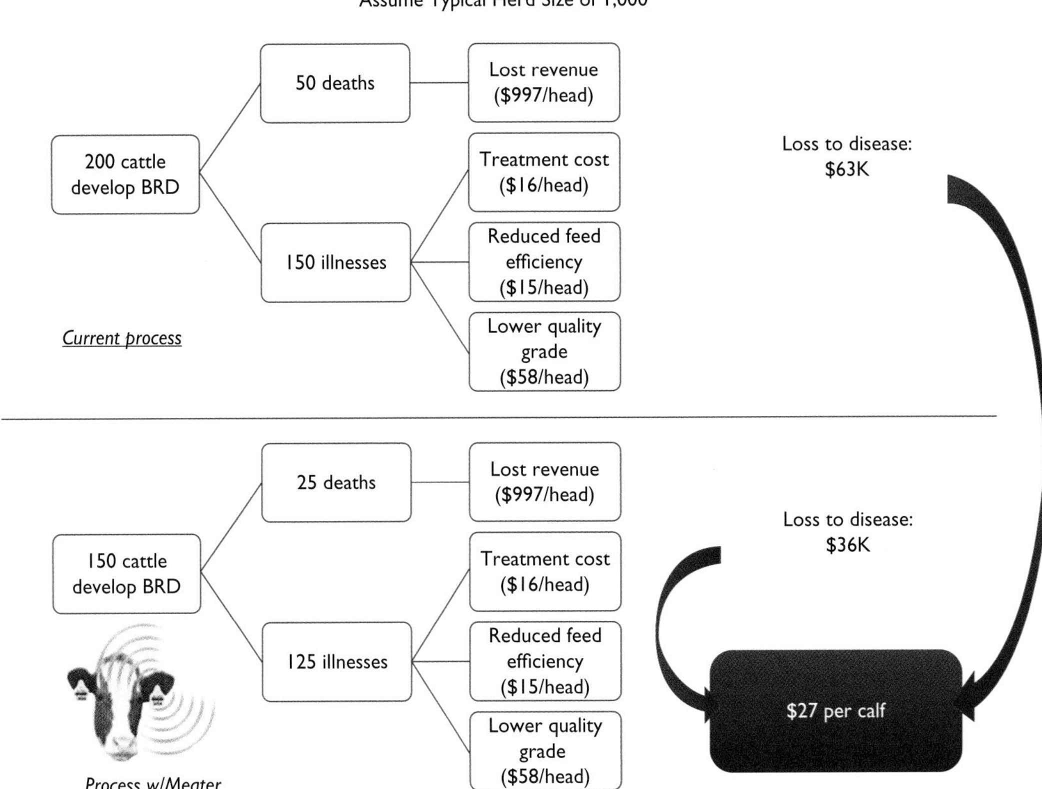

Figure 8.3 Meater loss-to-disease comparison.

rancher would save by using their product (Figure 8.3). The difference between these was their Quantified Value Proposition. This could easily be quantified because the Persona's top priority was something very measurable—money.

This was a compelling and highly specific Quantified Value Proposition that made it much easier to engage and quickly close their target customer on acquiring the product. It will also be of great help in later steps when the team looks to determine its Business Model and Pricing Framework.

SUMMARY

The Quantified Value Proposition is framed by the top priority of the Persona. You first need to understand and map the "as-is" state in a way familiar to the customer, using the Full Life Cycle Use Case. Then, map out the "possible" state of using your product, clearly indicating where the customer receives value based on the Persona's top priority. A visual, one-page diagram is best, because the customer can easily see the Quantified Value Proposition and can show it to others for validation. When done well, this will be of immense value to you throughout the process of launching your business, so extra effort spent to get this optimized is well worth it.

STEP 9

Identify Your Next 10 Customers

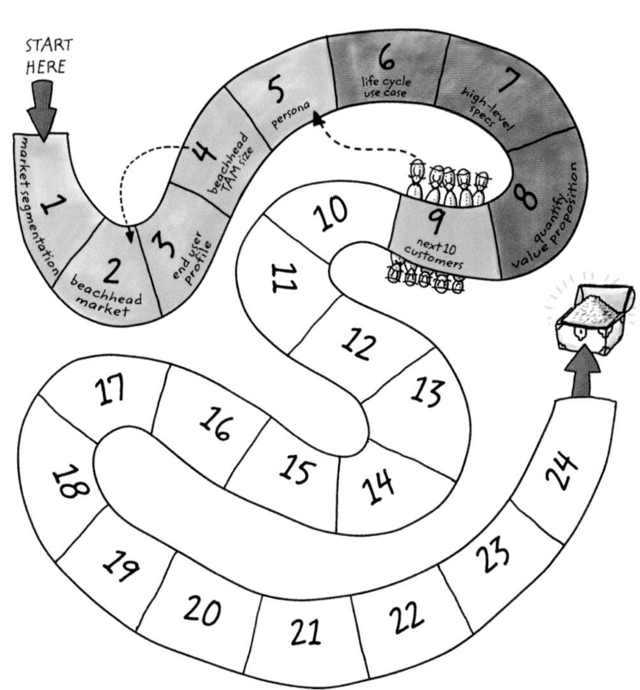

IN THIS STEP, YOU WILL:

- Identify at least 10 potential customers, besides your Persona, who fit the End User Profile.
- Contact them to validate their similarity to your Persona, and their willingness to buy your product.

Explicitly identifying the next 10 customers after the Persona increases your level of confidence that you are on the right path and may also help you refine earlier steps.

While it is important to identify and develop a Persona to represent your end users, you must also be sure to identify other potential customers to ensure your product's success. This will dramatically increase your confidence that you have identified a scalable opportunity, not just a one-customer solution, as well as your credibility.

One potential danger of focusing solely on your Persona is that you could build your business to be too specific, focused only on the Persona without the ability to sell to other customers. If the Persona is done correctly, this will not happen. The TAM calculation was the first checkpoint to guard against hyper-focus; this step is another one. Also, the output of this step, a list of 10 potential customers beyond your Persona, will be highly beneficial to you as you proceed.

In this step, you will list 10 high-potential customers that fit your End User Profile that are well-represented by the Persona. You will then contact them to verify and refine your primary market research. First, you want to verify that they are similar to the Persona. Then you will validate all of your work thus far, such as the Full Life Cycle Use Case, Quantified Value Proposition, and so on. If you are successful in this step, you can be significantly more confident that your business has a high probability of success—and you will be able to convince others, such as future partners, employees, customers, advisors, and investors. If you run into issues in this step, you will be able to go back and determine where the flaws in your plan are and improve them before going further.

By listing and interviewing 10 potential customers, you are directly testing every hypothesis you have built over the past eight steps. Your primary market research has been designed so that you continually stay aligned with the customer's needs; but this is your first big "systems test" where you are presenting the customer with everything you have worked on so far, so you may encounter some negative feedback at this step if your plan is not quite right. That is not only okay, but probably good. You are unlikely to have everything correct at this point anyway, so if the only feedback you get is "everything is okay," then it is likely that the customer doesn't care much about your product and its value to them. If the customer gives you detailed feedback, even if it is negative, it shows the customer cares about the problem you are trying to solve, and that it is worth your time to iterate with them to create a good product.

By explicitly identifying and contacting your first 10 customers, you will greatly lower the risk of your new business, getting you on a direct, focused, and fast path to success.

HOW TO COMPLETE THIS STEP

1. List more than 10 potential customers (aside from your Persona), and include any pertinent information you have about them from your existing research. There is no set number of customers you should list, because sometimes you can complete this step with a list of

12 customers, while other times you need to list 20–30 or more customers in order to get 10 customers who match your criteria and who are interested in your product. Each of these customers should be similar to each other and the Persona; if not, revisit the list, and potentially revisit your selection of Persona. It is important to have homogeneity in your list. They should all be powerful purchasing references for each other.

2. Contact each of the potential customers on your list and present your Full Life Cycle Use Case, High-Level Product Specification, and Quantified Value Proposition (Steps 6–8). Be sure while having these conversations that you are operating in "inquiry" mode, not "advocacy/sales" mode, as the latter will diminish the quality of your interactions. Determine whether the customer's needs and ideas are in line with what you've established thus far from your Persona, Full Life Cycle Use Case, Quantified Value Proposition, TAM assumptions, and so on. Especially validate with these customers the hypothesis you have regarding the Persona's top purchasing priorities.
3. If a customer validates your hypotheses from the previous steps, now is a good time to ask the customer if they would consider providing a letter of intent to buy your solution, once it is available. You are still in "inquiry" mode, so you are asking, "If a company were to offer this product, would you be interested in purchasing it?" rather than "Will you buy this product?" If they are extremely enthusiastic, you can even ask them to prepay for the product, which is a fantastic level of commitment. Before you take their money, however, make sure you can deliver what they want and also make sure there are no special conditions in their purchase order that you cannot or do not want to be expected to meet.
4. If a customer's feedback is not aligned exactly with your assumptions, take good notes and think how this affects your analysis. Do not overreact to each new interview, even if there is a major disconnect, unless you see a pattern. You will know intuitively if there is a major disconnect after a few interviews.
5. Now that you have contacted each customer, you may have new data. At this point, you can go back and modify your earlier assumptions and determine whether to contact additional customers. Your end goal is a homogenous list of 10 customers who are truly interested and aligned with your Persona and other assumptions.
6. If you find that you cannot create a list of 10 customers who are excited about your High-Level Product Specification, then you may need to reconsider your beachhead market.
7. While this step is conceptually simple, contacting customers and getting information from them will require a good amount of work, but will be invaluable as you move forward. Do not share this list of customers or the information you gather with others outside your company.

IS THE CURRENT PERSONA VALID?

In the process of determining the Next 10 Customers, you are testing to ensure that your Persona is truly a useful and credible representation of the target customer. If the Persona is a statistical outlier relative to the target customer group, it will not only be a poor source of information, but it will lead you to develop a product your target customer might not want. While validating the Persona, you may also uncover other interesting traits that customers share with the Persona, which will allow you to revise the description of the Persona to make it stronger. Often in this step, you find an even better Persona than you started with, which is a good thing. You are continually spiraling to the optimal solution.

DEALING WITH NEGATIVE FEEDBACK

Throughout the 24 Steps, your purpose is not to complete each step with 100 percent accuracy, but rather to test hypotheses and to learn from your potential customers. Getting negative results will happen and how the entrepreneurial team responds to them will be a fundamental factor to the team's success. Therefore, if any step returns negative feedback, meaning feedback that does not support your hypotheses, you have received valuable information that there may be an error in the research and data you have been using up to this point. Negative results at one step is not the end of the venture in most cases, but moving forward with a faulty plan that was based on hope and not facts is a recipe for failure.

"But why should I listen to the naysayers?" you may ask, pointing to Steve Jobs or other entrepreneurs who achieved success through seemingly counterintuitive methods. True entrepreneurs see possibilities that others do not and overcome obstacles that others cannot. But you cannot will a market to exist any more than you can change the laws of thermodynamics. Even the most powerful personalities with extreme "reality distortion zone" powers cannot do so, as history has shown with Dean Kamen and the Segway, or even Steve Jobs at NeXT Computer. This is where this customer-centered process comes into play.

EXAMPLES

Methane Capture of Landfill Sites

A very energetic and savvy student team was building a plan for a new venture that included creating a sophisticated technology to monitor and capture methane from landfill sites, thereby reducing the harmful emissions from these sites and converting them instead into valuable fuel to produce electricity.

They did all of the steps including the Market Analysis, Persona, Full Life Cycle Use Case, and Quantified Value Proposition. They felt like it all made sense but they had to verify this in the real world.

The team made a list of the 10 most promising landfill sites considering their location, size, ownership structure, and other factors. They then proceeded to contact the appropriate person at each site and found an extremely positive response from 8 of the 10. In fact, they got letters of intent at the end of the meeting from more than half of them, giving the team an incredible boost of confidence that they were on the right path (Table 9.1).

In this case, the process worked flawlessly and the results were extremely comforting and validated the team's plans.

Table 9.1 Methane Capture Next 10 Customers Table

	Project Owner—Location ***(names changed for this book)***	**Total Megawatts Installed**	**Name/Contact Info** ***(names changed for this book)***	**Contacted?**
1	Waste Management—City Name, State	9.8	Site owner	Y
2	Smith Waste Systems—City Name, State	4.8	Site owner	Y
3	Energy Systems, Inc.—City Name, State	18.4	Third-party operator	N
4	Waste Management—City Name, State	16.8	Site owner	Y
5	Waste Management—City Name, State	16.5	Site owner	Y
6	Energy Systems, Inc.—City Name, State	12	Third-party operator	N
7	Waste Management—City Name, State	9.8	Site owner	Y
8	Waste Management—City Name, State	7.9	Site owner	Y
9	Smith Methane Group—City Name, State	7.34	Third-party operator	Y
10	Smith Waste Management—City Name, State	6.9	Third-party operator/ Site owner	Y

Virtual Arts Academy: A B2C Two-Sided Market Example

Another illustrative case came from a team that came up with a concept of providing high-quality training in the arts to upper-class children in suburban locations over the Internet. The team did its marketing research and assembled a list of parents from Wellesley, Massachusetts. They quickly learned that getting the parents of rich, suburban children to pay for such a service was not the problem. The more challenging aspect of this two-sided market was identifying whether artists would be excited to participate in such a business opportunity. Did they have the patience to do this? Did they have the equipment? Did they need the money? Would they be willing, able, and reliable enough to provide the supply of instructors for the demand that existed? Even though they were not the paying customers, but would instead be paid by the venture, the artists had to be available to perform the services necessary at a price point that would make the new venture attractive enough for the founders to pursue it.

Taking on this challenge, the founders leveraged their networks, including social media, to find a group of potential artists and interviewed them. They documented their interviews and met to see what they had learned after each one.

The final result was that 8 of the 10 potential artists were very excited to participate in the Virtual Arts Academy; the other two could probably be convinced, but the team was short on time to do the research. This process of talking to real people and making sure the team's Persona was accurate was very valuable. The team became much more confident in its new venture and was much more focused in the steps that followed.

SUMMARY

Identifying and interviewing your Next 10 Customers now ensures that your Persona description and other assumptions hold true for an array of customers. If you have completed this step properly, and made modifications to the other steps from what you learned here, you should have great confidence moving forward to build the plan for your new venture.

STEP 10

Define Your Core

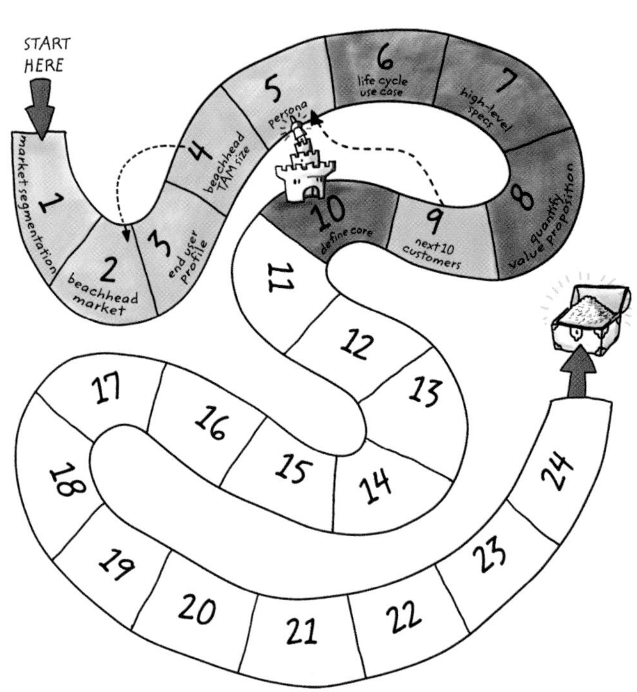

IN THIS STEP, YOU WILL:

- Explain why your business can provide customers with a solution that other businesses cannot nearly as well.

You need to figure out something that you do that will make you better than anyone else at producing a solution for your customers. This will be the new venture's eventual crown jewels.

So far, you have focused almost exclusively on meeting the needs of a well-defined target customer. Now you will start looking to the future by determining what about your business makes you special, what your "secret sauce" is.

The Core is something that allows you to deliver the benefits your customers value with much greater effectiveness than any other competitor. You are looking for that single thing that will make it very difficult for the next company that tries to do what you do. It could be a very small part of the overall solution, but without it, you don't have nearly as valuable a solution. What is it that you do better than anyone else?

The Core also provides a certain level of protection, ensuring that you don't go through the hard work to create a new market or product category only to see someone else come in and reap the rewards with a similar business of their own. What is it that your product does that your competitors can't duplicate, or cannot duplicate easily? That is your Core.

A FEW EXAMPLES OF CORE

Determining your core is a very situation-specific exercise. It requires great thought and there may be multiple options for a Core. Rather than prescribe how to determine your Core, I will give you some examples from categories that could inspire (or become) your Core.

- **Network Effect:** If this is your Core, you become the standard by achieving so much critical mass in the marketplace that it does not make sense for potential customers to use another product. The value to the user of this product falls under Metcalfe's Law, which essentially says that the value of the network to any individual on that network is exponentially related to the number of users on the network. The company with the most users is the most valuable; hence it is logical for new users to choose that network. As a result, the network becomes even more powerful; it is a positive feedback loop. Examples of businesses that achieved this are eBay (for both buyers and sellers), LinkedIn, Facebook, and Google for Advertisers. MySpace may have had some advantage from a network effect initially, but the company failed to recognize it and did not leverage it as its Core, which helps to explain why Facebook was able to rapidly gain market share to the detriment of MySpace. Today Facebook has achieved network effects and an almost unassailable position in the marketplace.
- **Customer Service:** By establishing processes and culture that focus on excelling at customer service, this potential core allows you to retain customers at a very high rate as compared to competitors, and thereby avoid costly churn. It will also allow you to attract and obtain

customers in a much more efficient way than others in the market, as your customers are thrilled with their experience with you and become salespeople for you by creating positive word of mouth. This core requires an incredibly strong commitment from the entire organization and a fanatical focus to execute a high level of customer satisfaction in a consistent fashion. It often involves extraordinary measures that are hard for others to follow, such as "no questions asked refunds" or other costly policies. Visible examples of this are Zappos, Warby Parker, Nordstrom, Commerce Bank, and at times in its history, IBM. This strategy is difficult to execute such that a competitor is unable to copy and negate your core, but when it works (and it does from the various examples I have just given you), it can be very effective.

- **Lowest Cost:** Another Core you may pursue is to develop the skills, relationships, processes, volumes, financial overhead, and culture to outcompete anyone else in the market on cost and become the long-term low-cost player. This has been a successful Core for Walmart and it is also part of the strategy behind many Asian companies, especially with Chinese companies that have recently entered the clean energy sector. It may be facilitated by achieving economies of scale. Often it is not a Core, but rather an entry strategy for companies who then choose to compete on something else. For example, Honda entered the U.S. market as a low-cost provider of weed whackers, scooters, motorcycles, lawnmowers, and cars; but, eventually they no longer were the low-cost option. In fact, their Core was the capability to build great motors, and the low cost was just a way to get into a new market.
- **User Experience:** There are a multitude of new strategies that have evolved into potential Core strengths and a common one now is user experience (UX). This seems to have been embraced by the market (or at least a significant part of it), which is a major contributor to the recent uptick in entrepreneurial activity and success in New York City, where there is a lot of design and fashion talent available to address this challenge. The strategy here would be to become the best at developing and continually improving the UX through the company's emphasis on it. One company's (Gemvara) relentless focus on this from the CEO on down has resulted in recruiting top talent, prioritization in operational reviews, and a culture where every employee knows that the bar is very high for this area and nothing less than excellence will be accepted. Clearly this has been Apple's Core as it produces products that leverage the company's capabilities and commitment to an insanely great user experience.

These are just a few examples of defining a Core. The key is that the Core be clearly defined, and your founding team aligned so that the Core is what the business will continually work to develop, and will always put first when planning and executing any strategy. The Core is your business's last defense against the competition.

HOW TO DEFINE YOUR CORE

Of all the steps thus far, defining your Core is more inward-looking and less research-based than the others. You will rely on this internal introspection, combined with external data gathering and analysis. While the process may seem broad and general at first, your end definition of your Core should be concrete and specific.

Defining your Core is not easy. It cannot stay an abstract intellectual exercise, but must integrate many different considerations (what the customer wants, what assets you have, what you really like to do, what others outside your company can do, and what the personal and financial goals of the owners are). At the same time, it must be done efficiently (i.e., not take too long) and very specifically such that you arrive at an answer you are highly confident is accurate. You cannot be changing your Core like other elements in this process; it has to remain fixed over time, once you lock in on it. If you change it, you do so at your peril as you will often lose whatever advantages you have built. That being said, it does happen that Cores change as you learn more about your market, your customers, and your own company assets. Google is a great example—they thought their Core was the technological excellence of their search engine algorithm, but in the end, it was their ability to embrace a new business model around keyword-based text ads in search, and to achieve network effects before anyone else.

WHAT ABOUT INTELLECTUAL PROPERTY? OR CULTURE?

One common starting point when determining your Core is to conclude it is your intellectual property. Its effectiveness as a Core depends heavily on your industry. In the medical industry, especially the biotech industry, patents are incredibly important in ensuring success of a product or a new company. In other industries, there may be some value, but often patents are insufficient for ensuring business success. They tend to be static and markets are dynamic. Capability is generally better than a patent—but it is best to have both for sure. For instance, teams with high levels of capability in an area will continually produce innovative goods, over time overwhelming a company that is built around one or a small number of patents (except in such specific cases as biotech).

Some companies find an advantage in the marketplace by creating a process and culture that innovates incredibly fast. They stay close to the customer and then use strong product management and agile development to translate their initial head start into a sustained and growing advantage as time goes on. However, this strategy is difficult to sustain as a unique Core as your organization scales, because as smaller companies enter the market and begin competing, they will have advantages that allow them to be nimble as well, perhaps surpassing your pace of innovation, once your business is large. Most companies wisely do not rely solely on their speed of innovation as their Core, but rather use it as a motivator and a moat around the castle before they finally settle on a Core. To put it simply, all businesses should aim to innovate quickly, regardless of their definition of Core; but, few businesses will find lasting success in rapid innovation without something else as a Core.

CORE IS DIFFERENT THAN COMPETITIVE POSITION

Your customers very likely will not see your Core as the reason they buy from you. They will instead look at your Competitive Position, which you will map in Step 11. Your Core will drive your ability to deliver certain benefits to the customer, which has to translate into value for the customer (based on the customer's top priorities), which then leads to a better Competitive Position. The Core is how you are building a capability to differentiate yourself from your competitors, and it cannot be easily replicated by others. It is the most concentrated way to gain differentiation from your current and potential competitors so you can really focus your small amount of resources to gain maximum value for your new venture.

FIRST-MOVER ADVANTAGE IS NOT A CORE

One of the most overused and incorrect terms used when defining a Core is "first-mover advantage." The term refers to a company being successful solely by being the first in the market. However, most companies that are first to market end up losing the market to a later entrant who outperforms the first company, so first-mover advantage by itself cannot translate into a sustainable Core and could be seen as a disadvantage. First-mover advantage can help a company with a well-defined Core, but it cannot win the market by simply by being first; this must be translated into something else like locking in key customers, achieving positive networking effects for your company, recruiting the best talent in a certain area, and so on.

LOCKING UP SUPPLIERS IS TYPICALLY NOT A CORE

One way to gain a competitive advantage is to anticipate the key elements of your solution and lock in vendors on an exclusive or a functionally exclusive arrangement. You can generally request exclusivity in return for meeting agreed-upon milestones and minimum order quantities, especially if the supplier sells its product to a much different market than yours, or if you are buying large volumes from a relatively small supplier. Apple has employed this strategy effectively, using it to maintain high profit margins that give the company lots of resources and flexibility, but its Core is actually maintaining a culture of perfection and transcending past mental models, both made possible by the late Steve Jobs.

Like intellectual property, locking up key suppliers is a good "outside the core moat" strategy to slow down your potential competitors and should be aggressively used when appropriate, but it is not your ultimate Core, just a trap along the way for those who might follow. It is a very valuable strategy to have multiple traps along the way to make it hard on your competitors; but, you should have only one Core. The Core is the Crown Jewel that is the final barrier through which the competitors should not be able to break through.

EXAMPLE

SensAble Technologies

When we thought about what the Core for SensAble would be, it seemed obvious to some. We had a unique hardware robotic device called the PHANToM, a device that was renowned for its clever design. In addition, we had an extremely fundamental patent for "force reflecting haptic interface" (U.S. patent #5,625,576) which was one of the most referenced patents of its time.[1] We also had Thomas Massie, the driving intellect behind the technology, and a rising engineering star at MIT, fully invested in the company. Surely that was the Core, right?

However, when we stepped back and thought about our priorities as founders, we realized that we were looking to achieve a high level of success in a relatively short period of time. Co-founders Thomas and Rhonda Massie wanted to return to Kentucky in four to five years, and I wanted to do something big that could scale quickly and be of interest to venture capitalists, which would be a five-year timetable.

If our focus were intellectual property, we would become dependent on others, with an unpredictable time frame, and would need to become legal experts to ensure others did not ignore or circumvent our patents, which was not interesting to us and not aligned with our personal goals and passions. This was not an attractive scenario for us, and so while we aggressively pursued building our intellectual property portfolio with our IP lawyer Steve Bauer and MIT, it was one of the outside

[1] Gregory T. Huang, "From MIT Entrepreneur to Tea Party Leader: The Thomas Massie Story," *Xconomy*, May 17, 2012, www.xconomy.com/boston/2012/05/17/from-mit-entrepreneur-to-tea-party-leader-the-thomas-massie-story/2.

moats of our castle (as in the cartoon at the beginning of this step), not the crown jewels (Core) that we would protect in the centermost part of the castle.

If our focus were hardware, it would take a lot of time and money to achieve success, and hardware companies were not as attractive to investors as software companies. Robotics in particular was extremely out of favor during the mid-1990s. After some thinking, it became clear we should not be a robotics company at all. After all, our beachhead market was not about robotics, but about design. So as with intellectual property, we aggressively protected and developed our PHANToM hardware, even though it was an outside wall, not the Core.

We had been able to lock up the supply of a key component (the high-fidelity motors) that made our hardware far superior to what other companies were offering, presenting a substantial barrier to entry. But if market conditions had been right, our competitors would have found a way to produce the key component themselves. We instead defined our Core as revolving around software, which was more scalable and would be more valuable. In talking with Thomas, we realized the software behind the PHANToM was very complicated (the hand is truly faster than the eye—we had to achieve update rates of 1,000 frames per second to simulate touch as opposed to the 20–30 frames per second that displays visual images on televisions and movie screens). It was not just the interface software but also how we represented weight, shapes, texture, deformations, and many other physical properties of the objects we rendered for touching in the computer and then how they interacted with them. We ended up defining our Core as "the physics of three-dimensional touch." This Core was to be embodied in a software engine that rendered 3D objects on the computer, not for visual representations, but for touching them.

With a formalized definition of our Core, we needed to translate it into a sustainable advantage that would grow over time. So we quickly identified the key people on our team who had the skills to support the Core. We then identified the people outside the company who were leaders in this field and moved quickly to build strong relationships with them and lock them in with us. We also identified the organizations and institutions where these people would be found (specific departments at MIT, Brown University, and Stanford University) and developed our visibility, reputation, and relationships there to recruit the best and the brightest future stars. This became a top priority of Thomas Massie as the CTO and he reviewed this at least quarterly in his technical strategy discussions. We made sure to have a strong skills development plan in this area and our incentive system reflected this as a priority with strong compensation and large stock option grants.

In this way, we determined a Core that would protect us and give us a huge competitive advantage as we successfully developed the market. It was certainly not obvious in the beginning, and the obvious answer would have been a far less optimal Core, so the extra attention paid to determining a Core was well worth the effort in the end. It paid dividends many times over going forward.

SUMMARY

Defining the Core is the first step where you spend a lot of time looking internally, in contrast to the strong customer focus of many of the other steps. The Core is what you have that your competitors do not, that you will protect over time above all else, and that you continually work over time to develop and enhance. Once you agree on a Core, it should not change without a great deal of thought; instead, you should continually make your Core stronger. If it changes often, this is a bad sign because it means you are likely not building it effectively. However, it can change as you discover what your customers value most and what you do best. Defining your Core is not easy and may seem abstract, but it is an essential step to maximize the value of your new business.

STEP 11

Chart Your Competitive Position

IN THIS STEP, YOU WILL:

- Show how well your product meets the Persona's top two priorities.
- Show how well the Persona's priorities are met by existing products in comparison to your product.
- Analyze whether the market opportunity you have chosen fits well with both your Core and your Persona's priorities.

How does your core map to what your customer really wants?

The Competitive Position is where you take your Core and translate it into something that produces real value for the customer, something that they will care deeply about.

When you are looking to create a new market, you build from the customer back with a clean slate, rather than picking an existing product and making a better version of it. In their book, *Blue Ocean Strategy*, W. Chan Kim and Renée Mauborgne argue that if you focus on an underserved customer and make a product for that customer that truly meets the customer's need, there is no need to focus on the competition because your unwavering focus makes the competition irrelevant.

While the point is a valuable one and is true to some extent, the reality is that customers usually make purchasing decisions on a comparative basis, considering all options and determining which solution best fits their priorities. The Competitive Positioning Chart helps you analyze how much better you are vis-à-vis your competition; it can also highlight areas of weakness. Taken together with the Quantified Value Proposition, it shows that your product is needed and you are the right organization to provide it.

In the Competitive Positioning Chart, you show visually how well you fulfill your Persona's top two priorities versus how well your competition does so. The goal is to show that your Competitive Position both leverages your Core and that your product satisfies your Persona's priorities far better than existing or logical future products. If both of these are not true, you may need to revisit your market selection or your Core. While there is some flexibility with your Core, it is usually limited. Inability to translate your Core into benefits for your customer does not necessarily mean your Core is wrong, because the Core is a reflection of your team's assets and capabilities; instead, there may be a better market opportunity where your Core is more suited. The Competitive Position is the link between your Core and your Persona's priorities, and shows that they logically make sense for the target market you have chosen.

THE TOUGHEST COMPETITOR OF ALL: THE CUSTOMER'S STATUS QUO

Often, your largest obstacle will be convincing customers to make a change from their status quo. When the Sony Walkman was first created, there were few comparable devices, but the biggest competition for Sony was selling to consumers who did not listen to music on the go. The status quo for these customers would have included listening to music at home or going to concerts.

Your Quantified Value Proposition should have picked up any problems with your product versus your Persona's top priority; but, comparing your product to the status quo here ensures that you have a valid real market and not a conceptual, fictitious one.

Often when my students come up with an idea, only to find another company doing something similar, they first fear they are too late. Then their competitive mindset kicks in and they believe they can and must crush the other small startup company. They invest a lot of energy in beating what they believe to be their direct competitor, rather than delivering a product that meets the customer's needs. Yet they and the perceived competition combined probably have an infinitesimally small market share. The much bigger share of the TAM comes from getting people to change what they are doing today, overcoming natural human and organizational inertia. It is far better to address the untapped market of "customer doing nothing" than focusing on some other brand-new startup.

In the end, if you have a good Core and people convert from the status quo to a new solution, the market will take off and both you and the other small competitor will win big. In such an outcome, it is likely that the two of you will merge, both get bought by bigger firms, or both go public. Once you have your Core and Competitive Position, don't focus too much precious time on competitors; rather, spend most of it working with customers, developing your Core, and getting products out the door.

HOW TO CHART YOUR COMPETITIVE POSITION

As with the other steps, this is a pretty simple logical step—the key is getting the right information from your primary customer research. This process will allow you to return to the customer and validate your position as well.

Charting your Competitive Position starts by identifying the top two priorities of your Persona and then assuming that these two priorities are all that matter. Your Core is probably inspirational and thoughtful, and your product's features are great, but they do not dictate the customer's priorities.

Next, create a simple matrix/graph as follows:

1. Divide both the x-axis and y-axis into two halves.
2. On the x-axis, write the number-one priority of your Persona.
3. On the half of the x-axis closer to the origin, write the "bad state" of this priority (e.g., if the priority is "reliability" then write "low" here).
4. On the other half of the x-axis, write the "good" state of this priority (e.g., "high" for "reliability").
5. On the y-axis, place the number-two priority of your Persona. Write the "bad state" on the half of the y-axis closer to the origin, and the "good state" on the other half of the y-axis.
6. Plot your business on the graph, along with those of your competitors (current and future). Also include the customer's "do nothing" or "status quo" option.

The chart in Figure 11.1 lists the Persona's status quo, as well as other companies whose products potentially address one or both of the Persona's top two priorities.

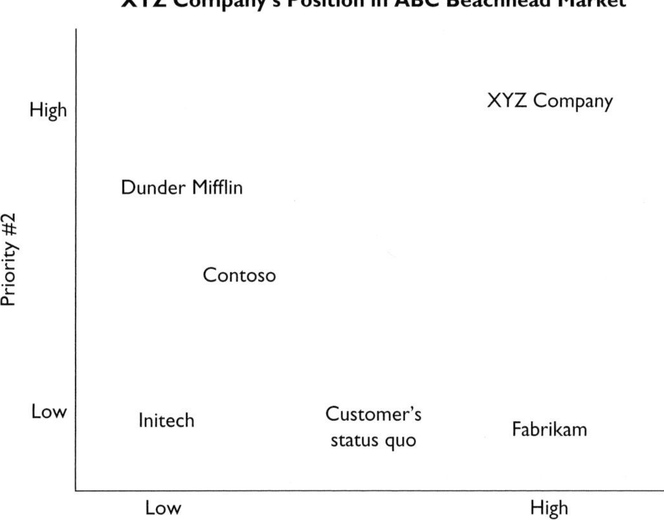

Figure 11.1 Competitive Positioning chart.

If you have done good primary market research, your business should be positioned in the top-right quadrant of this graph, at the high end of the "good" states of each priority. The bottom-left quadrant is where you absolutely do not want to be. Other locations on the chart are not necessarily bad. But if you find yourself somewhere other than the top-right of the chart, you should reevaluate your product compared to your competition.

Then, review this chart with your target customers for feedback; refine it as needed until the chart accurately describes your product and the competition relative to the Persona's top two priorities.

EXAMPLES

SensAble Technologies

For SensAble, there were some who believed our Competitive Position was based on the PHANToM device or the ability to feel things in the computer. These, however, were the features of the product that technical people were interested in; it was not the reason our target customer would buy our product, FreeForm. Our Persona work indicated that their first priority was speed to market; second was ability to convey design intent.

Essentially, the design team managers wanted a solution that had the ease of use and ability to convey design intent like clay, but had the benefits of flexibility and communications of a digital asset like the CAD/CAM (Computer Aided Design/Computer Aided Manufacturing) software tools. The CAD/CAM tools that management was pushing were not being successfully adopted by the designers we were targeting because those tools were not built with the priorities of the designers in mind. The CAD/CAM and Alias/Wavefront CAID (Computer Aided Industrial Design software) tools had impressive underlying mathematical representations of the shapes that were created, which gave the final model great precision, but they limited what could be done and were very nonintuitive for the designer. It was like squeezing an inflated balloon—when you made changes in one part of the design, it could very well automatically make changes in other parts of the model, whether or not the user intended to.

The chart in Figure 11.2 quickly and succinctly captured the difference between the status quo of clay as well as the competitive offerings from CAD/CAM and CAID companies. It also leveraged the Core of SensAble with its 3D software engine as well as the unique PHANToM hardware. Because of

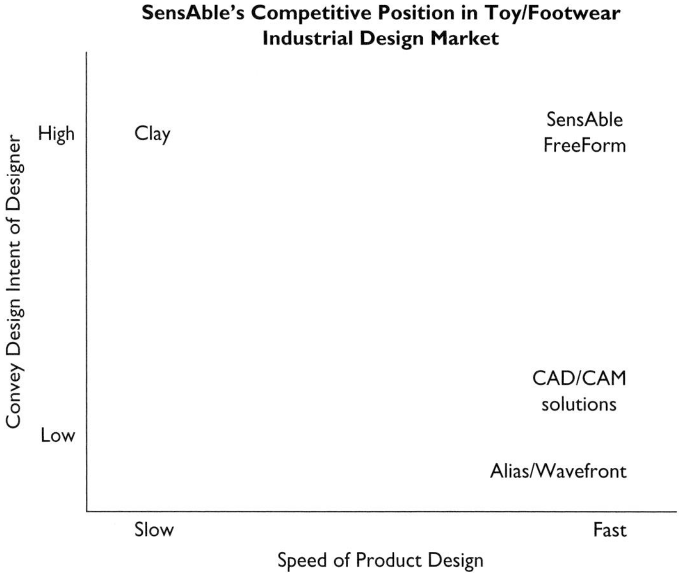

Figure 11.2 SensAble's Competitive Position.

this, no one else could legitimately make the claim that they could address the customer's priorities as well as SensAble's FreeForm product.

SunSpring

This team of MIT and Harvard students from my Energy Ventures course had access to a unique technology that used solar energy to filter water. They had identified a beachhead market of filtering drinking water for military teams stationed in places that were off the grid or lacked access to reliable electricity.

In this case, cost was not a top priority for the military. Rather, the key elements were reliability and efficiency, since teams needed to carry the product on remote missions where there were no opportunities for repair or for procuring additional sources of water. Any product fulfilling the military's priorities had to work all the time, and had to deliver as much filtered water as possible. These priorities fit well with the team's Core, which was its technological capability, but their Competitive Position is expressed by how the product met the customer's needs, as seen in Figure 11.3.

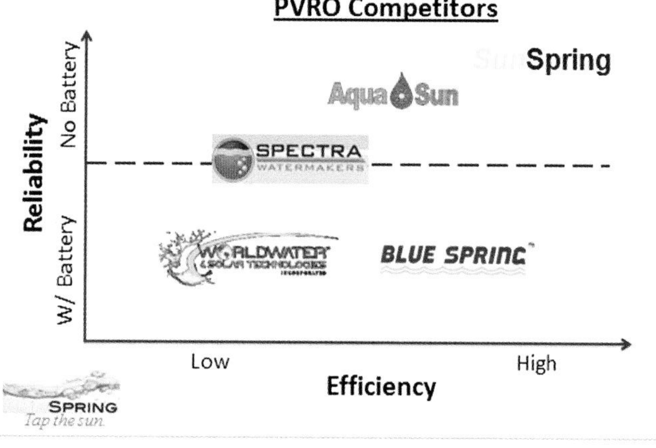

Figure 11.3 SunSpring's Competitive Position.

SUMMARY

Defining your Competitive Position is a quick way to validate your product against your competition, including the customer's status quo, based on the top two priorities of the Persona. If you are not in the top right of the resulting chart, you should reevaluate your product, or at least the way you are presenting it. This will also be a very effective vehicle to communicate your qualitative (not quantitative) value proposition to the target customer audience in a way that should resonate with them.

STEP 12

Determine the Customer's Decision-Making Unit (DMU)

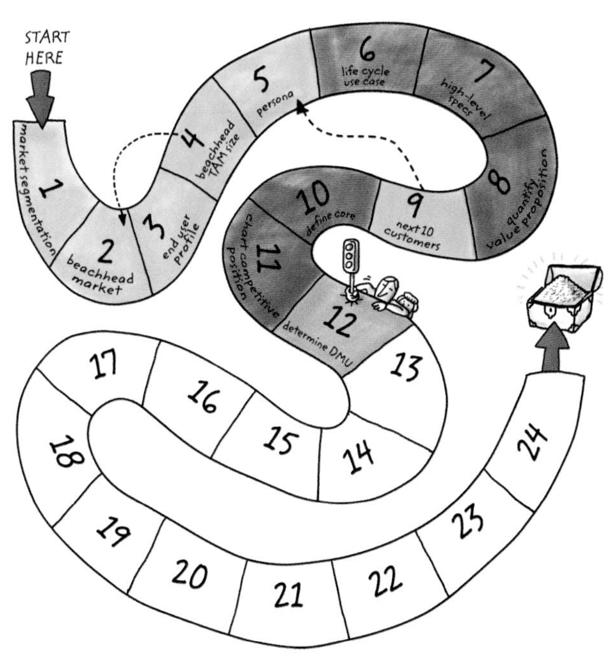

IN THIS STEP, YOU WILL:

- Learn who makes the ultimate decision to purchase your product, and who will be advocating for purchasing it.
- Meet the influencers who have sway over the purchasing decision.

Your target customer almost surely has a decision-making group of more than one person. Understanding this group and explicitly mapping out each person's role and interest is of critical importance not just for the sale, but also much earlier in the process when you are developing the product and all of its attributes.

At this point, you should be confident that your Persona will get substantial value from your product and that your offering is unique. Now, you need to become equally confident that your Persona and Next 10 Customers can buy your product. Rarely is the purchasing process simple. When almost any product of significance is acquired or adopted for use, whether in a B2B or consumer market, multiple people will have to be convinced that your product is worth purchasing.

To sell your product successfully, you will need to identify all the people who will be involved in the decision to acquire the product for the end user. Some people will actively approve or block acquisition, while others will present opinions that can sway the acquisition process.

This process, or some variant of it, has been presented in many different ways in sales training programs and put to practice for decades. For the sake of this book, I will use a simple common language to describe this process and integrate it into the 24 Steps. This process works for both B2B cases and B2C cases, though B2C cases may involve fewer people, each of whom may have multiple roles.

PRIMARY ROLES IN THE DECISION-MAKING UNIT

- **Champion:** The champion is the person who wants the customer to purchase the product, typically but not necessarily your end user. Multiple people can play this role. The champion is the "straw that stirs the drink." The champion can also be referred to as the "advocate."
- **End User:** This is the person who will actually use the product to create the value that is described in Step 8, Quantified Value Proposition. Hopefully this person is your champion as well; regardless, the end user typically plays a significant role in the purchase of a product.
- **Primary Economic Buyer:** This is the primary decision maker, as everyone else looks to this person to sign off on spending money to purchase your product. Most often, this person controls the budget. Sometimes, the primary economic buyer is also the champion and/or the end user, which makes your job easier, but does not completely neutralize influencers or individuals who object to the purchase.

ADDITIONAL ROLES IN THE DECISION-MAKING UNIT (DMU)

- **Primary and Secondary Influencers:** These individuals often have a depth of experience in the subject matter, and can influence the rest of the DMU, including the champion and end user.

Typically, influencers can be sorted into primary (plays a major role in the decision-making process) and secondary players (plays some part in the decision-making process). Sometimes, the influencers may also have formal Veto Power, but other times, the influencer is trusted enough that his or her word acts as a de facto veto. Other influencers in the decision-making process may include media publications, individual journalists, outside contractors, friends and family, industry groups, websites, blogs, and anyone else who the Primary Economic Buyer turns to for information and feedback.

- **Person with Veto Power:** These individuals have the ability to reject a purchase for any reason. Often, in a B2B environment, this individual outranks the advocate or end user in a corporate hierarchy.
    - In a consumer market, an individual rarely has Veto Power; rather, the primary influencer(s) may have the authority or be well-respected enough to exert a de facto veto. One example of true Veto Power in a consumer situation would be a homeowner's association or town zoning law that requires your customer to obtain a special variance from the association or town before being able to install or use your product. In that case, the association or town would be part of the Decision-Making Unit. In a corporation, the IT department often has veto power over acquisition of computer hardware and software if it does not comply with corporate standards.
    - Unions and collective bargaining agreements may also block purchase of your product because of certain provisions that have become essentially regulations in the business in question.
- **Purchasing Department:** This department handles the logistics of the purchase. They can be another obstacle, as this department often looks to drive prices down, even after the decision to purchase has been made by the Primary Economic Buyer. They can try to disqualify you based on certain purchasing rules that the company has set. In general, they are a link in the chain that you should neutralize but not sell to.

Understanding the Decision-Making Unit of your customer is integral in determining how you will develop, position, and sell your product. It will give you great insight into what your odds of success are and importantly, how much resource, skill, and time it will take for a new customer to acquire your product.

You will gather more information about the acquisition process, both in the Process to Acquire a Paying Customer and throughout the 24 Steps, but this is a great place to start your research.

HOW TO DETERMINE THE DECISION-MAKING UNIT

Once again, operating in "inquiry" mode rather than "advocacy/sales" mode is how you get helpful information about the DMU. If the customer believes that your product provides a strong value proposition, the conversation will flow naturally. This is an excellent time to ask the customer, "Assuming we could produce the product we have described, what would need to be done to bring a product in to test out? Who besides you (make sure you make them feel good!) would be involved in the decision to bring our product in? Who will have the most influence? Who could stop this from happening? Assuming the product does what we believe it will do, whose budget will the money come from to pay for it? Does this person need anyone else to sign off on this budget? Who will feel threatened by this and how will they react?"

You will also want to refer back to the research you have already done. When you built the Persona initially, you should have found some information about who or what influences the Persona, from people and organizations, to websites, publications, and media gurus.

If the Advocate or Primary Economic Buyer are not your Persona, you will want to build a fact sheet similar to your Persona fact sheet for the individual in each role. You will have to think about how you will appeal to them, so you get a "yes" or at least a "neutral" response.

Once you have gathered this information, plot it out visually so the information is unambiguous. You can then show this map to your Persona and Next 10 Customers to get feedback quickly, helping you revise the map until it accurately reflects the DMU for your first set of customers. The map also helps communicate the gathered information within your team. The DMU for each customer should be similar, and you should see patterns start to emerge. If you do not, either your customers do not match the Persona, or you have not segmented the market enough.

EXAMPLES

B2B Example: Mechanical Water Filtration Systems

Previously we looked at the Mechanical Water Filtration Systems venture, which chose to focus on producing a water purification solution for data centers and ended up with the Persona of Chuck Karroll.

While determining the DMU for their Persona, and validating that DMU with their Next 10 Customers, the team behind Mechanical Water Filtration found out that Chuck was the Primary

Economic Buyer and Advocate as well as the end user, but there were a number of other key players to consider.

Determining secondary influencers was also straightforward; this group included the Hamilton and Manos blog, the AFCOM meetings Chuck attended, and the occasional Uptime Institute events that he was involved with (including their newsletter). The DMU within the company, however, turned out to be rather complex.

First of all, the team explored the relationship between the facilities manager, the data center manager, and the chief information officer (CIO), both for the Persona's company and the Next 10 Customers. The team found out that the typical data center manager was generally more involved in the purchasing process than Chuck's data center manager was. Data center managers typically viewed themselves as secondary buyers, since the facilities manager's budget was contained within the data center manager's budget, providing the data center manager with veto power. However, if the facilities manager made a strong and convincing case for purchasing something, it would be unlikely the data center manager would veto the decision.

The CIO of the organization was involved in a tangential way. The CIO would never drive the decision, but if a purchase ran counter to his goals or he saw the purchase as risky, he would veto it. He would ask questions to test the proposal but had little influence. He was also very unlikely to block a decision jointly supported by the facilities manager and the data center manager.

The team initially thought the company's Chief Green Officer (CGO—a playful name they gave him) would be an advocate for the product. However, the research showed that the CGO was not taken seriously by the facilities manager. The CGO could advocate to the CEO of the company to secure some one-time funds in support of the purchase, but the CGO was a secondary player who was more helpful as a source of information to the company on how they could adjust their sales strategy, rather than a driver of the process.

The team, however, underestimated the influence external contractors had on the decision-making process. As it turned out, external contractors had a heavy influence on the facilities manager because they built and retrofitted data centers on a regular basis, while the facilities manager did not. Therefore, the facilities manager looked to them as a major source of information on water cooling solutions. The team realized that they needed to build a Persona-like fact sheet on the contractors and come up with a value proposition as to why their solution was a positive event for them too. The team also needed to understand the internal group within the company who recommended and handled outside consultants on a regular basis.

Not understanding any of these constituencies could lead to mystifying delays in the sales process; offending them or proposing something counter to their interests would likely kill the proposed acquisition.

Other players that you see on the map in Figure 12.1 had to be kept in mind as well, despite not being primary players in the process. The mechanical contractor did not have a lot of influence, but the team was wise to touch base with him to make sure that he did not propose replacing their solution with a cheaper one. The purchasing department did not have much influence, either. It was at the end of the chain, but the team had to be aware of their procedures and policies, and make sure not to make mistakes at that point in the process.

All of this is shown in the DMU map in Figure 12.1.

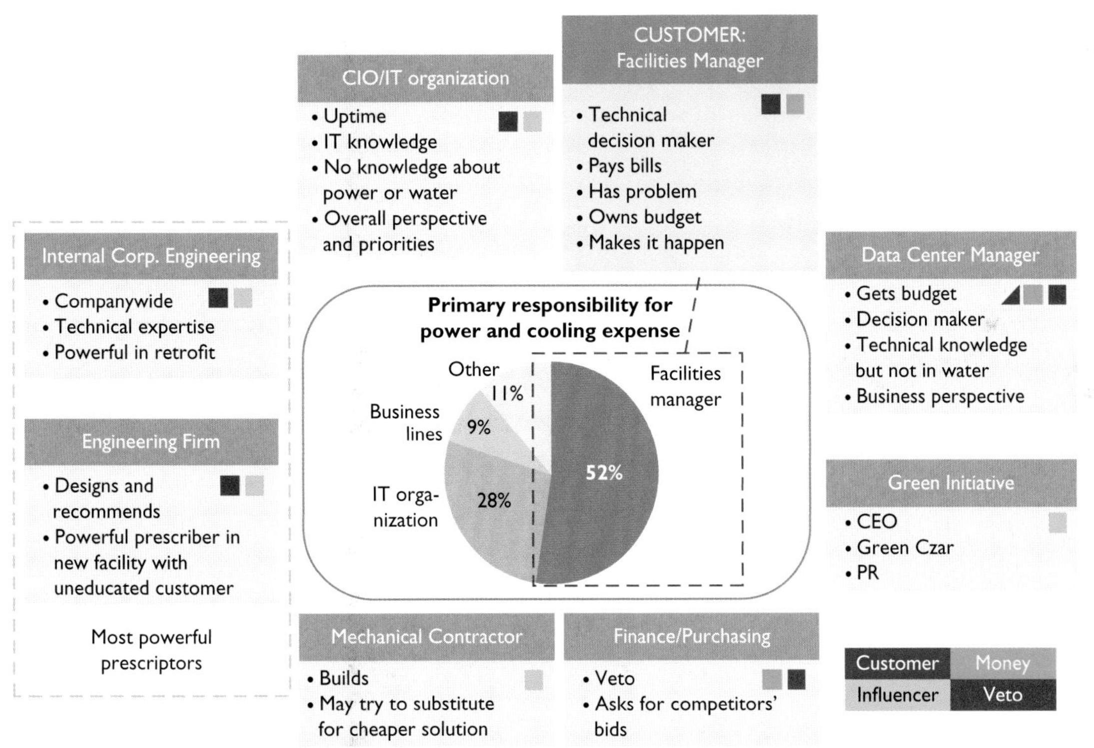

Figure 12.1 The Chuck Karroll decision-making unit.

B2B Example: The Curious Case of Healthy Air

The Decision-Making Unit analysis can also help you troubleshoot issues with previous work you have done in the 24 Steps. Some of my students decided to create a product with new technology that killed airborne germs more effectively than previous methods. When it came time to identify the beachhead market, one team member, who was a parent, thought that day care centers would be an excellent beachhead market. The team let the parent's excitement carry the day, and did not do a rigorous analysis of the market on their first pass through the process. This misstep led to them defining a Persona around the owner of a day care center, and defining the value proposition as parents being more inclined to send their kids to such a center, paying more money for their care. The team demonstrated that parents saw value in the product.

However, when the team analyzed the Decision-Making Unit, they came back with ashen faces, saying they needed a new beachhead market. When the team had gone to day care center owners, the owners deferred the decision to the individuals who ran the individual centers, deeming the decision not important enough to handle themselves. The first time the team pitched to these individuals, they were lukewarm at best about the idea. One was openly hostile, and let the team in on a secret. Preventing children from getting sick was not a motivator for day care centers since it did not impact the business or revenue; parents were required to commit and generally pay in advance for child care. So the center did not lose money when children stayed home sick. Further, children sick at home meant fewer children at the center, making the child care providers' jobs easier. While the centers did not want to encourage illness, they had perverse incentives to not discourage it.

The team thought about various ways to overcome these objections, but ultimately went back and chose another beachhead market.

Consumer Example: LARK Technologies

One of our star students, Julia Hu, started a company where the initial concept of the product was a silent alarm clock for consumers. The device consisted of a vibrating wristband linked wirelessly to an iPhone app that controls what time the alarm goes off. The idea was that for couples who sleep in the same bed, a silent alarm allows those couples with differing sleep requirements to keep separate schedules rather than be awoken by the earlier riser's alarm.

The Decision-Making Unit for their target customer turned out to have two members—the early riser was the end user (often male); the late riser was the advocate (often female). While the early riser was also the Primary Economic Buyer, the late riser was the one who wanted the early riser to stop waking her up. The late riser would put pressure on the early riser to find and pay for a solution.

It turns out that the end user/Primary Economic Buyer was a frequent visitor to the website Urban Daddy, which served as a primary influencer both by providing ideas for items to purchase and by offering special discounts to encourage a purchase (i.e., flash sales).

Julia and her team targeted Urban Daddy to get to the Primary Economic Buyer. Once their product was on Urban Daddy, they began to receive orders at a rate of one per minute.

SUMMARY

Having determined how you create value for the customer, you must now look at how the customer acquires the product. To successfully sell the product to the customer, you will need to understand who makes the ultimate decision to purchase, as well as who influences that decision. The Champion and the Primary Economic Buyer are most important; but those holding Veto Power, as well as Primary Influencers, cannot be ignored. B2B situations are easier to map out, but the process is still important in a consumer situation; large consumer goods companies like Procter and Gamble have been doing this process for many years.

STEP 13

Map the Process to Acquire a Paying Customer

IN THIS STEP, YOU WILL:

- Map out the process by which a customer decides to purchase your product.
- Estimate the sales cycle for your product.
- Identify any budgetary, regulatory, or compliance hurdles that would slow down your ability to sell your product.

After knowing who will make the decision, it is critical to know how they will make the decision and what is involved in each step so that you can design your product to optimize for this process.

Determining the Decision-Making Unit of your customer is a big step toward figuring out how to get your product into your customer's hands and money into yours. However, the process by which you convert a potential customer into a paying customer, and from initial contact to final payment, is more complicated than asking your Advocate to pressure your Primary Economic Buyer.

By creating a map of the Process to Acquire a Paying Customer, you will:

- Understand the length of the sales cycle. The length of the sales cycle is a crucial determinant in how expensive it will be for you to acquire new customers. It is also critically important to project cash flow accurately. You will need to go from initial contact to paying customer quickly enough for you to create a sustainable business.
- Build the foundation for the Cost of Customer Acquisition calculation. You will need to reach a point where you make more money from current customers than you spend attracting new customers. It always costs more than you would think to acquire customers.
- Identify hidden obstacles that will inhibit your ability to sell your product and get paid. If something about your business will be a deal breaker, you want to know now, rather than once you have fully committed to the business, raised money, and hired employees.
- Be able to show your potential lenders and/or investors that you understand the customer's buying process, which for many is a prerequisite to investing in your business.

HOW TO MAP THE PROCESS

The following items from the Full Life Cycle Use Case (Step 6) will be the basis for mapping the process to acquire a paying customer. You do not need to do additional work on these items in order to use them in this step.

- How customers will determine they have a need and/or opportunity to move away from their status quo and how to activate customers to feel they have to do something different (purchasing your product).
- How customers will find out about your product.
- How customers will analyze your product.
- How customers will acquire your product.
- How customers will install your product.
- How customers will pay for your product.

By mapping the process to acquire a paying customer you will capture more detail about each of these items especially now considering the DMU, as well as map out the internal purchasing mechanisms of your target customer. A seasoned entrepreneur with extensive industry experience may be able to build a map of the process relatively quickly; but the first-time entrepreneur will find the task tougher, with lots of educational moments on how the real world works. It is always good to find someone with deep experience from your target customer group as an advisor to learn about very specific and critical information such as this.

Some elements in your map will vary depending on the industry, but the basic components of the process will include lead generation, access to influencers, pre-purchase planning, purchasing, and installation. Many of these elements will also have multiple subcomponents. For instance, talking with the end user may be one component; talking with the end user's supervisor may be another component.

Be sure to factor in any regulations from governmental or quasi-governmental organizations that would potentially impact your ability to sell your product. You should have uncovered in the DMU (Step 12) whether any governmental officials hold Veto Power over a project—such as when a regulator must approve an element or milestone in the process. By mapping this process, you will also outline what regulations you and your customer are required to fulfill in order for the product to be sold. One example of regulations proving too onerous for a business idea is presented later in this step. Similarly, there could be internal standards for your target customer's company that must be complied with, rather than regulations; but the process is still the same.

For each component in the process, include:

- Who are the key players from the DMU that will be involved?
- What is their influence on the process? Again, this is hopefully information you have already obtained in Step 12 when you built the DMU; but now we are putting it in temporal order and developing educated estimates on how long each component will take.
- What is their budget authority (amount and type)?
- How long will it take to complete each component you identify? List them in temporal sequence noting any that can run in parallel. (Be diligent. You need to have at least 80 percent certainty in each step. Make conservative estimates because entrepreneurs almost always underestimate the time to complete each step.)
- What are the inputs and outputs of this step?

Through this process, you will better understand the customer's business as it relates to your product. Mapping out this process is important because you will need to navigate the same process over and over to sell to more customers; so understanding this process will pay dividends later, when you can more easily acquire new customers.

BUDGETING/PURCHASING AUTHORITY

A key factor in each component of this Step is to identify the budgeting/purchasing authority of each individual involved in that component of the process as appropriate. One common limit you will find is that an individual can only purchase items up to a certain dollar amount, such as $5,000, without approval from a more senior person. Sometimes, this approval comes directly from one decision maker, while other times, it kicks off a long and involved process with the purchasing department and its regulations. Identifying these limits may help with your Pricing Framework later on, because a price lower than an individual's limit means you can eliminate certain players from the DMU who would otherwise be involved in the process. This could dramatically reduce your sales cycle, which could be the difference between success and failure for your new venture.

Another important consideration is whether payment will come from the yearly operating budget or the longer-term capital budget. Identify which budget your customer would use to pay for your item, and what that budgeting process is. In some companies, it may be much easier and faster to get approval to include an expense in the operating budget than in the capital budget; but with other industries and companies it may be exactly the opposite. While seemingly a small item, this could mean the difference between a three-month sales cycle and a one-year sales cycle, which could mean the success or failure of your new venture, especially if you are not aware of it a priori.

TIME IS OF THE ESSENCE

Make sure you take into consideration the time it takes to move through each step in the process. Once you have made all your time estimates, go back and validate whether the estimates are reasonable. Are you accounting for delays? Are you being aggressive or conservative in your estimates?

CONSUMER VERSUS B2B

The process map for a consumer will likely be simpler than the map for a B2B environment, but there is still plenty to learn from it. Think of the gains as online retailers who are determined to finds ways to streamline the purchasing process, such as in Amazon's famous "one-click" system. Entrepreneurs were able to look at a failure in the process—where buyers would abandon their electronic shopping cart prior to checkout—and determine from the customer's viewpoint what needed to be improved to help the checkout process along.

EXAMPLES

Mechanical Water Filtration Systems

The team working on this product was looking to sell to facilities managers new water purification systems that would help their data centers to be more energy efficient. They were initially planning to sell their system to new data center constructions because that would not involve having to replace an existing system or sell against a solution that already worked for the data center. Besides, they were getting more inquiries from new data center constructions as opposed to retrofit situations, so it seemed to make logical sense to pursue the new constructions market.

After extensive interviews, they mapped the Process to Acquire a Paying Customer at new data centers as well as retrofitting existing centers. In the process, they uncovered something interesting that changed their focus from new centers to retrofit opportunities, which caused them to revisit their Persona (Figure 13.1). As I described in Step 5, the team selected Chuck Karroll as their Persona.

The team had secured its first pilot program in a new data center in less than nine months, so they could have assumed that this was the sales cycle. But upon performing an analysis of developing the map of the Process to Acquire a Paying Customer more generally, they realized that the way they had secured the pilot was not repeatable for other customers. When they looked at the length of the acquisition process for new data centers after the pilot, they discovered that the sales cycle would take an average of 2.5 years, which was way too long for a startup to survive week-to-week, with the ups and downs of cash, employee morale, and product stability. While the revenue from the pilot could help pay bills and minimize cash burn, the team looked toward retrofits as a better way to enter the market due to its shorter sales cycle. Such a long sales cycle could be managed to some degree by excellent (and likely experienced) entrepreneurs, but is usually the kiss of death for the first product of a brand-new business and new entrepreneur.

The middle range for installing the product in retrofit projects, by contrast, was just over a year, which was much more manageable than a 2.5-year time frame. (Even a year-long sales cycle is challenging for a startup, so even shorter would be ideal.)

However, the team had not seen many inbound queries about retrofits, so they revisited their Persona and did brand-new primary market research on the retrofit market. They found that existing data centers received the idea well, but they were much less likely to be shopping for a solution because they already had one that worked.

The team decided to focus on retrofits to get going, but once cash-flow positive, they would begin selling to new data centers as well. This was an extremely important insight that came out of the analysis.

Description of the Acquisition Process

NEW PROJECT

- Contact CIO to get approval and gain access to internal company specialist
- Contact internal company specialist/green czar/Corporate Facilities Manager to influence Engineer
- Contact design engineer to work together in definition of water system, give specifications, and have them prescribe MWFS
- Contact general contractor and Purchasing to ensure purchase and proper installation

RETROFIT

- Contact Facilities Manager and help him sell to Data Center Manager
- If necessary, contact CIO to get approval and gain access to Data Center Manager and internal company specialists
- Contact Facilities Manager/Data Center Manager/Purchasing to ensure purchase of our product and proper installation

NEW PROJECT

Lead Generation	Access to Influencers	Access to Design Engineers	Design Phase	Construction Phase: Actual Sale to Contractor	Installation
1–2 months	2–4 months	2–4 months	6–12 months	12–15 months	1 month

RETROFIT PROJECT

Lead Generation	Access to Facility Manager	Access to Influencers	Negotiation with Purchases and Budget Owners	Installation
1–2 months	4–6 months	2–4 months	2–3 months	1 month

Figure 13.1 Chuck Karroll's acquisition process.

When Regulations Make a Market Difficult to Enter: "PayPal for Kids"

One of my star MBA students, Frederic "Freddy" Kerrest, who also had a computer science degree from Stanford, entered MIT with the determination to found a major new venture upon graduation. He aggressively pursued opportunities to build his knowledge and experience in how to create new ventures. He even ran the legendary MIT $100K Entrepreneurship Competition.

He methodically evaluated ideas to start his company in his second year and settled on an idea that I will simply call "PayPal for Kids." The market opportunity centered around online commerce opportunities for children, an area that was constrained by the need for a parent to approve every transaction, no matter how small, because the parent's credit card was needed to make transactions.

Freddy's premise was that he could create a service expressly for kids where parents would place a set amount of money—say $50—in an account that kids could use to purchase items online, anywhere that credit cards are accepted, without parents needing to preapprove every purchase.

Parents could prevent money from being spent on sites and purchasing categories they did not approve of, and they would be able to see after the fact what their child had spent money on. Part of the value proposition to the Primary Economic Buyer (the parents) in this case was the ability to teach their children about personal budgeting and financial discipline.

From the excellent primary market research that had been done, it would appear that this was a great business opportunity. Then it came time to outline the Process to Acquire a Paying Customer. It was at that point that things began to change.

Freddy aimed his venture to serve parents and children throughout the United States. But he discovered that to collect money and distribute it as his model dictated, with his company getting a percentage of each transaction as revenue for his business, he needed to be registered as a bank or financial institution in any U.S. state he wanted to do business in. For his venture to be successful, he would therefore have to register as a financial institution in dozens of different states. The cost, time, and bureaucratic mentality needed to properly do this killed the idea, as Freddy did not want to start a business that needed to deal heavily with government regulations.

Freddy quickly used his newfound knowledge to continue to pursue ideas and partners with more wisdom. Based on his prior experience in enterprise software (deep market knowledge is always a great place to start as an entrepreneur), Freddy founded a company called Okta, which helps enterprises manage and secure web-based applications; the company is doing very well.

Here, the key hang-up in the Process to Acquire a Paying Customer was not the length of the sales cycle but rather the complexity of it and certain requirements that had been overlooked previously.

SUMMARY

Determining the Process to Acquire a Paying Customer defines how the DMU decides to buy the product, and identifies other obstacles that may hinder your ability to sell your product. From elongated sales cycles to unforeseen regulations and hidden obstacles, selling a product can sometimes be far more difficult than simply meeting the Persona's needs. This step makes sure you have identified all the potential pitfalls in the sales process.

STEP 14

Calculate the Total Addressable Market Size for Follow-on Markets

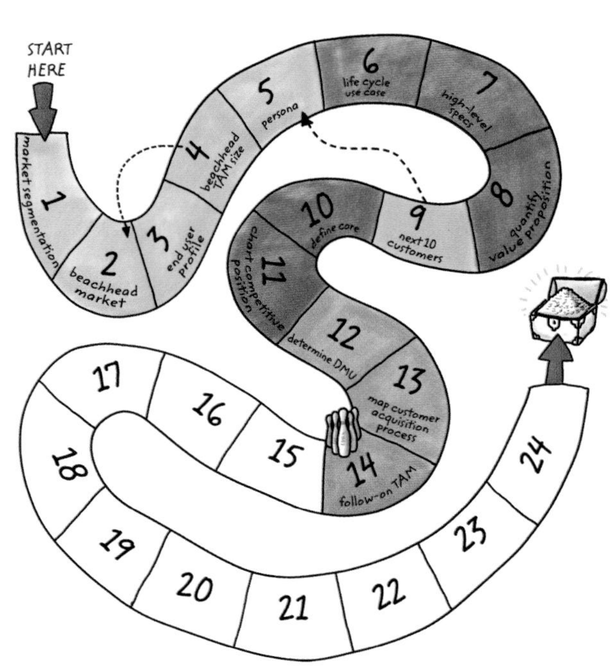

IN THIS STEP, YOU WILL:

- Briefly consider which "follow-on" markets you will expand to after dominating your beachhead market.
- Calculate the size of these follow-on markets.

While maintaining a relentless daily focus on your beachhead market, you should also do some small amount of analysis on what happens if and when you win the beachhead market; from a general standpoint and without a great deal of detail, what do you project will be your next markets and how big will they be?

So far, you have focused on customers in your beachhead market, and rightly so. At this point in the process, though, you will take a step back and briefly and quickly validate the existence and size of other, similar markets ("follow-on markets") that you will target once you have dominated the beachhead market. This is a check to make sure you are heading in the right direction to build a scalable business and also a reminder of the size and nature of the bigger opportunity.

There are two types of follow-on markets. One involves selling the same customer additional products or applications, which is often referred to as upselling. Since you already have a keen awareness of your target customer's needs and priorities from all of your research, this knowledge can be used to determine what additional products you could create for or even resell to the customer. One benefit is that you can use existing sales and distribution channels to sell the new products, leveraging the investment and positive relationship you have built with the target customer. However, making additional products will likely stretch your business beyond your Core, which may hurt your Competitive Position in those markets, unless your Core is something related to customer relationships.

The second market, and the path often taken by innovation-based startups, is to sell the same basic product to "adjacent markets," which are markets similar to your beachhead. While selling to these new markets usually requires additional features, product refinement, and/or different packaging, marketing communications, or pricing, you are leveraging the same Core, and building off the expertise and scale developed in the beachhead market. The challenge is that you will have to establish new customer relationships in each adjacent market, which can be risky and expensive.

While the Core of innovation-based startups often naturally leads to the latter strategy, you can pursue either strategy, or a mixture of the two, after dominating your beachhead market. Geoffrey Moore in *Crossing the Chasm* uses an analogy of bowling pins, where the "1" or lead pin is your beachhead market, the pins on the left side of the set are adjacent markets; the pins on the right side of the set are additional applications for the customer in a particular market (Figure 14.1).

In this step, you will identify some follow-on markets and determine the Total Addressable Market (TAM) for those markets. You need not and should not spend much time at all on this step right now—probably one-tenth or less of the effort and analysis you did for your beachhead market. Likely, much of the information you need for this Step was already gathered when you did your initial Market Segmentation.

What good does this process do? It keeps you cognizant of the long-term potential of your business as you begin to design your product and build capabilities. You will excite management, employees, and investors by showing that the business has the potential to be overwhelmingly successful. You will also get a better sense of other potential markets if your beachhead market turns out to be much more problematic than you envisioned and you have to either abandon it or revisit other options.

However, it is very important that you do not let this broader market and subsequent TAM calculation distract you and your team from the beachhead market. The broader TAM calculation

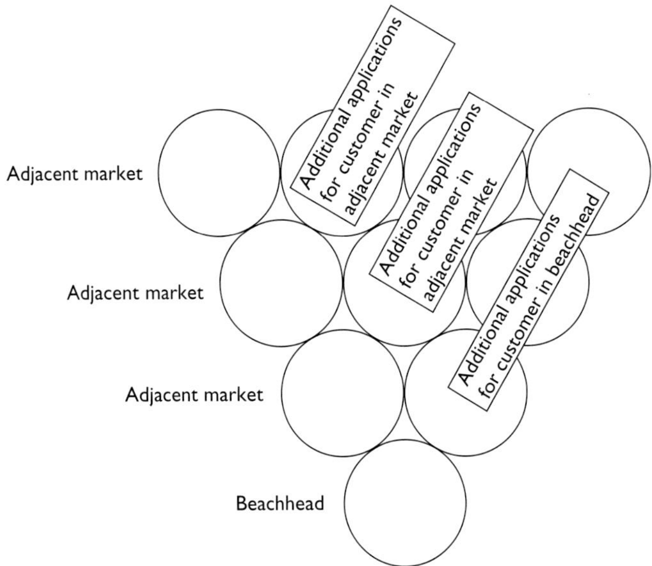

Figure 14.1 Modified Moore bowling pins.

should galvanize the team to conquer the beachhead market first, while keeping the team thinking about the importance of developing and growing the Core. As the cartoon at the beginning of the step illustrates, success in the follow-on markets only happens after you win your beachhead market.

HOW TO CALCULATE BROADER TAM

Think through the various adjacent markets and upselling opportunities that logically make sense with your product. You should be able to identify at least five or six follow-on markets. Use the same general methodology to calculate the TAM for each follow-on market that you did for your beachhead TAM in Step 4.

If you want to attract venture capital and/or build a big business, the general rule is that the broader TAM (for 10 or less follow-on markets), plus your beachhead market TAM, should add up to over $1B.

Use all the techniques I mentioned in Step 4, like making sure the units are correct; but you need a lot less primary market research for now.

EXAMPLE

Smart Skin Care

This team started with a beachhead market of sunscreen for extreme athletes, with a $20M per year TAM. Considering that their gross margins would be very high, this was a good-sized market to get started in and build up some momentum to attract much bigger markets—such as sunscreen to general consumers, potentially a multibillion dollar per year TAM.

They looked at other follow-on markets as well to see where they could use the underlying technology to easily enter markets and gain a large market share. Each of the market opportunities in their simple flow chart (Figure 14.2) were $100M or more per year and the TAM for the follow-on markets added up to around $2B per year. You don't need to get into a lot more detail than a

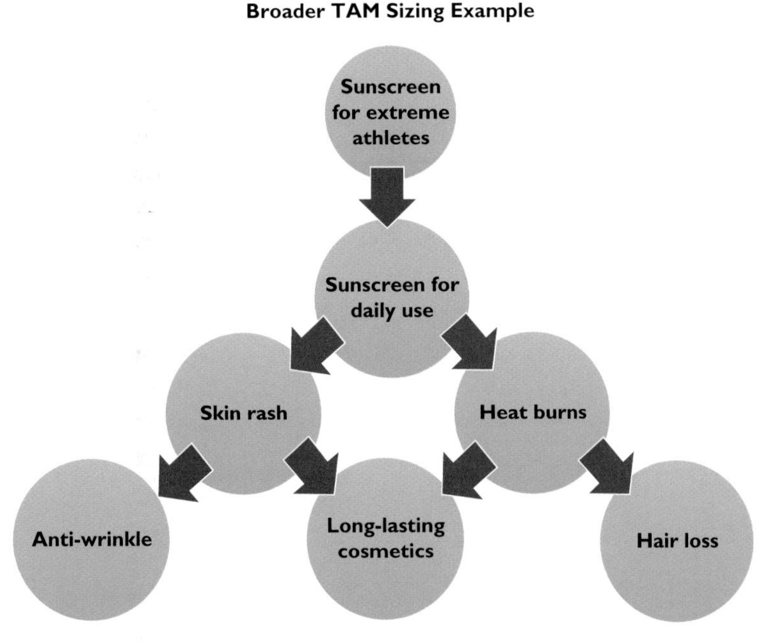

Figure 14.2 Broader TAM sizing for Smart Skin Care.

flowchart, though you should include the dollar amount for each follow-on market and the total TAM, neither of which are included in the flowchart shown.

SUMMARY

The Calculation of the Broader TAM should be a quick validation that there is a bigger market and should reassure team members and investors that your business has great potential in both the short term and long term.

STEP 15

Design a Business Model

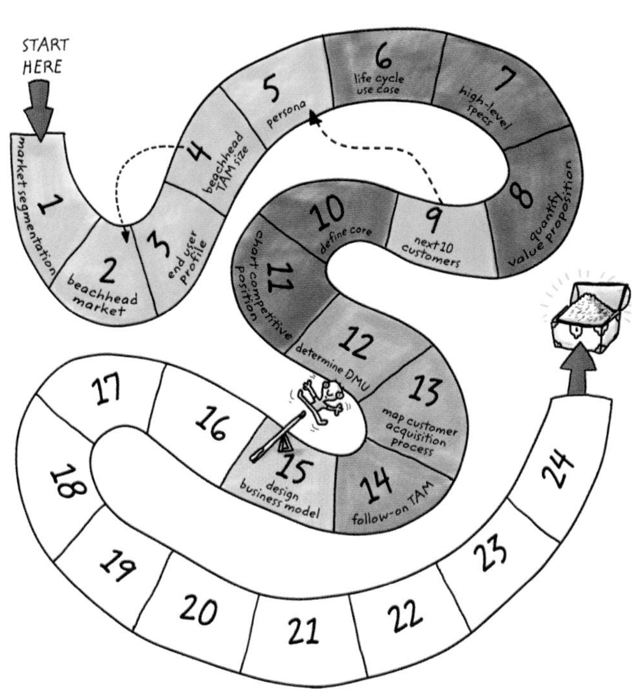

IN THIS STEP, YOU WILL:

- Examine existing models across industries for capturing some of the value your product brings to your customer.
- Use the work you have done in other steps to brainstorm an innovative model for your venture.

Methinks you need to get things more in balance!

How you will capture your share of the value you create is a topic that deserves more attention than entrepreneurs usually give it.

Entrepreneurs often spend a disproportionately small amount of time on their business model. They invest a lot of time in developing the End User Profile, the product definition, and the value proposition, showing how they will create value for the customer, but barely any time figuring out how that value translates into a profitable business. They are so excited to bring the product to market that they just default to adopting whatever business model is popular in similar markets.

Why spend all this time focusing on innovation related to technology and product design without a commensurate amount of time on innovating with your business model? The track record shows that companies that spend time and effort on innovative business models can see enormous payback.

Google's search product is an excellent example of an innovative business model. Prior to Google, the business model or "value capture framework" of search engines was to fit as many banner advertisements on a page as possible, and to charge as much as possible for them. Google, by contrast, used simple text ads and targeted them based on the keywords used in a particular search. Advertisers found this technique more attractive than banner ads, because they had better data on the effectiveness of individual ads, and could make more effective ads based on the data. This highly innovative business model is what made Google the juggernaut it is today, not the technical proficiency of its search algorithm.

Ironically, this idea of commercially viable contextual search was not Google's but rather came from Overture, an Idealab company that was the first to bring to the commercial market a credible keyword-based advertising solution under the name of GoTo.com. Google simply embraced the idea more enthusiastically and executed a rollout plan that made it the de facto leader in online advertising.

It is a similar story for Apple's iTunes. Before iTunes, the standard method of capturing value for digital music was to charge a monthly subscription fee for access to a library of music, where failure to pay the fee meant access to the music was cut off. Apple successfully differentiated itself with a one-time $.99 per song charge, after which the user could keep the digital song forever. Initially, this model was perceived as risky, so Apple had to put a lot of effort into getting music labels to agree to the model and to educate users on the model's benefits. The model ended up being a major factor, if not the major factor, in the success of iTunes relative to other music services, with a tremendously positive return on the investment Apple made in carefully and innovatively thinking through the value capture model.

Therefore, make sure to spend time on deciding what your business model for value capture will be and don't just default to the current standard in your industry.

As a new business, you will have many options for business models; but it is very difficult to change a business model once you have established a base of customers. This is one advantage you have over the current entrenched vendors in your industry area. Therefore, evaluate your business model through your customer's perspective when you launch and consider testing different options before you settle in on the business model you will use to capture value.

A BUSINESS MODEL IS NOT PRICING

A business model is a framework by which you extract from your customers some portion of the value your product creates for them. It is the idea that the amount of money your venture gets paid is based on how much value the customer gets from your product, and not some arbitrary markup based on your costs. You should constantly be working toward achieving business models and pricing that are value-based even if you have to make temporary shifts along the way to get there (e.g., joint development contracts, government projects, pilot projects where the scope is unclear and the risk is high). However, pricing matters surprisingly less than designing an effective business model, because the latter has a more direct influence on your ability to extract value over the lifetime of your business.

KEY FACTORS WHEN DESIGNING A BUSINESS MODEL

When thinking about an appropriate business model for your business, there is no one universally right answer, as it depends on your specific situation. There are four key factors that I always make sure entrepreneurs consider:

1. **Customer:** Understand what the customer will be willing to do. The knowledge you gained from mapping the Decision-Making Unit and Process to Acquire a Paying Customer will be valuable here.
2. **Value Creation and Capture:** Assess how much value your product provides to your customer and when. Then determine which ways of capturing value match up well. Your Quantified Value Proposition will help here.
3. **Competition:** Identify what your competition is doing.
4. **Distribution:** Make sure your distribution channel has the right incentives to sell your product.

FREE IS NOT A BUSINESS MODEL

There are two types of "business models," especially common among web companies. One, "freemium," is based on the idea that users get the basic functionality of the product at no charge and pay for premium features, whether through a subscription charge or by purchasing add-ons. The second is "we'll come up with something later," relying on investor money to get a sizeable user base before coming up with ways to be profitable. But neither of these are business models, because you do not have a business until you have someone actually paying money for your product.

In *Predictably Irrational*, author and respected behavioral economist Dan Ariely says that people will behave very positively toward your product when the price is zero because there is no friction to purchasing, as compared to a product priced at any amount above $0. Free will get many people to try your product, and can be part of an overall strategy to reduce your Cost of Customer Acquisition. However, that is about it, because you have not shown that any of your "customers" would actually pay for your product at any price, even a penny. And while these "customers" are using your product for free, you are still incurring costs to provide your product, so you will need some source of money to keep your business going, such as paying customers.

Instagram is a good example of a "business" that was not actually a business in my mind until it got its first paying customer, Facebook, which acquired the company whole. Such "lottery tickets" can gain a lot of users and can sometimes result in successful acquisitions, but they do not represent a sustainable model for actually staying in business. "Freemium" and "we'll come up with something later" can be a means to an end, but are not business models, because there is no proven business there.

GENERALIZED CATEGORIES OF BUSINESS MODELS

Thinking through some of the common types of business models will help you get a better sense of which is the best fit for you. You will likely decide on a hybrid business model that includes elements from multiple categories. It is a good idea to look at business models in industries other than your own; such lateral innovation often results in creative, effective business models. This list is designed to give you some exposure to the many options available, but you should also think beyond the list when designing your business model.

1. **One-time Up-Front Charge plus Maintenance:** This is the most common business model, where a customer pays a large up-front charge to obtain the product, with the option to secure ongoing upgrades or maintenance of the product for a recurring fee. The up-front charge may need to come out of the customer's capital budget, especially if the expense is large, and spending from the capital budget requires a potentially long and formal approval process. The ongoing maintenance charge would come out of the customer's operating budget. For your business, a large up-front infusion of cash is good because it helps offset your high cost of capital, but with this decision you will very likely minimize your ability to secure a recurring revenue stream.

2. **Cost Plus:** In this scenario, the customer pays a set percentage above the cost of producing the product. This is common in government contracts as well as situations where you and your customer want to share the risk of producing the product. The challenge with this model is that it requires agreement on the accounting assumptions, trusting that the numbers are correct and will continue to be correct. This model might also be attractive when your product is immature and there will almost surely be scope creep, but in that case, the offering should mature and you can then migrate to a different business model. It can also create incentives that reward activity rather than progress, which is bad for both you and your customer.
3. **Hourly Rates:** This model also tends to reward activity as opposed to progress, which can be the wrong incentive, but when a project is poorly defined or very dynamic, this might well be the preferred model. A common business model for services firms, it is similar to scenario number 2, but the rates are set by the market demand rather than costs.
4. **Subscription or Leasing Model:** This is a set payment each month or another predetermined and agreed-upon time period. It is a great way to get a recurring revenue stream. There are a number of variations, including:
    a. *Annual or Multi-Year Commitment:* This locks the customer in and provides them with predictable lower payments as opposed to a one-time up-front payment. One type is a subscription prepayment such as what MIT senior lecturer Howard Anderson used when he founded Yankee Group. He charged an annual fee for a monthly newsletter that would be delivered over the course of the year; the resulting up-front cash flow created less need for capital. (Note: Getting prepayments, even if you have to provide discounts, is generally good for startups.)
    b. *Month-to-Month Commitment:* This method gives the user great flexibility and you can often extract a much higher monthly payment for this arrangement, compared to an annual or multi-year agreement.
5. **Licensing:** Licensing your IP address to customers and receiving a royalty can result in a very high gross margin (gross margin is the difference between marginal revenue and marginal costs). In addition, if you are licensing your product, you do not have to make big investments in production and distribution capability for a whole product. However, there are many downsides to the strategy. Licensing generally only works when the IP is extremely strong. Another major consideration is that you are relying on existing companies to take your IP and create new disruptive products, which they may be hesitant to do as it threatens their short-term and medium-term interests of maintaining their existing products. Your

customer will be incented to find ways to make products that do not require use of your IP because if they can avoid paying you license fees, they can improve their gross margins. Another downside is that you are not spending time with the ultimate end user learning their needs, so your ability to continually innovate will be limited. Additionally, your royalty rate will generally be equivalent to one-twentieth or less of the revenue per sale; and hence the TAM will as well, because a five percent royalty rate is about the best you can hope for. Still, licensing can be an attractive option in areas like biotech, where re-creating the infrastructure necessary to make whole products is extremely costly.

6. **Consumables:** Another value capture framework that can be advantageous to both the customer and your business is the consumables model. For the customer, the benefit is a low up-front cost, with ongoing costs based on usage, which the customer can usually control. The customer might not have an easy way to pay for a large up-front cost but has much more capability to procure once usage has started. Once usage has started, they can justify the purchase of some consumable product the solution uses. The amount of consumable that needs to be purchased is directly related to usage; and, in many cases, your customer can pass the cost on to their own customers. For your business, it might very well be a way to reduce the friction to capture new customers and thereby reduce the sales costs and also substantially increase the amount of money you will get from that customer over the long term. This is a very popular model for medical devices, but it is also used frequently in the consumer space. A highly visible and well recognized example is the razor/razor blade model made famous by Gillette. HP is another example, where almost all if not all of their profit on printers comes from selling inkjet cartridges.
7. **Upsell with High-Margin Products:** Similar to the consumable business model, the central product is sold at a very low margin, but the overall margin is increased from the sale of very high-margin add-on products. This business model is often used in consumer electronics stores or websites and frequently in new car sales. In a consumer electronics retailer, frequently an item like a camera might be sold at just above cost, which attracts the customer, but then they buy add-ons that have a higher margin and customers are sold a warranty extension for one, two, or three years that also has a very high margin. Like buying a car, it is the additional items like warranty extension, accessories, rustproofing, and the like that are the high-margin products where sellers make the lion's share of their profits.
8. **Advertising:** As with newspapers and magazines in their heyday and now with websites, the ability to attract and retain a desirable demographic can be monetized through third parties who want access to the customers you have attracted. When done properly and on a sufficient scale, this can be a very lucrative model, as Google and others have shown; but many

startups have fallen substantially short when they attempt to rely solely on advertising. For businesses like LinkedIn, advertising is part of a broad portfolio of revenue streams.

9. **Reselling the Data Collected—or Temporary Access to It:** Somewhat similar to the advertising model, reselling user data requires first attracting end users with a free product, then receiving money from third parties who pay for access to demographic and other information about your users. This is a major source of revenue for LinkedIn, which sells a special package for recruiters that gives access to a wide array of LinkedIn user data. The medical industry also resells access to user data for market research.
10. **Transaction Fee:** Online retailers often pay or receive a commission for referrals that lead to sales. One obvious example is eBay, which receives a fee from each successful auction, paid by the seller. The model is similar to how credit card companies work, where a percentage of each transaction goes to the credit card company.
11. **Usage-Based:** A usage-based model—similar to how electric utilities are metered—has been used across various other industries. Cloud computing products, such as Amazon's cloud service that hosts websites, charge by the amount used. This allows customers more control over their expenses because they only pay for the amount of bandwidth used, rather than paying for extra capacity they don't use.
12. **"Cell Phone" Plan:** This is a predictable, recurring base fee charged in exchange for a certain amount of committed usage, with additional charges, often at much higher marginal rates, if the customer uses more than their allotted amount. The base charge is generally far less per amount of usage than the overage charge. You get predictability from the base charge, as does the customer, because they know what they can use; but they also have flexibility if they need additional usage. MIT senior lecturer Jim Dougherty, when he was at IntraLinks, used this strategy to effectively monetize its principal product, an online interface for lawyers and investment bankers to securely share documents with clients, in a manner his customer base greatly favored.
13. **Parking Meter or Penalty Charges:** When I lived in Cambridge, Massachusetts, I had always found it curious that the city had incredibly large and expensive parking meters that had to be put in the sidewalk extremely securely. And yet for a long time, the hourly parking rate was only $.25. It seemed to defy logic that a quarter per hour justified the significant purchase and installation costs of a meter, along with the expense of paying someone to collect the quarters. Of course one day it occurred to me how they made money when I came back to my car and found a $25 parking ticket that became a $40 ticket if I did not pay it in 10 days. What a business model! No wonder they have so many parking enforcement people.

But this is the same business model used by credit card companies and (for a while) Blockbuster by charging late fees. The problem that Blockbuster discovered, however, is that loyal customers can become alienated by such late fees, so when Netflix emerged with the tagline "no late fees," Blockbuster lost significant market share and never recovered. The lesson is, do not take advantage of your customer's naivete as a central pillar of your business model.

14. **Microtransactions:** A new successful model that came into vogue with online computer games, and is now being tested to try to save newspapers, is microtransactions. In this model, the customer is asked to provide their credit card and then they make very small (defined as less than $12; often they are $1 or less) transactions for digital goods (which have virtually no marginal cost because they are electrons). There are many of them so they can add up.
15. **Shared Savings:** This business model is often brainstormed, but rarely used because of the complexities in implementing it, despite its conceptual elegance. In this scenario, the customer pays only once they have realized savings or benefits from the product. One area where this has been used with success is the Energy Efficiency Service Companies (ESCOs) such as Ameresco. It is generally not implemented because it is hard to determine how much savings to attribute to the product, especially over a multiyear time period. One area where this model works, because the accounting is clear, is venture capital, where the general partner gets around 20 percent of the profits from their investments (this is termed the "carry").
16. **Franchise:** If an entrepreneur comes up with a good idea and is able to implement but does not have the desire, skills, or money to roll it out, they can use the franchise model and get paid a percentage of sales and/or receive a large initial startup fee in return for providing the knowledge and brand that has been developed. You can also make money by selling your brand-name products to the franchises to be distributed.
17. **Operating and Maintenance:** A new business might not want to really sell a product but rather get paid for running a plant or other operation for a fee. While this is similar in some ways to a consulting agreement, the customer has more incentives to control or cut costs, as it will directly impact the customer's income. This model is common in the energy sector.

This is nowhere near an exhaustive list of business models, but it will help you think about different ways to capture value for your business. There are many options, including crafting a hybrid of the above models or, as you will see in the next section, innovating a new type of business model. Brainstorm and, if possible, experiment with different variations.

THINK OUTSIDE THE EXISTING CATEGORIES

A Rhode Island company called Amie Street used an innovative business model to capture value from song downloads based on demand. The very first downloads would be free, but as the number of downloads increased, the company would increase the charge to the customer. Customers were incented to go and listen to music and see if they could pick songs before they became popular. If they recommended a song when it sold for a low dollar amount, and the song later gained popularity and increased its price, the recommender would be given 50 percent of the price difference.[1] Amie Street was bought by Amazon for an undisclosed price in September of 2010; what made Amie Street attractive to Amazon was the company's variable pricing and clever incentive schemes.

Be careful, though, not to spend so much time being clever with your business model that you lose focus on creating value. The two sides to a business, creating value and then capturing value through a business model, should be in balance.

SUMMARY

The business model is an important decision that you should spend time focusing on. The decisions you make here will have a significant impact on your profitability, as measured by two key entrepreneurship variables: the Lifetime Value of an Acquired Customer (LTV) and Cost of Customer Acquisition (COCA). Do not focus on pricing in this step, as your choice of business model has a far larger influence on profitability than your pricing decisions.

Once you have established a business model, it is possible but generally not easy to change to a different model. Therefore, choose a business model that distinguishes you from competitors and gives you an advantage over them, because they cannot easily change their business model to match yours.

[1] Michael Arrington, "Amie Street: Awesome New Music Model," *TechCrunch*, July 23, 2006, http://techcrunch.com/2006/07/23/amie-street-awesome-new-music-model.

STEP 16

Set Your Pricing Framework

IN THIS STEP, YOU WILL:

- Use your Quantified Value Proposition and Business Model to determine an appropriate first-pass framework for pricing your product.

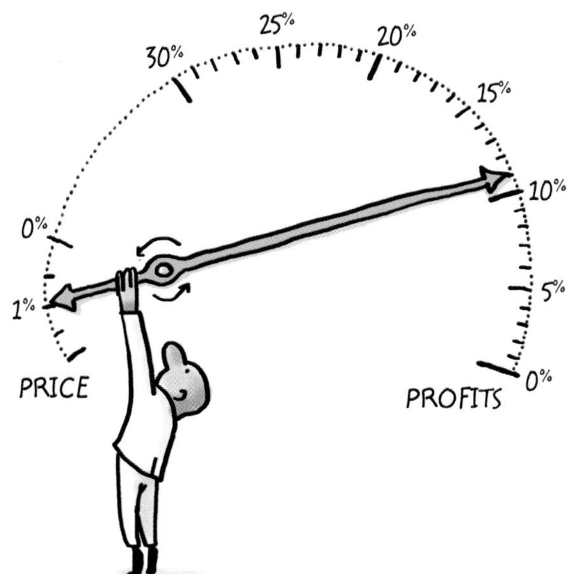

Improving pricing
can have a big effect on profits . . .
but be patient until the market
matures and you have enough info

Now that you have settled on a business model, it is time to start coming up with a pricing strategy. Fine-tuning the strategy can have a huge impact on your earnings.

With a business model in hand, you can now make a good first estimate on your Pricing Framework, understanding that it will likely change as you continue through the 24 Steps. This step is the beginning of a pricing process, because you will likely end up with multiple price points and pricing strategies, and you will iterate as you experiment and get feedback from the market about price points. Whereas your Business Model is much less likely to change, price points are often subject to change based on market conditions. Some businesses even change pricing on a daily basis (e.g., gas stations) or, even more dramatically, on a real-time basis (e.g., dynamic pricing of airline tickets).

Your goal for the moment is to create a first-pass strategy that will allow you to calculate the Lifetime Value of an Acquired Customer, which along with the Cost of Customer Acquisition is an important variable that indicates the profitability of your business. You will find it easier to go back and change your Pricing Strategy once you have gone through and made your other calculations, as opposed to trying to get everything right at first. Much like many of the other steps in this book, getting pricing right is an iterative and ongoing process where you start at some point that is the best guess for that moment and then you spiral closer and closer to a better answer.

The Pricing Framework is extremely important in influencing your profitability, so it is important you price your product correctly. In his book *The 1% Windfall*, Dr. Rafi Mohammed cites a McKinsey & Company study that shows that for companies in the Global 1200, a price that is 1 percent higher would lead to an 11 percent increase in overall profits, because once costs have been paid, the remaining revenue is all profit. Of course, there is always an upper limit to your price due to the dynamics of the Decision-Making Unit, Process to Acquire a Paying Customer, and sales cycle. The Pricing Framework is your attempt to strike a balance between attracting as much revenue as possible and attracting as many customers as possible.

BASIC PRICING CONCEPTS

1. **Costs Shouldn't Be a Factor in Deciding Price.** Set your pricing based on the value the customer gets from your product, rather than on your costs. Cost-based strategies almost always leave money on the table. In software, for instance, the marginal cost (the cost of producing one more copy of the software) is virtually zero, so pricing based on cost would make it extremely difficult to make any money. Instead, use your Quantified Value Proposition, determine how much value your customer receives from your product, and charge some fraction of that. The exact fraction depends on the competition and the industry, but 20 percent tends to be a reasonable starting point, leaving 80 percent of the value for the customer, who is taking a risk by incorporating your product into their infrastructure. Some companies,

like Microsoft and Intel, have been able to take advantage of monopolistic positions to price even higher, but short-term gains through this strategy may create long-term problems for your business if your customers think you are gouging them and other companies emerge with different or lower-priced products.

a. The percentage of customer value that you can capture with your pricing depends on your business model and how much risk you are pushing onto your customer. A monthly subscription model, where a customer is paying over time, but can also cancel at any time, will allow you to price higher than an up-front charge model, where the customer is taking additional risk by paying for the product in full before knowing how beneficial the product will be for them.

b. If costs come up in conversations about your product, make it clear that your price is not based on cost. Immediately turn the discussion around to how much value you create for the customer. As Steve Walske, the successful CEO of Parametric Technologies, is reputed to have said, "My business is very simple. My customers give me two dollars and they get back ten. That is why we are so successful."

c. Don't give out your cost numbers to anyone who does not have a real need to know. Definitely do not tell your sales group, because any good salesperson will use any and all of their resources to make a sale, even if it means driving the price down to costs. This mentality is in fact why you hired them, love them, and what makes them effective. (If you doubt this, read about the behavior of real estate agents in *Freakonomics* by Steven Levitt and Stephen Dubner.) If you open yourself up to conversations about costs it can lead back to inappropriate conversations about your pricing, which will lead to decreased morale, productivity, and potentially profitability.

2. **Use the DMU and the Process to Acquire a Paying Customer to Identify Key Price Points.** The Decision-Making Unit and Process to Acquire a Paying Customer provide invaluable information about how your customer's budget works. Knowing an individual's purchasing authority limits can help reduce friction in the sales process. One example of using this information to inform your pricing comes from Kinova of Montreal, Quebec. Kinova sells the Jaco assistive robotic arm for disabled people in wheelchairs (Figure 16.1). When Kinova entered the market in the Netherlands, their primary market research found that consumers could get reimbursed up to 28,000 euros from their health insurance for purchasing the product. If the price went above 28,000 euros, Kinova would need the consumer to pay the extra amount out of pocket, creating friction in the sales process. Despite an extremely strong value proposition that could have supported a higher price, Kinova priced its product at

Figure 16.1 Kinova's Jaco assistive robotic arm.

28,000 euros, which dramatically decreased the company's sales cycle length and Cost of Customer Acquisition. As a result, the company quickly ramped up sales and enjoyed a much larger market share than it would if it had priced the product at a higher amount.

3. **Understand the Prices of the Customer's Alternatives.** It is imperative to understand, from the customer's perspective, the alternative products available, and how much the customer would pay for each, including the customer's status quo. Carefully research what other alternatives would achieve similar benefits for the customer, what the prices of those alternatives are, and how much better your solution is. Data collection and analysis is very critical in this step.
4. **Different Types of Customers Will Pay Different Prices.** When I was getting one of my companies off the ground, I got some sage advice after presenting to legendary entrepreneur Mitch Kapor. "The bad news," he said, "is you will sell half as many units as you think you will. But the good news is you will be able to sell to the first group of buyers at twice the price you think you will." He was spot-on. Geoffrey Moore explains why in *Crossing the Chasm*. Different types of customers will pay different amounts, depending on how early or late they are buying relative to other customers, so a differentiated pricing strategy and structure for these distinct customer segments will mean substantially higher profits for your business.

Moore breaks customers down into five waves:

a. **Technological enthusiasts** are the first people to buy a product. They love technology and will buy one of anything. Some are consumers, while others work in university R&D labs, national labs, or companies like General Electric. They will only buy one (hence half the number you expect) but since they want to have it right away, before anyone else, they are willing to pay a much higher price (hence twice the price).

b. **Early adopters** are also price-inelastic but are very interested in feeling like they got a special deal and will require lots of attention and extra service; so make sure to build that into your pricing model.

c. **The early majority (pragmatists)** is where you will make yourself a great and truly scalable company. That is the price point that most of us think about when we are talking about and planning for a pricing strategy.

d. **The late majority (conservatives)** are later in the process and your pricing strategy will be very clear by then; they like well-defined, conservative plans.

e. **Laggards/skeptics** come so late in the process that you may have already sold your company at this point.

5. **Be Flexible with Pricing for Early Testers and "Lighthouse Customers."** These two types of customers are beneficial to have early on. Early testers will collaborate with you to improve your product, and lighthouse customers strongly influence the purchasing decisions of others in the industry. Allow for flexibility on pricing with these two groups of customers, whether through discounting an up-front charge or through a free or low-cost trial period, as it is important to get them committed and satisfied. These customers may help you create case studies or do on-site seminars where you can promote your product, or otherwise be strong references in the market. However, do not give your product away to these customers, and do not discount any ongoing revenue streams, because that would signal that your product has a very low value, setting a dangerous precedent. Have early customers sign an agreement where their pricing terms be kept confidential, and be firm with other, later customers who try to secure the same pricing terms, because you do not want your early one-time-only deals to define your general pricing strategy. Additionally, if you have the option to discount hardware or software, I much prefer to discount the hardware and hold the line on software pricing. Customers can more easily understand hardware value versus software value, and it will be easier to reestablish higher hardware pricing as opposed to reestablishing software pricing.

6. **It Is Always Easier to Drop the Price Than to Raise the Price.** It is best to price high and offer discounts initially, rather than price too low and find you need to raise the price later. Usually, your first customers will have larger budgets than your later customers who are more likely to accept less-than-cutting-edge technology in exchange for a lower price. Also, you will find it difficult to convince customers to accept a higher price when they are used to paying a lower price. Sometimes, a price increase is necessary as you learn more about the market, but successful price increases do not happen frequently.

EXAMPLE

Helios

This student team was working on developing an exciting new thin-film technology that captured solar energy and could release the energy on demand. The team's beachhead market was remotely deicing windows on corporate and government fleets of automobiles.

The team factored in that the primary alternatives to their product were drivers manually deicing their individual cars, or maintenance employees manually deicing a fleet. Union rules and desires also had to be included. To get to a good educated guess on pricing, the team had to clearly understand its Quantified Value Proposition, as well as the rational and emotional qualities of the Decision-Making Unit.

The team created a first-pass Pricing Framework, and then once they calculated their Lifetime Value of an Acquired Customer and Cost of Customer Acquisition in later steps, they went back and revised their Pricing Framework based on those calculations. In the revised pricing framework, they set the price at $100 per unit, which would provide $100K in the first year of sales (based on the target customer's average vehicle fleet size of 1,000). With average 20 percent fleet turnover, they would net $20K per year afterward. As part of their framework, they compared their technology to window tinting, concluding that customers would judge their pricing against what they were used to paying for tinting. The strategy also discussed a discounting strategy for pilot customers to jump-start positive word of mouth.

This case is a good reminder that different steps depend on each other, and you should continually revisit and revise your assumptions based on work done in later steps.

SUMMARY

Pricing is primarily about determining how much value your customer gets from your product, and capturing a fraction of that value back for your business. Costs are irrelevant to determining your pricing structure. You will be able to charge a higher price to early customers as opposed to later customers, but be flexible in offering special, one-time-only discounts to select early testers and lighthouse customers, as they will be far more beneficial to your product's success than the average early customer. Unlike your business model, pricing will continually change, both as a result of information you gather and as you progress throughout the 24 Steps, as well as in response to market conditions.

STEP 17

Calculate the Lifetime Value (LTV) of an Acquired Customer

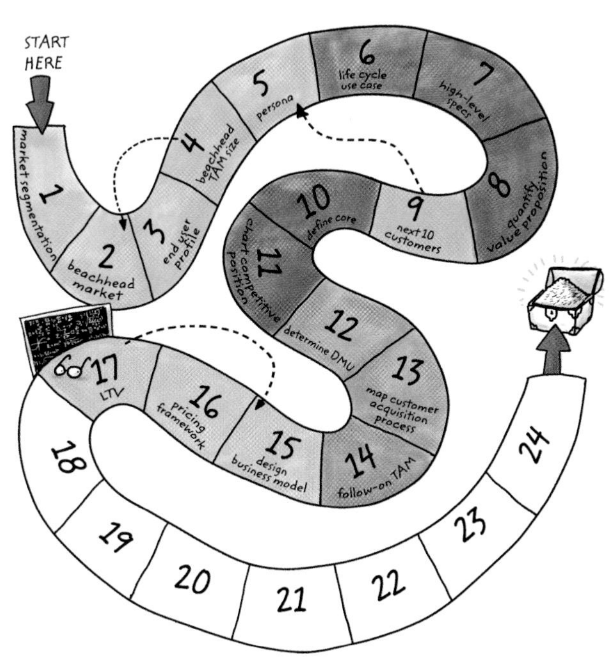

IN THIS STEP, YOU WILL:

- Add up the revenue that you can expect to receive from an individual customer.
- Discount the revenue based on how much it will cost you to repay investors over time.

Now that you have determined at least a first pass on your value capture model and specifics, you can start to do the simple fundamental math for a new venture. Can you acquire customers at a cost that is substantially less than their value will be to your new venture over the customer's lifetime?

So far you have done a lot of very important analysis grounded in real-world customer interaction to see generally if and how your new venture would work. Now you will do the math or "unit economics" to discern whether it is a sustainable and attractive business from a microeconomic standpoint. The Lifetime Value of an Acquired Customer (LTV) calculation, along with the Cost of Customer Acquisition (COCA) calculation, will help you determine how profitable your business will be in the beachhead market. The LTV serves as the most fundamental checkpoint both to determine how viable the business is, and to make sure you clearly understand what will drive the sustainability and profitability of the business so that you stay focused going forward.

A very expensive case study regarding the importance of LTV, COCA, and unit economics can be seen in Pets.com. The company was founded in August 1998 to sell products over the Internet to consumers for their pets. The concept was that people spent a lot of money on their pets and that this new company could capture those sales and become very large and profitable with a new business model that did not involve the costs of maintaining brick-and-mortar retail stores.

The concept and the strength of the management team allowed the company to easily raise millions of dollars from investors. In their drive to build a brand and acquire customers, they aggressively advertised their website, including a high-profile Super Bowl commercial in 2000. They were acquiring customers but had not rigorously analyzed the unit economics.

When they finally did so, they realized that because of the low margin on the products they were selling and the very high costs of customer acquisition, which had stayed relatively constant rather than decreasing as they should, the company was losing money with each new customer it captured. The company was bleeding cash but management doubled down and said it was simply a matter of volume, that when the customer base was large enough, the company would be cash-flow positive. This was wishful thinking rather than genuine economic analysis because management had not developed a clear path to increase the LTV, nor had they developed a clear path to significantly reduce the COCA. So the bleeding of cash just increased as they got more customers.

Soon the investors woke up and realized that the math for Pets.com did not work. In November 2000, the company was shut down and assets were liquidated. Three hundred million dollars of investor money had been lost, but, to put a positive spin on it, it can be viewed as a $300 million educational lesson to make sure people are disciplined and intellectually honest about their unit economics analysis before they invest too much time, money, or energy into a new venture.

One would think that this education would prevent future mistakes along this line, but this has not been the case. In what will most likely prove to be an even more costly example of not paying attention to the unit economics of a new venture, Groupon has failed to focus sufficiently on these fundamentals. The company, founded in 2008, grew slowly at first, but then began rapidly expanding with its product, which in a large number of regions offered a deep discount every day for a different business. The company leveraged word-of-mouth advertising through social media to become a fast-growing company—in terms of revenue. It became the darling of many, including investors, the press, and its customers, but there was a problem. Groupon had not established a viable Core, so as competition increased, its LTV would likely go down and its COCA would go up as it fought in a crowded marketplace to find more customers. They never figured out the unit economics and once the buzz wore off and people started to look at their financials, this problem became clear. As of this writing, the story has not come to closure like the Pets.com case but I can assure you that many people wished they had spent more time on unit economics early on in the company's life cycle.

Over the next three steps, you will work to determine the LTV and COCA, starting with the LTV. Both are important, because if there is not a clear way to end up with the LTV substantially higher than the COCA, you will not be able to cover your business costs such as product development, finance, administration, and overhead.

All the work you have done in the previous steps, like defining the DMU, mapping the customer acquisition process, identifying a Core and a plan to grow it, will help you to logically estimate the unit economics over time. Big changes in these factors, like the DMU, could dramatically affect your unit economics; so it is crucial to keep a close eye on making those as real as possible and noting any changes in them over time.

KEY INPUTS TO CALCULATE THE LTV

Now I will take you through precisely how to calculate the LTV of a customer. While the final number will likely be a range and not necessarily correct the first time you do it, it is very important to understand what drives the value of LTV. In other words, you need to know much more than just a number; you need to understand the underlying factors so you can understand your risks and how you can increase LTV over time. It will also help you when you get real paying customers and you need to analyze what their LTV is and how it is trending. This is how and when you will make adjustments to continually monitor whether your unit economics are on track to a viable, sustainable, and attractive future. Here are the key inputs that you will need to understand to estimate the LTV:

1. **One-time Revenue Stream, If Any.** Typically, if there is an up-front charge for your product, it is a one-time source of revenue.
2. **Recurring Revenue Streams, If Any.** Subscription and maintenance fees, as well as repeated purchases of consumables, are all recurring revenues.

3. **Additional Revenue Opportunities.** If there are opportunities to "upsell" the customer, where the customer purchases additional products with minimal additional effort from your sales team, include these as revenue streams. Remember to consider the DMU and the sales cycle you calculated earlier. Underestimating either of these could lead you to a distorted view.
4. **Gross Margin for Each Of Your Revenue Streams.** The gross margin is the price of your product minus the production cost of making an individual product. Cost does not include sales and marketing costs (which is factored into the COCA) or overhead costs like R&D or administrative expenses.
5. **Retention Rate.** For each recurring revenue stream, this rate is the percentage of customers who continue to pay the recurring fee for the product. This usually expressed as a monthly rate or a yearly rate. (The opposite of retention rate is "churn rate," which is the percentage of customers you lose.) Assume, for simplicity, that once the customer has stopped paying a recurring fee, the customer will no longer be receptive to upselling. Do not assume that on a multiyear or multimonth contract customers will make all of their payments. Early termination of a contract by the customer should be incorporated into the retention rate.
6. **Life of Product.** For each one-time revenue stream, this is the length of time you expect the product to last before the customer will need to either purchase a replacement or discontinue use of the product.
7. **Next Product Purchase Rate.** For each one-time revenue stream, this rate is the percentage of customers who will buy a replacement product from you when the current product has reached the end of its life.
8. **Cost of Capital Rate For Your Business.** Expressed as a yearly rate, this is how much it costs you, in debt or equity, to get money from investors for your business. For a new entrepreneur who lacks a track record and is just getting started, the appropriate number is most likely between 35 and 75 percent per year.[1] This number is so high because an investor gives you money he cannot get back for years at a time (an illiquid investment). The investor is also taking a great risk because you are a brand-new business. These two factors mean that investors will charge you quite a premium for capital.

[1] William A. Sahlman, "A Method for Valuing High-Risk, Long-Term Investments," *Harvard Business School*, Case 9-288-006, August 12, 2003.

HOW TO CALCULATE LIFETIME VALUE

The LTV is the Net Present Value of your profits from year 0 through year 5. As a brand-new business, you will calculate the LTV over a five-year period. When projecting more than five years out, the compounded cost of capital for a startup is so high that it negates what value your customer provides you beyond five years. The customer still has value to you beyond five years, but you also have to factor your cost of capital rate into the calculation.

The LTV is expressed in dollars per customer, so to calculate this you will use the prices that an individual customer pays.

For each revenue stream, you will use the gross margin and the retention rate to calculate your profit for the first year your customer buys the product from you ("Year 0"), as well as the subsequent five years. (Use the next product purchase rate instead of the retention rate for the years the customer would be expected to replace the product.)

Then, you will total the profit across all revenue streams for each year. You will need to do one more thing before you can add up the profit numbers and get the LTV, though. The last calculation is called the Present Value at Above Cost of Capital, which discounts the profit to take into account that your investors will need to recoup with interest their investment in your business. The present value for year 0 is equal to that year's profits. To calculate the present value for each year's profits beyond year 0, use the following formula:

$$\text{Present Value} = \text{Profit} \times (1 - \text{Cost of Capital Rate})^t$$

where t = number of years after year 0.

The LTV by itself will not tell you how attractive your business is; for this, you will also need to calculate the COCA, which you will do in the coming steps. An LTV of $10,000 per customer, for instance, is great if your COCA is $1,000 per customer, but is poor or at best "challenging" if your COCA is $50,000 per customer.

Venture capitalist David Skok has written brilliantly about unit economics on his blog www.forentrepreneurs.com; he simplifies things down to their essence. For software as a service (SaaS) companies, he believes a sound rule of thumb for the ratio of LTV to COCA should be 3 to 1. That might sound aggressive but isn't for at least three major reasons. First, consider that COCA does not include many other costs in your business such as research and development, finance and administration, and other overhead (not to mention profit). Therefore, there needs to be a significant allowance for these factors. Secondly, there is also usually at least some over-optimism built into the LTV and COCA calculations despite your greatest efforts to make it real;

so a 3:1 ratio ensures there is plenty of room for error. Third, a new venture is a highly variable system, so having a high ratio of 3:1 or greater will ensure that you have the ability to manage through the tough times when the unexpected happens (e.g., product delays, competitive reaction, recession).

HOW TO CALCULATE THE LTV: "WIDGET" PLUS YEARLY MAINTENANCE FEE

The following is an example of how to calculate the LTV based on a conceptual case of company that makes a "widget." In the business model, there is a one-time charge for the widget, with an annual recurring charge for maintenance.

- One-time revenue: The widget is priced at $10,000.
- Recurring revenue: Yearly maintenance fee of 15 percent of the widget's price after a six-month warranty period. The fee would therefore be $750 in year 0 and $1,500 in subsequent years.
- Additional revenue opportunities: None.
- Gross margin for each revenue stream: Widget: 65 percent. Maintenance: 85 percent.
- Retention rate: Maintenance: 100 percent per year in the first year; 90 percent per year in subsequent years.
- Life of product: Five years.
- Next product purchase rate: 75 percent of those customers who are still paying the maintenance fee at the time of next product purchase.
- Cost of capital rate: 50 percent.

As you can see from Table 17.1, all the above factors matter in determining an estimate for LTV. Some key drivers, however, are the very high cost of capital that new companies have because their limited ability to attract investments gets very expensive. This means that profits tomorrow are much less valuable than today's profits. This makes the subscription and consumables business models not as clear a winner as one would think. The other big drivers are the gross profit margin for your various streams of revenue and your customer retention rate. It is typically cheaper to keep an existing customer than to find a new one, making this a big leverage point.

Table 17.1 Widget LTV
The line items "Retention rate" and "Cost of capital rate" are not a direct part of the calculations, but should instead be factored into the "Cumulative retention rate" and "Net present value factor," respectively.

	Year 0	Year 1	Year 2	Year 3	Year 4	Year 5
Revenue Time Series: Widget						
Price of widget	$10,000					$10,000
Next product purchase rate (beyond year 0)						75%
Gross margin for widget	65%					65%
Profit from widget	$6,500					$4,875
Revenue time series: Maintenance						
Price of yearly maintenance contract	$750	$1,500	$1,500	$1,500	$1,500	$750
Retention rate	*100%*	*90%*	*90%*	*90%*	*90%*	*n/a (see next product purchase rate)*
Cumulative retention rate	100%	90%	81%	72.9%	65.6%	65.6%
Cumulative retention rate = r^t where r = retention rate and t = no. of years after year 0						
Next product purchase rate						75%
Gross margin for maintenance	85%	85%	85%	85%	85%	85%
Profit from maintenance	$637.50	$1,147.50	$1,032.75	$929.48	$836.40	$313.65
Sum of profits	$7,137.50	$1,147.50	$1,032.75	$929.48	$836.40	$5,188.65
Cost of capital rate	*50%*	*50%*	*50%*	*50%*	*50%*	*50%*
Net present value factor	100%	50%	25%	12.5%	6.25%	3.125%
Net present value factor = $(1 - r)^t$ where r = cost of capital rate and t = no. of years after year 0						
Present value above cost of capital	$7,137.50	$573.75	$258.19	$116.19	$52.28	$162.15
Net present value of profits (LTV)	$8,300.06					

Likewise, there are many factors that entrepreneurs initially overlook in determining the Lifetime Value of their customers, but the biggest one is the cost of capital. If you have access to low-cost capital, it can make a huge difference. When entrepreneurs do this calculation, they are usually surprised at how low the Lifetime Value of a customer is for their business.

It must also be noted that while we use the cost of capital to determine LTV, there is also value in knowing the absolute number of the revenue stream and users in the out years. This will be a key determinant in the value of the asset you have created, which will make it much easier for you to get lower-cost money and potentially make you an attractive and valuable acquisition target. So while LTV is critically important to make you sustainable and ensure your lack of dependence on others, a deeper understanding than just the single number is important as well.

Overall, it is important for you as a disciplined entrepreneur to operate not with blind optimism but rather with real numbers and to understand what drives those numbers.

IMPORTANT CONSIDERATIONS

There are many other secondary factors to consider when determining the Lifetime Value of your customer. Even if your LTV is too low for your product to be viable you should consider whether these elements are correct first; then consider whether you can positively impact your LTV with some adjustments.

1. **The Business Model Decision Is Very Important.** Your choice of business model can greatly affect your LTV and the amount of revenue you earn. Recurring revenue models such as subscription models often increase revenue but require additional capital from investors up front, and thus have a very high cost of capital. A one-time charge up front can reduce the amount of capital you need to get started, but is not as lucrative on an ongoing basis.
2. **LTV Is about Profit, not Revenue.** Your gross margin and cost of capital rates are integral to determining an accurate LTV. The most common mistake entrepreneurs make on LTV calculations is they simply tally up the revenue streams; but it is the profit that matters.
3. **Overhead Costs Aren't Negligible.** To simplify the LTV calculation, overhead is excluded; but to account for this, the LTV must be substantially higher than the COCA. These overhead costs, which may include R&D and administrative expenses, are not included when determining the gross margin of a product. These costs can be spread out over the total units of a product sold; so as volume sold goes up, the overhead cost per item goes down.

4. **Gross Margins Make a Big Difference.** Wrapping your lower-margin core product with high-margin add-on products will substantially help your LTV. LARK Technologies started out selling a silent alarm clock, which is a hardware solution; but their business model was not sustainable until they developed an additional revenue stream from a subscription business that produced an expert sleep analysis report for the user. Not only did this increase overall revenue, it produced a much higher-margin recurring revenue stream and allowed LARK to stay in touch with their customers to potentially sell more products to them in the future.
5. **Retention Rates Are Very Important as Well.** The longer you can keep a customer, the better your LTV becomes. This is one of a few levers you can easily control to improve the profitability of your business. A small increase in customer retention rates will mean significant improvements in your cumulative profits.
6. **Finding Additional Real Upselling Opportunities Can Be Very Attractive.** Upselling additional products to your customer can significantly improve your profit as we see in the LARK Technologies example above. Make sure to drive upselling based on the needs of your Persona, not just to improve your numbers. Companies that over-upsell can lose track of what value they are creating for their customer and also lose the trust and confidence of the customer.

Example: Helios

As we discussed in Step 16, Helios had created a coating that deices windshields. They had determined the price should be $100 per unit. This price (the expected net price after discounts) included the window cover and the software to remotely control the deicer on a smartphone for one year.

Based on their business model, pricing decisions, and research on how much the average customer would buy in a typical transaction, the team determined that the yearly revenue per customer in the first year would be $100,000. The typical customer fleet they targeted had 1,000 vehicles (some had more and some had less, but 1,000 was the average fleet size of their target market) and hence the $100K net revenue per new customer estimate for the first year. In subsequent years, an average of 20 percent of the fleet would be replaced, so the new vehicles would need coating to be applied as well, providing a recurring revenue stream.

As you see in the model in Table 17.2, it is expected there would be a 5 percent price increase each year, a 90 percent customer renewal rate (an aggressive assumption), 97 percent gross margin because there will be additional marginal service and maintenance costs for each fleet, and a 40 percent cost of capital, as the business happens to have access to some lower-costs funds to get

Table 17.2 Lifetime Value Calculations for Helios
Numbers may not add up exactly to LTV per Fleet due to rounding.

	Year 0	Year 1	Year 2	Year 3	Year 4	Year 5
Revenue per Year (Assumes 5% Yearly Price Increase) =	$ 100,000	$18,900	$17,861	$16,878	$15,950	$15,073
Gross Margin Profits from Revenues =	$ 97,000	$18,333	$17,325	$16,372	$15,471	$14,620
Net Present Value at Above Cost of Capital =	$ 97,000	$11,000	$ 6,237	$ 3,536	$ 2,005	$ 1,137
NPV of Profit Stream or LTV per Fleet =	**$120,915**					
Pricing (Unit Price)	$100	Business Model is a one-time charge with no recurring revenue				
Average Yearly Revenue per Fleet in Yr 1	$100K					
Gross Margin	97%					
Price Increase per Year	5%					
Life of Product	5 years					
Retention Rate	90%					
Cost of Capital for Company (est.)	40%					

started. As you can see from the calculations, when the customer unit considered here is a car fleet customer (which is appropriate), the LTV from these assumptions is estimated to be between $100K and $125K.

The Helios example raises many interesting points, as is usually the case when doing LTV calculations; they vary greatly and understanding the underlying drivers and leverage points is extremely important.

This new venture was driven to make a big initial sale to a fleet and move on, rather than building a "sticky" product that leveraged happy existing customers to gain additional sales. The business would collect its largest payment in the first year (the $100K to outfit all of the vehicles in an average fleet, a figure that they did not have to discount for cost of capital), so it had weak incentives to continue to work with customers and gain follow-on orders for the 20 percent annual turnover of vehicles. Further, the 90 percent retention rate figure, assuming that 90 percent percent of the customers who initially installed the product would continue to purchase it for new vehicles added to their fleet, seems aggressive based on other companies' experiences.

It was also surprising that the LTV was not higher; but the choice of the business model and pricing left the company with these economics for LTV. To sell a new fleet would take a lot of time, effort, and ultimately cost. The COCA would be in excess of $30K and probably in excess of $50K because of the high number of sales calls required.

After Helios did their LTV calculation, they saw they would need to revisit their business model and pricing to find if there was a better way to monetize, as well as potentially expand their value proposition by adding more functionality and thinking about new ways to leverage the smartphone app that would activate the deicing system on vehicles.

Extreme Example of LTV: Pet Rock

One example I use to illustrate why hardware without recurring revenue streams can be a difficult business at the unit economics level is Pet Rocks. In 1975, advertising executive Gary Dahl invented the idea of a Pet Rock. It was a pet that required no maintenance and no cost after the initial purchase. Such was the attraction of this "product" (some might refer to it as a fad, or worse, a bit of a scam). It sold for $3.95 each.

This was simple enough and made our calculations easy. Gary got $1 per product placement and that was it. There was no recurring revenue nor product obsolescence where the customer would buy a new product. There were no consumables involved with this product either. This was the value proposition to the target customer; but it presented a real dilemma for the company providing the product, as demonstrated below:

- One-time revenue: The widget is priced at $3.95.
- Recurring revenue: None.
- Additional revenue opportunities: None.
- Gross margin for one-time revenue (which is the only revenue): 25 percent.
- Retention rate: Doesn't matter because there is no revenue stream and they won't buy more.
- Life of product: Infinite.
- Next product purchase rate: 0 percent (they would not buy more—the joke doesn't scale).
- Cost of capital rate: 50 percent.

So Gary Dahl got $1 per rock sold and the company (really just Gary Dahl) made $1 million. There was no Core for the company and competitors moved in; within the year the fad was over. The LTV was $1 and the TAM very limited. It was not even a social or interactive fad that had much of a viral component, and as such, might not only increase the TAM but also make it more likely it would come back, like a yo-yo or hula hoop. The LTV was $1 and it was a one and done phenomenon. This is not a model for the type of innovation-driven new ventures that we are teaching here how to create. Don't be a Pet Rock business model.

SUMMARY

The Lifetime Value of an Acquired Customer calculation is the profit that a new customer will provide on average, discounted to reflect the high cost of acquiring capital that a startup faces. It is important to be realistic, not optimistic, when calculating LTV, and to know the underlying drivers behind LTV so you can work to increase it. You will be comparing the LTV to COCA. An LTV: COCA ratio of 3:1 or higher is what you will be aiming for.

STEP 18

Map the Sales Process to Acquire a Customer

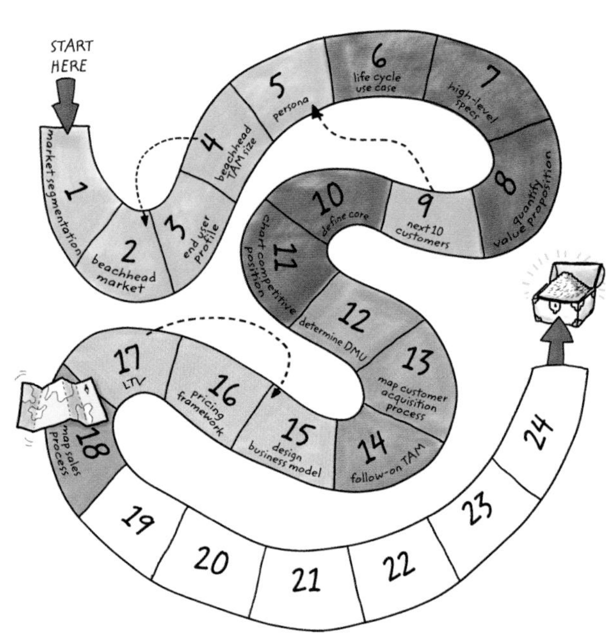

IN THIS STEP, YOU WILL:

- Develop short-term, medium-term, and long-term sales strategies for your product.

Understanding the details of customer acquisition will make clear to you the drivers of costs so that you will know over time how to make the sales process shorter and more cost-effective.

Now that you have done a first-pass estimate on the lifetime value each customer brings to your business, the question becomes "How much it will cost to bring a new customer to your product?" Determining the LTV might have seemed complicated, but the Cost of Customer Acquisition (COCA) is generally even more challenging and often much more grossly miscalculated.

The concept of COCA is relatively simple; but entrepreneurs (myself included) tend to dramatically underestimate how much it costs to gain a new customer when they first start.

To truly understand how much you will have to spend on your sales process in order to gain customers, you will conduct a rigorous, honest assessment based on facts, not hope, starting by mapping out your expected sales process.

Therefore, over the next two steps you will take a methodical approach to make a first-pass estimate of the COCA. You will not attach dollar amounts to the sales process at first so that the numbers do not distract you from being comprehensive about what your sales process will include.

In this step you will focus on the sales process, mapping out your short-term, medium-term, and long-term sales channels. In the next step, you will use this information to calculate what the cost of your sales and marketing initiatives are per customer. Once you calculate your COCA in the next step, you will likely go back and change your sales process to lower the COCA.

The COCA, in combination with the LTV, helps you understand the dynamics of your business and gives you enough data to make a meaningful first-pass analysis on the sustainability and profitability of your business.

FOUR FACTORS ENTREPRENEURS OFTEN OVERLOOK ABOUT CUSTOMER ACQUISITION COSTS

Entrepreneurs are inherently optimistic, and tend to remember only customers who responded positively to information about their products or offer to buy their products relatively quickly. They often fail to account for many factors and scenarios common to the customer acquisition process. The most commonly overlooked include:

- The cost behind all of the sales and marketing efforts required to reach their prospects. These may include the salaries of salespeople, printing of brochures, creation of websites, costs of trade show exhibits, advertising in industry publications, development of white papers, and so on.
- Long sales cycles that cost a lot of money. Entrepreneurs tend to remember only the shortest sales cycles.

- All the customers who did not buy their product, and the sales and marketing costs associated with reaching those customers. How many frogs did you kiss before you found your prince (i.e., your first customer)?
- Corporate shake-ups that affect the customer's Decision-Making Unit. New managers bring in new products and people to accomplish their goals, which can hamper the effectiveness of an entrepreneur's efforts to sell to the customer.

YOUR SALES PROCESS CHANGES OVER TIME

For almost all new ventures, the COCA will start very high and decrease over time. The sales process necessary to reach and close customers at the founding of a new business requires much more time and investment than the same process does once a business has matured and begins to scale.

The sales process is typically broken into three time periods for the sake of analysis. You will use different sales methods or combinations of methods in each period.

1. **Short Term:** In the short term, the primary focus of your sales process is to create demand for your product and to fulfill orders for the product. While your customer-centric focus means you have created a product the customer wants, your product is still new to the world, so you will need direct interaction with the customer to explain your value proposition and why your product is unique. The market will not be aware of your product otherwise. Another important reason for direct contact with initial customers is so that you can rapidly iterate to improve the product based on customer feedback, which is more difficult if you funnel sales through intermediaries such as distributors. This is the missionary sales stage and it ends when you start to see demand for your product that you did not directly generate.
   - Direct salespeople—often called "business development" people—are traditionally a wise and effective investment here. However, they are very expensive and they take time to get up to speed. Good ones are hard to retain, and identifying good versus mediocre salespeople is hard to do prior to hiring them. Be sure they are good at this stage, the missionary sales stage, not just the later stage when the company has more of a track record. Despite these challenges, they still might be your only and therefore your best option.
   - Web-based techniques such as inbound marketing, e-mail, social media marketing, and telemarketing can help lessen the need for direct salespeople, even at this stage. Some products, particularly web apps, can do well with a free trial and robust documentation rather than relying heavily on direct salespeople. One of the great benefits of this tool is that you can get extensive analytics on your customer that are not possible through the human channel.

2. **Medium Term:** At this point, focus shifts more from demand creation toward order fulfillment as word of mouth and distribution channels take on some of the demand creation burden. At this stage, you will also begin client management, which means ensuring you retain existing customers and creating additional sales opportunities for them. Distributors or value-added resellers (VARS) are often used, especially to serve more remote markets, or smaller customers who have a lower LTV. This way, your direct salespeople (who are more costly to you) can focus on larger customer opportunities with a higher LTV. Using distributors or VARS substantially lowers your cost of customer acquisition but requires you to give up some of your profit margin to the distributor—between 15 and 45 percent or higher depending on the industry. The decreased profit margin per unit is presumably more than offset by the reduction in COCA that results and the speed at which you can enter new markets through these already-existing distribution channels. When this happens will depend on the LTV of your product. The bigger the LTV, the longer it may take to reach this stage; but it is always best to move through these three stages as quickly as possible, especially if you have a low LTV.
3. **Long Term:** Your sales group focuses on fulfilling customer orders. Your business will do very little demand creation, and will continue client management where appropriate. Internet and telemarketing avenues are commonly employed in a long-term strategy. There will have to be adjustments made as competitors come into the market, which will affect your ability to get to this stage and what you do once you get there.

HOW TO MAP YOUR SALES PROCESS

To develop this short-term, medium-term, and long-term sales strategy, you must understand which sales channels you will use and how your use of sales channels will change over time. You can draw on the work you have already done in the Full Life Cycle Use Case.

Key questions that your sales process should address include:

- How does your target customer become aware that they have a problem or an opportunity?
- How will the target customer learn that there is a solution to this problem they have, or learn there is the opportunity they did not previously know about?
- Once the target customer knows about your business, what is the education process that allows them to make a well-informed analysis about whether to purchase your product?
- How do you make the sale?
- How do you collect the money?

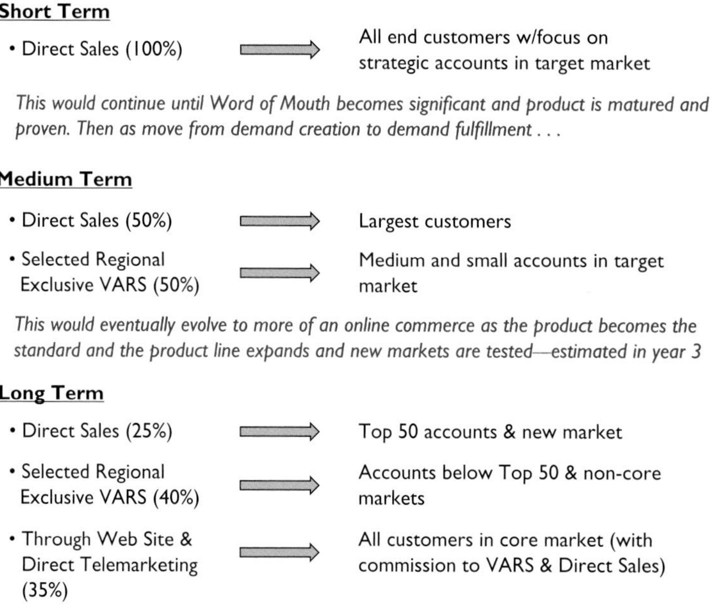

Figure 18.1 Example map of sales process.

Once you have developed the sales process, vet it with experienced professionals in the industry. Figure 18.1 shows a pretty typical traditional sales and distribution strategy for B2B companies.

SALES PROCESS COMPARISONS: ZYNGA, GROUPON, LINKEDIN, FACEBOOK

Looking at web companies, you can see that a variety of strategies can be employed to reach customers, ranging from fully involved salespeople to no salespeople at all. FarmVille maker Zynga chose a viral approach to greatly reduce the need for salespeople. Groupon's model, by contrast, required heavy direct sales involvement to acquire merchants as customers, resulting in a high and steady COCA that affected the company's profit margin; however, on the other side of its two-sided market, Groupon has had its daily deals spread virally by effectively incenting consumers to spread word of deals to their friends.

LinkedIn has a more refined model. They started with highly selective online ads and some direct salespeople (to sell their recruiting package). Once they got market traction and a reasonable critical mass, they started to rely much more heavily on users recruiting their colleagues to join the site through a well-developed system of easy-to-send invitations, coupled with an effective algorithm suggesting possible new connections. This system quickly started sending e-mails to people outside the network to join if they were not already in. Once the company achieved high levels of market penetration, it focused its algorithm on making recommendations of people already on the site, to encourage more connections the user can make, keeping the user coming back and more deeply invested in the site so that switching would be more and more difficult. Facebook has similarly been able to leverage a network effect to bring in new users at very little cost, then increasingly tie them to their network with a similar algorithm to suggest likely people the user would like to be linked to.

EXAMPLE

LARK Technologies

Silent alarm-clock manufacturer Lark Technologies realized in mapping out its sales process that it would need to educate users about what a silent alarm clock and sleep-coaching product was all about (Figure 18.2). It would take some hard work to get the market moving. CEO Julia Hu developed the following short-term, medium-term, and long-term plans.

Short Term: With no alternative, Julia started by engaging in one-on-one selling to potential customers, even setting up a table on the MIT campus on Commencement day to explain her product and its value. Julia also sought and won lots of public speaking opportunities to create awareness of her product. This strategy had a significant cost associated with it because it pulled her away from the core operations aspects of her business.

Many of the first units were sold to family and friends who could spread the word about the product. Julia also engaged her Persona's primary influencers, such as the website *Urban Daddy*, a daily e-mail newsletter specifically targeted at wealthy young urban professionals.

The company created a website where customers could purchase the product. They also experimented with the search engine optimization (SEO) to help drive traffic to the site. It also started to experiment with social media like Twitter, though with marginal results.

Medium Term: The company signed a deal with Apple to distribute its product in the Apple Store without requiring exclusivity. The strategy gave the Lark product instant credibility, in that it had been approved for sale in the Apple stores by Apple itself, as well as much broader exposure; but the company had to give up a lot of margin. Since the product sold in the store was the hardware component and the store had to carry inventory, LARK's gross margin was significantly affected.

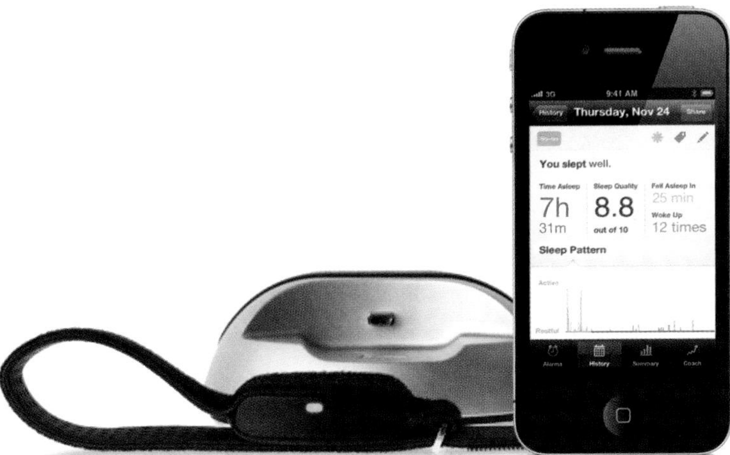

Figure 18.2 LARK's display.

However, Julia no longer had to do one-on-one sales, instead focusing on recruiting distributors and improving LARK's website.

Long Term: The website is the key place to get info about the product and purchase it. Julia expects 40 percent of her orders to come through the website (and other direct online channels), 50 percent from the retail distribution channel, and 10 percent from other channels.[1]

SUMMARY

Mapping the sales process is a thoughtful first pass at how you will enter the market, refine your sales strategy over time, and ultimately establish an inexpensive long-term strategy for customer acquisition. The sales process includes creating awareness, educating the customer, and handling and processing the sale. The sales process drives the COCA, one of the variables—along with the Lifetime Value of an Acquired Customer—that shows your business's profitability.

[1] These numbers were changed to illustrate the point and are not Julia's actual long-term projections.

STEP 19

Calculate the Cost of Customer Acquisition (COCA)

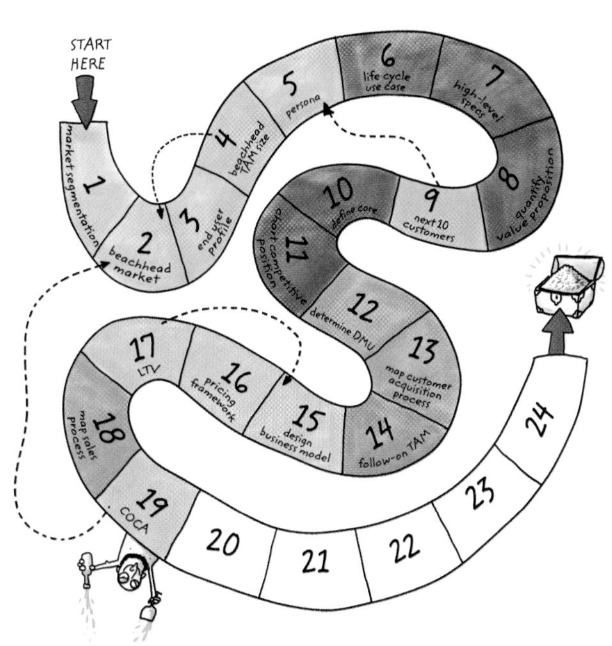

IN THIS STEP, YOU WILL:

- Determine how much it costs to acquire a customer over the short term, medium term, and long term, based on your sales process.

We love the entrepreneurs and their optimism but it almost always blinds them to the real costs of customer acquisition. It is essential that you do realistic calculations and then make appropriate adjustments over time.

Caution: The Cost of Customer Acquisition (COCA) is an extremely important metric and can be difficult at first to understand and calculate. This step explains the COCA in detail, but you will need to pay close attention to the details to calculate it correctly. It requires a significant amount of effort and systematic thought. Do not skip or skim this step because getting COCA right is both critical and challenging.

The sales process you defined in the previous step (Step 18) directly influences your Cost of Customer Acquisition (COCA). In determining the COCA, you must quantify all the sales and marketing costs involved in acquiring a single average customer in steady state. Your COCA does not include any fixed production costs or expenses outside of the sales and marketing department, such as research and development, finance and administration, or overhead. It does include all the sales and marketing costs, even when a potential customer chooses not to purchase your product. In this step, you will calculate your COCA for three contiguous time periods, where the first time period begins with your initial sales costs.

You will refine the COCA calculation as you get farther along in the sales process. To determine your starting COCA, you must identify what factors influence your COCA, assign realistic values to the various factors, and understand what actions you can take to ensure your COCA decreases over time.

WHY COCA MATTERS

Typically, in the early stages of the sales process, the COCA exceeds the Lifetime Value of an Acquired Customer. In sustainable businesses, the COCA decreases over time until it is significantly less than the LTV. One of the key questions for your business is how long it will take for the COCA to drop below the LTV of a customer, because until you reach that point, your business is spending more money than it is taking in (Figure 19.1).

HOW *NOT* TO CALCULATE COCA: A BOTTOM-UP PERSPECTIVE

Let's say we are selling a widget with a sales cycle of half a year, and it takes one twentieth of our salesperson's work time to identify, engage, track, support, close, and collect payment for selling to

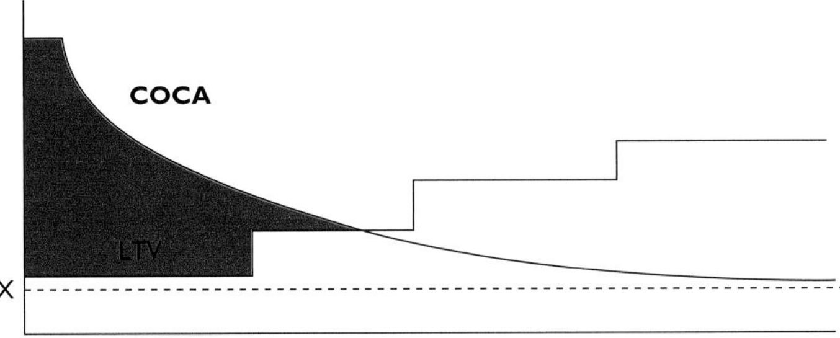

Figure 19.1 In a sustainable business, the cost of customer acquisition (COCA) will eventually drop below the lifetime value of an acquired customer (LTV). During the long-term stage of the sales process the COCA will level off, and will continue to require an ongoing investment (represented on this chart by the dotted line X), but costing less than the LTV of the customer. The LTV will often increase over time as well, due to upselling opportunities with existing customers (or "negative churn" as David Skok calls it). Pricing power will sometimes increase as well, if your product becomes a standard with little forceful competition. This graphic representation has a particularly aggressive LTV increase, which is usually not the case but it does add some drama to the chart. The red area indicates your cash burn before reaching cash-flow positive.

one customer. We pay the salesperson $150,000 per year if they make 100 percent of their quota (often called on-target earnings). For this example, we will assume the salesperson meets their quota.

Therefore, how much does it cost to pay one salesperson to acquire one customer? To determine the cost of one salesperson per sales cycle, we multiply their yearly salary by the length of the sales cycle: $150K * ½ year = $75K per sales cycle. Then, if the salesperson devotes one-twentieth of their time to closing one sale, the cost of the salesperson's salary on each sale is $75K * 1/20 = $3,750. While all of this seems logical, it does not nearly represent the actual Cost of Customer Acquisition. It's merely the cost of one component of the sale—the salesperson.

First, the calculation above does not take into consideration all the other costs associated with closing this deal. The salesperson's benefits package (health care, vacation time, 401(k), etc.) typically costs you the equivalent of 25 to 30 percent of their salary. Then there are costs for travel and entertainment, demo units, tech support, mobile phone bills, trade show expenses, marketing campaigns to generate leads, Internet data charges, and more. We could do a bottom-up analysis, painstakingly scrutinizing the receipts and invoices and assigning expenses to each customer. We also have to take into account the other expenses associated with having a salesperson: the office furniture, computer, Internet and phone charges, the cost to rent or purchase the building the salesperson works from, and more. Let's say that all these costs, added up and divided by the number of new customers equals another $2,500 per customer. So is our COCA actually $3,750 + $2,500 = $6,250? No!

Also, when we said it takes the salesperson one-twentieth of their time to close one sale, and divided the salesperson's salary for that sales cycle by 20 to get the cost per customer, we were assuming that the salesperson closes 100 percent of the sales they work on, totaling 20 sales per six-month sales cycle. This assumption is extremely unlikely because no salesperson closes every deal. If a salesperson is closing even 50 percent of the customers he engages, the person is probably getting paid much more than $150,000 per year and therefore would not be working at your company.

Even assuming a salesperson closes 25 percent of sales, which is very aggressive, meaning the salesperson is actually selling five units during each sales cycle, rather than 20. So for every one-twentieth of a salesperson's time spent on a customer who makes a purchase, another three-twentieths of the salesperson's time is spent with potential customers who do not buy. These costs have to be factored into the COCA as well.

A bottom-up analysis that factors in all these other expenses tends to get messy very quickly and can create a false sense of accuracy. In my experience, this method does not work. A completely accurate estimate of the cost to acquire one new customer is hard to project. What we can be sure of is that estimating a COCA of $6,250 would be dramatically understated, and merely the tip of the iceberg of the COCA cost. Realistically, the COCA in this example is probably closer to 10–20 times that number (Figure 19.2).

THE RIGHT WAY TO CALCULATE COCA: A TOP-DOWN PERSPECTIVE

A more effective way to calculate an accurate COCA is to tabulate your aggregate sales and marketing expenses over a period of time; then divide that by the total number of new customers you acquire within that time period. Since your COCA(t) will vary over time as your sales process changes and your organization is in the learning curve and you develop strong positive word of mouth within your target customer group, you should calculate it over time. I recommend three time periods in order to show how the COCA is trending.

Appropriate time periods depend on the life cycle of your product, which is directly related to the amount of time it takes for your customer to realize the value proposition from your product. A typical way to define the first three time periods for a COCA calculation is by taking your first year of sales, your second and third year or sales, and your fourth and fifth year of sales. Depending on your new venture, these time periods could be different. If in doubt, use year 1, years 2 and 3, and years 4 and 5 as your three time periods.

Figure 19.2 Be careful with bottom-up COCA calculations as they tend to be significant underestimations.

When aggregating your sales and marketing expenditures, be sure to include costs for all the key items in your sales and marketing plan: sales reps, auto, travel and entertainment, phone, Internet, demo units, technical sales support, website development, consultants, trade shows, real estate, administrative support, computers, and so on. Also calculate the cost in time that the executives on the team spend on sales as these are very real and expensive costs.

This calculation requires that you understand your sales process well. Do not worry if your calculation is not exactly right; but be sure to enlist an experienced person to help develop budget projections, and be sure to understand how adjusting costs affects the profitability of your business.

Dividing the cost of your sales and marketing expenses by the defined time period will yield the Total Marketing and Sales Expenses over Time or TMSE(t) where t is the first, second, or third time period. If a sizeable portion of your TMSE(t) is the cost of retention of existing customers, rather than acquiring new customers, subtract this from the TMSE(t). We will refer to the cost of retention as the Install Base Support Expense over Time or IBSE(t). Then, determine the number of new customers you will close during that time period (which means delivering the product and collecting their money), referred to as New Customers over Time or NC(t).

Given these definitions, we can explicitly define the COCA calculation for any given time period to be as follows:

$$\mathrm{COCA}(t) = \frac{\mathrm{TMSE}(t) - \mathrm{IBSE}(t)}{\mathrm{NC}(t)}$$

$$\text{Cost of Customer Acquisition} = \frac{\text{Total Marketing and Sales Expenses}(t) - \text{Install Base Support Expense}(t)}{\text{Number of New Customers}(t)}$$

Once you have numbers for each of your first three time periods, plot them on a graph where the x-axis is time and the y-axis is COCA for that period. You can also draw a best-fit curve.

The graph in Figure 19.3 illustrates a good COCA, where it decreases over time. The horizontal line at X represents the COCA's steady state, once sales volume ramps up and the product, company, and market mature, typically achieved during the longer-term stage of your sales process.

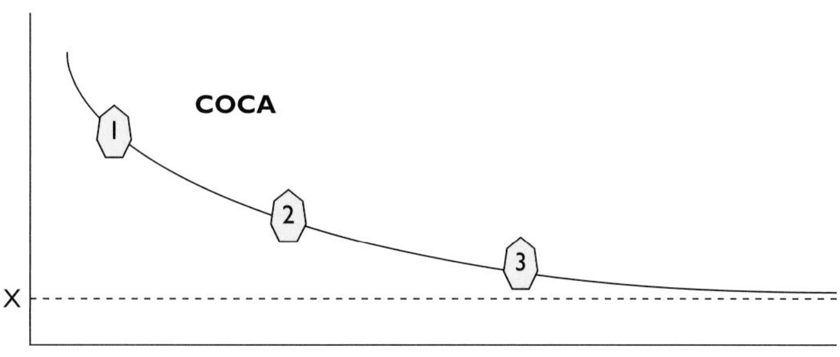

Figure 19.3 Graph of COCA over time.

HOW TO REDUCE COCA

As you can see in Figure 19.3, the COCA will almost always start at a very high point (i.e., well above the final COCA and likely higher than the LTV) because you need to first create the market. Your organization will seek ways to reduce these costs to make the business much more attractive. Here are some of the common ways this can be done.

1. **While Very Powerful, Use Direct Sales Judiciously as It Is Very Expensive:** Hiring a team to do direct sales may be necessary to start, but it is very expensive. As an alternative, consider investing instead in technological enablers, from telemarketing to having an effective web presence to engaging through social media in order to decrease costs as much as possible.
2. **Automate as Much as Possible:** Whenever possible, try to automate the customer acquisition process even if it requires significant investments. If you can promote your product through sites where there are big networks and opportunities to make your message go viral, from Facebook's and LinkedIn's network effects to Amazon.com's preference engine, these are great channels through which details about your product can be shared. You might also automate your marketing by creating incentive schemes for your users similar to the ones made famous by Avon, or the one Groupon used to reach a multibillion-dollar valuation.
3. **Improve Conversion Rates in Sales:** Always focus on improving the conversion rates from your leads. As you see in the bottom-up calculations, there is a huge cost associated with chasing deals that you don't close. Getting higher conversion rates on leads opens up the funnel so more deals get through, increasing your revenue and decreasing your COCA.
4. **Decrease the Cost of Leads and Improve the Quality of Leads:** Getting a bunch of business cards at a trade show may get you a lot of leads (less cost per lead), but they are probably poor-quality leads. You can reduce the cost of leads without sacrificing the quality of the lead with techniques like HubSpot's inbound marketing strategy. Incorporating tools and techniques into your sales process that increase the quality of your leads, and paying attention to where your leads are coming from, will improve your conversion rate.
5. **Speed through the Sales Funnel:** By focusing on the speed at which prospects are moving through the sales cycle, you can decrease the sales cycle, which will have a dramatic positive effect on reducing the COCA.
6. **Choose Your Business Model with COCA in Mind:** The design of your Business Model can dramatically affect your COCA, as Jim Dougherty learned at IntraLinks, the company

providing a secure online space for investment bankers and lawyers to share documents with their clients. His business model was based on usage, but it was hard to sell to customers because they could not easily plan how much they would spend on the product. When he switched to a "cell phone" type of model, where customers paid a fixed amount each month for an agreed-upon type of service, with the flexibility to buy additional service on a usage basis, it became much easier to sell the product to customers, and the sales cycle length decreased dramatically.

7. **Word of Mouth:** The biggest driver of reducing COCA is positive word of mouth about a company and its product. This tends to dramatically decrease the sales cycle, decrease the customer's desire to push you for discounts, and bring in well-qualified customers who already are good fits for the product, so salespeople can be much more productive in dealing with them. Many companies today, large and small, attempt to drive this by measuring it using the Net Promoter Score index and system.[1] They carefully track this and report it in their operations, executive, and even board meetings. Bonuses are tied to it with the belief, validated in real life, that this is a good proxy for the strength of word of mouth from your customers.
8. **Stay Focused on the Target Market:** Staying focused on your beachhead market from the earliest steps of this process, and not getting distracted by customers outside of your chosen market, will help improve word of mouth and also make your sales reps much more productive. They will become experts in their industry and the sales cycle length will decrease (repetitive selling to the same DMU and Process to Acquire a Paying Customer makes the sales rep much more productive), thereby decreasing the COCA.

EXAMPLES

Associated Gas Energy: Using a Direct Sales Model

Oil drilling typically produces "associated gas" as well, and dealing with its disposal is costly and problematic for the environment. Often, no infrastructure exists at the drilling site to transport the gas to where it could be sold. Associated Gas Energy was a new venture plan developed by my students to enable oil producers to transform this operating cost into profit. Using GTL (Gas To

[1] Find out more about the Net Promoter Score and System at www.netpromoter.com. It is a systematic way to measure and then drive Word of Mouth.

Liquids) technology, associated gas is converted into crude oil at a cost to the customer of $70/barrel. The customer can sell this oil at market prices. If market prices are around $100/barrel, the customer gains $30/barrel. Reinjection cost savings yields approximately $10/barrel extra for the customer.

This was a very clever idea with seemingly compelling financials; but the COCA needed to be carefully considered. The target customer was a very conservative buyer who had to be sold to with old-fashioned direct sales methods, especially at the beginning. The new venture would require a lot of missionary work to get off the ground.

It was believed that the sales cycle for this expensive product ($300K for the initial installation plus annual maintenance fees) would be about one year even though it had a compelling value proposition. The company had good technology but needed to hire an experienced salesperson as well as a tech sales support person who had credibility and understood the sales dynamics. In addition, they were going to hire a consultant the first year to help them break through the initial customer inertia to be the first to have this system (remember, this is a conservative market!) and to get all the regulatory issues taken care of that come along with energy and environmental associated projects like this. They anticipated there would be a ramp-up time for the sales rep to become effective in selling the product, and so in the first year they were realistically projecting one system would be sold. The first sale would be the hardest; after that one, they would not need the consultant again. After they had gone up the learning curve, the new venture's team would have the capability to do the selling themselves. In addition, with a successful installation as a reference, the sales cycle could be dramatically reduced.

While the COCA for the first year was very high, if the product worked the way they anticipated, they would have validated the value proposition, taken away great risk, gained a reference site, and brought their sales rep and process up to speed.

In year two, they would be able to hire a second salesperson as well as a tech support person to increase their sales. In Table 19.1 you can see how they accounted for the full marketing and sales budget and how it scales over time. Ultimately, the COCA gets down to about $150K, which is still high, but it will continue to decrease in future years.

FillBee

The team behind FillBee did an outstanding job on their COCA calculation. Their plan showed how to develop a creative, comprehensive, and actionable marketing strategy that also allowed the team to track COCA in a quantifiable manner. This was extremely well-done and represents a plan and calculation that effectively uses the tools and tactics available today to drive COCA down over time in a systematic way (Figure 19.4).

Table 19.1 Associated Gas Energy COCA Calculation (a direct sales example)

	Year		
Items from Marketing & Sales Budget	**1**	**2**	**3**
Number of Salespeople = Number of Tech Support People	1	2	3
Sales Salary ($175K/year fully burdened)	$ 175,000	$ 350,000	$ 525,000
Tech Support Salary ($125K/year fully burdened)	$ 125,000	$ 250,000	$ 375,000
Travel	$ 24,000	$ 40,000	$ 52,500
Entertainment	$ 15,000	$ 24,000	$ 30,000
Events	$ 30,000	$ 35,000	$ 40,000
Website Cost	$ 10,000	$ 10,000	$ 10,000
Consultant	$ 15,000	$ —	$ —
Total	$ 394,000	$ 709,000	$ 1,032,500
Number of Customers	1	3	7
COCA for Year	$ 394,000	$ 236,333	$ 147,500

Example of Using Benchmarking: Speakeasy

Here is another technique to determine whether your COCA is reasonable. Speakeasy's plan was to teach people how to speak more effectively via tutorials over the internet. There was to be no direct sales force; rather they would count on their target customer finding out about them through social media platforms. They had the following COCA calculation, which I thought was excellent:

> **Speakeasy Cost of Customer Acquisition**
> In determining our cost of customer acquisition we benchmarked the cost against other SaaS companies that employ inbound marketing, mainly Zynga and Groupon. We realize that our venture is not as mature as these companies but the numbers still provide a reasonable benchmark.

A detailed visualization of the Company's overall marketing strategy—including estimated costs and consumer leads generated for year 1—is displayed below:

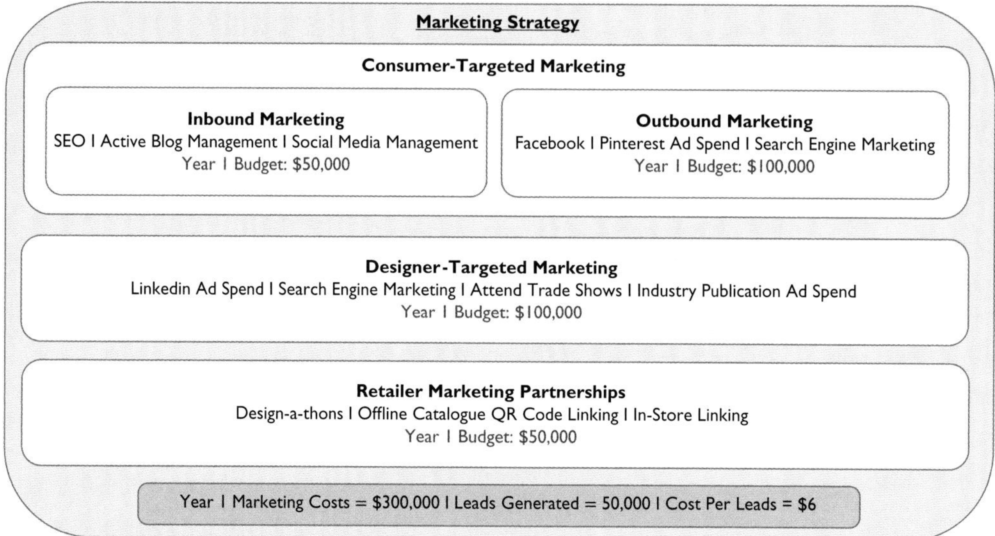

FillBee ascribes to a technology-driven sales strategy with an aim toward dynamically optimizing the user experience. The Company focuses on delivering highly targeted content and offers to its consumers, thereby maximizing purchase conversions of both furniture and custom designs.

A detailed visualization of the Company's sales strategy and accompanying funnel is displayed below:

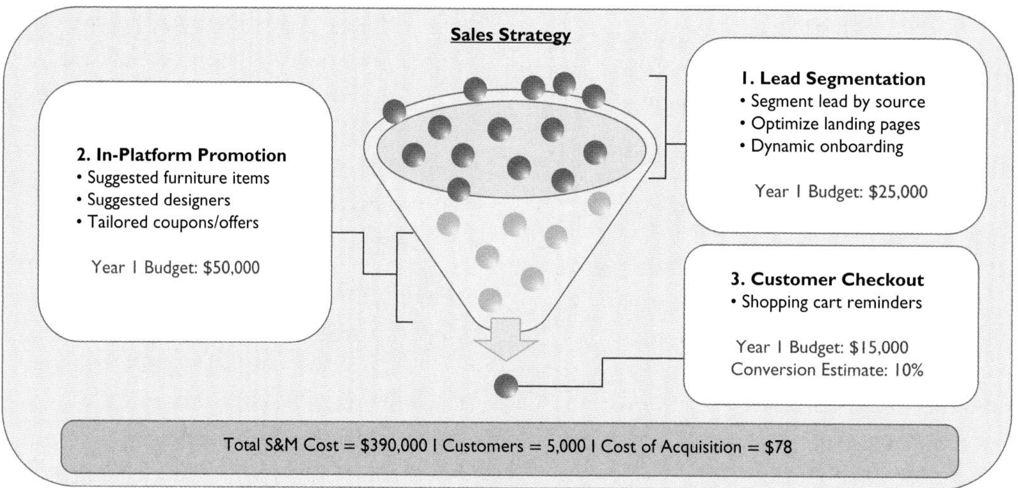

Figure 19.4 FillBee's COCA calculations.

Table 19.2 Groupon versus Zynga COCA Table

Company	COCA (2012)
Groupon	$5.40
Zynga	$0.85

Table 19.3 SpeakEasy COCA

Marketing Cost Assumptions			
	Y1	*Y2*	*Y3*
COCA/User	$1.60	$0.85	$ 0.85

As our customer acquisition strategy is more similar to Zynga's than Groupon's, we used Zynga's figures as the basis for our estimates [see Table 19.2]. Over the past quarters, Zynga's COCA has ranged from $.30 [to] $.85. To be conservative, we used the higher end of Zynga's range. Our company's COCA estimates in earlier years are higher due to an increased reliance on outbound marketing in addition to inbound. In years two and three, we will utilize a purely inbound marketing strategy and word of mouth. Lastly, we believe using per unit COCA as a driver to total marketing costs is reasonable since it allows us to provide an "apples to apples" comparison to other SaaS companies [see Table 19.3].

Example of a Way to Creatively Drive Down COCA: Dollar Shave Club

One of my favorite examples of how to potentially and creatively drive down COCA is from the company Dollar Shave Club. Founder and CEO Mike Dubin saw a significant opportunity to gain significant market share in the shaving industry by being a low-cost provider. Through eliminating middlemen such as retail stores and using a razor without fancy features, he could deliver on low cost. His value proposition for customers was not just cost, but that customers would save time by having razors delivered to them rather than going shopping. This value proposition was bolstered by his innovative business model, which applied the subscription and delivery model for the first time to the shaving industry.

All of this represented a beautiful Blue Ocean type of new product strategy, but there was still one problem. He needed to get the word out to customers, and the existing companies in the market had enormous marketing budgets that could drown him out and overwhelm him. As a new entrepreneur, he could not afford direct sales or even distributors, nor was this going to be his model. Through advertising he could try to create awareness but this would be cost-prohibitive and likely to invite a swift response from the established players. Mike's COCA was going to be too high. He needed to be creative.

So Dollar Shave Club fought back with the assets they had. Mike had a background in comedy and filmmaking and had some friends in the business. As a startup, he could create a quirky video beyond the bounds of what a company like Procter & Gamble could do. So Mike allocated the lion's share of his resources to make an outrageous and well-done 90-second video about Dollar Shave Club (Figure 19.5). Mike starts by describing the purpose of his company ("for a dollar a month we send high-quality razors right to your door") with the on-screen tagline "Shave Time. Shave Money." All is in alignment with his value proposition.

But then he starts walking toward the camera, about to create the moment that everyone will remember. He asks, "Are our blades any good?" The camera pans to a poster that answers that question, and defines the tone for the rest of the video: "No. Our blades are F**king Great." Mike continues to use humor and boldness throughout to mock current razor vendors, positioning himself

Figure 19.5 Dollar Shave Club screenshot.

to his target customer (young, digitally savvy, time-pressed urban males) as the lovable David taking on Goliath.

The video went viral immediately. The time and energy Dollar Shave Club spent on this video was probably the best money the company will ever spend. While this did not necessarily reduce COCA (because watching the video does not equate to "acquiring the product"), the video produced many very low-cost leads, and now the question is whether Dollar Shave Clubs can ultimately convert them into paying customers.

To see the final product, you can go to www.dollarshaveclub.com and use it as inspiration to think of creative ways you can reduce your COCA acquisition.

SUMMARY

At this point, you have completed the important steps of determining whether the financials of your business will work. The LTV and COCA analysis can kill many new businesses by identifying problems early in the process; but more often it highlights the importance of keeping an eye on key factors to make the business successful. It provides a simpler scoreboard than financial statements and allows you to make adjustments and refine your business. It makes your path to success more transparent. Don't let your optimism blind you in doing the calculations. Make the numbers real and not what you want them to be.

STEP 20

Identify Key Assumptions

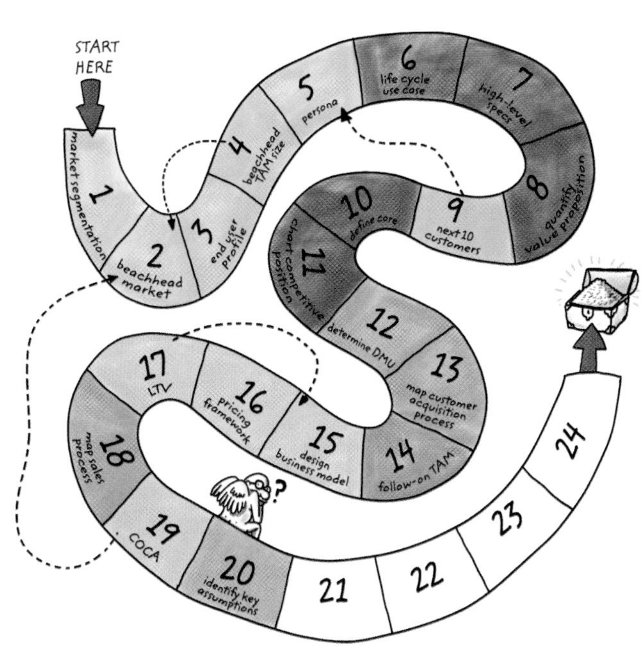

IN THIS STEP, YOU WILL:

- Determine which assumptions about your business have not been thoroughly tested.
- Rank your top 5 to 10 assumptions in order of importance.

Everything is looking and feeling good but before you go and build, step back and revisit again with the benefit of greater wisdom—what are the key assumptions that need to go right for your new venture to work?

You now have an understanding of who the customer is, what value you bring to them, how they will acquire your product, how much it costs to acquire a customer, and how much profit the customer will bring to you. However, yours is a new business with a product that has not previously existed. You are making certain assumptions based on logic and research, but without identifying and rigorously testing your assumptions, you will not know if they are valid. You have initially tested some of these assumptions already in the course of earlier steps; but in this step you will directly and rigorously test your key assumptions.

Yes, you have spoken to customers, you have observed them at work, you have queried them on each step along the way by talking to them and seeing if they find your plan consistent with their needs. But now you will step back and think about your big assumptions and test whether they are consistent with how the world works, not how you think or your customer says the world works.

Identifying and breaking down your key assumptions is not difficult, but entrepreneurs tend to skip over this step, trusting intuition or research to substitute for actual testing of business and customer behavior assumptions. But until you have tested your business assumptions and you have shown you will take a specified action, there is too much of a leap of faith for our disciplined entrepreneurial approach. Actions speak louder than words.

Those of you familiar with lean startup methodology will see similarities to the concept of a "minimum viable product" or MVP. However, in the 24 Steps framework, a "product" should always be complete enough that a customer can gain value from it. The MVP framework, by comparison, includes in its definition of "products" actions that merely test individual assumptions about the new venture idea. Therefore, I detail the process of identifying and testing assumptions in Steps 20 and 21, which will be followed in Step 22 by establishing what I call the "Minimum Viable Business Product" (MVBP)—a different concept than the MVP as used in Lean Startup language. The process of establishing an MVBP provides a "systems test" of whether your customer will pay money for what you are offering, not just a channel through which to test an assumption. Much as you do not have a meaningful business until you have a paying customer, your business does not have a product until someone purchases it, gets value from it, and can provide meaningful feedback to you about it.

Over the next two steps, you will unpack your assumptions, breaking them down into a prioritized list to test empirically before you launch your MVBP.

HOW TO IDENTIFY YOUR KEY ASSUMPTIONS

First, review each step of the framework and make a list of the areas in which you have made logical conclusions based on your primary market research. Have you correctly identified your Persona's priorities? Will your customer find the value proposition attractive when it comes time for them to make a purchase? Will the customer make the time and effort to integrate your product into their workflow?

One key area in which you should question assumptions is your gross margin. Are your cost targets accurate? If your product is hardware, review the bill of material and carefully analyze the cost of the most important items in the bill of material. If yours is a software development effort, you will do a similar thing, listing the key development challenges, assumptions, and cost items. Identifying and taking a closer look at these easily testable hypotheses provides an additional level of analysis to the most significant areas.

Two other key areas to test are the Next 10 Customers list and the Decision-Making Unit. Out of the customers you have already identified, are any of them "lighthouse" customers, where other customers will buy if they do? Are any "linchpin" customers, where if they don't buy, others will not? Are there other linchpin customers who you have not yet identified? And, most importantly, are the lighthouse and linchpin customers interested in purchasing your product?

EXAMPLE

Sasa

Started by three dynamic young female entrepreneurs—Ella Peinovich, Gwen Floyd, and Catherine Mahugu—Sasa is a for-profit social venture empowering women in Africa by allowing them to sell

Producers Assumptions

1. Craftswomen (i.e., Producers) want to be economically empowered.
2. Craftswomen will adopt the Sasa platform into their market practices.
3. The vendors will earn a sustainable income.
4. Vendors will trust the Sasa technology and services.
5. Existing infrastructures will be consistent and expand with demand.
6. Vendors will earn more using Sasa than by selling in the open-air markets.
7. A vendor can afford to buy a simple feature phone, which is camera-enabled.
8. A vendor is familiar with using SMS.
9. A vendor is able to leverage their knowlege of SMS to quickly adopt the use of MMS.

sasa Customer—Assumptions about the producers

Figure 20.1 Sasa customer assumptions about the producers.

Web Consumer Assumptions

1. Consumers not only value, but prefer handmade goods.
2. Consumers want to know who made their products and how.
3. International consumers will trust the Sasa technology and services.
4. International consumers will be compelled to buy products on the Sasa platform.
5. Sasa customers will return to Sasa to buy more products.
6. International consumers will happily wait for up to three weeks to receive products from Africa.
7. Sasa can profit greatly just from selling jewelry to start.
8. The necessary infrastructure and policy will be consistent and expand with demand.

sasa Customer—Assumptions about the web consumer

Figure 20.2 Sasa customer assumptions about the web consumers.

their art worldwide using mobile phones. As the team looked to launch and grow their business in a capital-constrained situation, they were very careful to identify their assumptions and test them so as not to waste any precious money or time. As a two-sided market, with the producers being the African artisans and the consumers being customers worldwide (with a beachhead market in the United States), they identified several key assumptions for each side of the market (Figures 20.1 and 20.2).

Note that some of the assumptions for the consumer side are not specific enough and will need to be decoupled into multiple assumptions.

SUMMARY

Identifying key assumptions is the first part of the process to validate your primary market research by looking for customers to take specific actions, which will happen in the next step. Before the assumptions can be tested, they need to be broken down into their component parts, so that each assumption represents a specific, narrow idea that can be empirically tested in the next step using a single experiment design. Do not worry about how you will design the experiment yet. Focus on breaking out all the key assumptions, because if you skip over an assumption fearing that testing it is difficult, you will neglect a potentially important factor in your business's health.

STEP 21

Test Key Assumptions

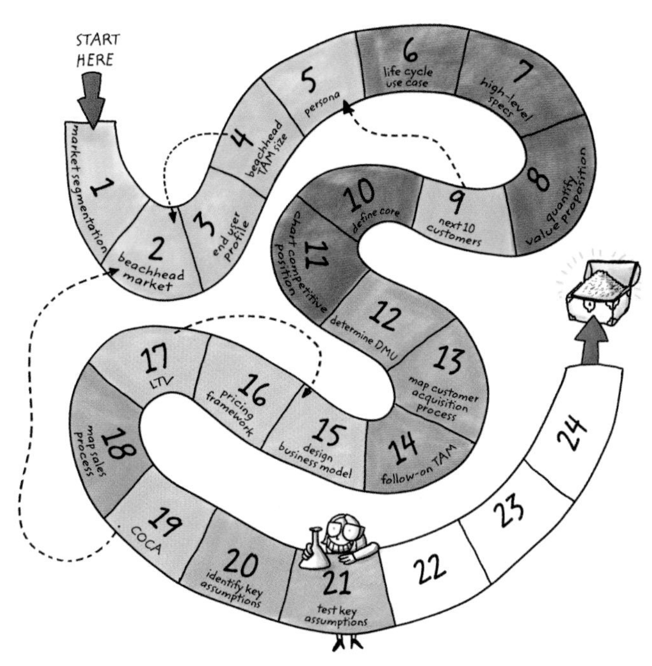

IN THIS STEP, YOU WILL:

- Take your list of key assumptions and design empirical tests to validate or refute them.
- Perform the empirical tests, moving quickly and efficiently to decrease the risk of your startup.

Now that we have identified those key assumptions, let's use a scientific approach to test them individually before just smashing them all together and seeing if they work.

With key assumptions identified, you will now design experiments to test these assumptions in the cheapest, quickest, and easiest ways possible. The goal is to gather empirical data that either supports or disproves your assumptions. These experiments will not require much, if any, in the way of building physical goods or writing code, but rather logical thinking to design simple yet effective tests. The rigorous primary market research you have done thus far and the single-minded focus on your Persona focuses you so that when you do test assumptions, they will be highly relevant to your business.

With the value of hindsight, some of these experiments may seem simple enough that they could have been conducted earlier in this process. But don't worry about this because what you have learned to this point will more clearly point you to the key assumptions. With all of the knowledge you have and the focus of product–market fit, you should be able to design and run efficient experiments.

Furthermore, if you run a bunch of experiments with different hypotheses off the top of your head, and some of the experiments seem to succeed, that by itself does not guarantee success. Remember, in social science research, you do not prove hypotheses so much as disprove hypotheses; so a successful experiment only suggests a successful venture. The combination of your primary market research and the empirical experiments you will perform in this step will lead you to more fully understand your customer and increase your likelihood of being successful.

NOW THAT WE HAVE IDENTIFIED THE ASSUMPTIONS, LET'S TEST THEM

Once we have identified the key assumptions, it is often not hard to test them. For instance, to test cost targets, send an informal request for quotation (RFQ) or spec to vendors to see if your cost projections are accurate at the volume you will be purchasing or developing. You should be able to quickly identify any cost targets that are out of whack.

To test the interest of lighthouse and linchpin customers, see if they will do any of the following:

- Prepay for your solution (best)
- Put down a deposit (good)
- Provide a letter of intent (okay)
- Agree to a pilot (acceptable)
- Express a strong interest in purchasing if certain conditions are met (not too reassuring but may be acceptable)

If you are meeting customers in person, bring along an experienced outsider to help you determine whether the customer is really excited about your product and will buy it, or is just being polite or collecting information.

To test whether certain customers are lighthouse or linchpin customers, repeat the above process but with other customers; see if they will attribute any of their purchasing decisions to certain other customers, and look for patterns.

EXAMPLES OF EASILY TESTABLE ASSUMPTIONS: STUDENT TEAMS

Assumption: Smartphone Users Aged 25–34 Access Weather Forecasts on Their Phone to Decide What to Wear

A team proposed this as a single assumption, but within it are two assumptions that must be decoupled. Assumption 1 is that people with smartphones use them to obtain weather forecasts. Assumption 2 is that people consult smartphone-based weather forecasts to decide what to wear.

To test the first assumption, the team approached their target customers (in a health club or restaurant, or on the sidewalk near where the target customer worked) and asked if they had a weather app on their phone and whether they used the app. Over 90 percent said yes, validating this first assumption. The team also looked at the general market research and found that weather apps were one of the most popular applications for smartphones further validating this assumption.

The results were mixed when testing the second assumption. In one distinctive group, less than 30 percent consulted weather forecasts on their phones for the purpose of deciding what to wear, while in another different sampled group, more than 70 percent did so. The team realized that the first group had the distinguishing characteristic of being male. The second group was female, showing that the team had identified an important segmentation factor and that they had not previously segmented their market enough, given they found such significantly different priorities existed along gender lines. The experiment provided the team with valuable information they didn't have before that was inexpensive and quick to obtain. Once they had done this, they then validated their assumption to be true but for a much more well-defined target customer group.

Assumption: "Neohippies" Aged 25–35 Use Their Smartphones to Help Them Shop in the Grocery Store

This team wanted to offer a smartphone-based personal shopping assistant to young people who shop at health food stores like Whole Foods Market. The students on the team used their smartphones when they shopped, so they assumed that others did so as well. This was a key assumption that needed to be tested.

To test the assumption, the team went to a Whole Foods and observed shoppers who fit the description of their demographic. Virtually none of the shoppers used a smartphone while in the store. The team was incredulous, but confirmed the result at a different Whole Foods location. The team interviewed shoppers and found that while many of them owned iPhones (the experiment was conducted around the time the iPhone was first released), they were not interested in using them while shopping because they already had a way of shopping that worked well for them and did not want to change. As a result, the team changed its focus completely and worked on a different mobile app for a different target customer. Maybe someday there would be a market for such an app, but the timing was not right yet.

Assumption: Conducting Opinion Polls Is Much Better on Facebook Than with Traditional Telephone-Based Methods

One student, a political science major, was concerned about political opinion polls and the possibility that the accuracy of polls would be affected by the growing number of people who were canceling landlines in favor of cell phones. American laws prohibit contacting cell phone users with autodialing machines, so pollsters who want to call cell phones have to individually dial each number, making it much more expensive to contact cell phone users versus landline users.

Polls risked being skewed because certain demographics were more likely to be cell phone-only users than others. The student assumed that since Facebook allows you to target ads at certain demographics and access the demographic data for clicked ads, he could use Facebook ads to quickly and cheaply conduct polls that are more accurate and less labor-intensive than telephone-based polls.

The student was able to test his hypothesis overnight with less than $100 in Facebook ads. His initial experiment compared his ad click-through rates against the 2012 New Hampshire presidential primary and the aggregate of the professional polls done of the primary. His click-through rates did not accurately predict the outcome of the primary, so he hypothesized that if he changed the design of the ads, he would achieve more accurate results. Less than a week later, with another $50 in ads, he tried a different format for the headlines of the ads (Figure 21.1).

This second attempt was compared to a different state's presidential primary, and achieved results similar to the professional polls that cost $100,000 and several days to produce. Interestingly, while validating his hypothesis, he found an even more interesting use for his idea—pollsters were interested in using Facebook's demographic targeting of ads to organize hypertargeted focus groups, a market opportunity with much broader application than simply predicting the results of an election.

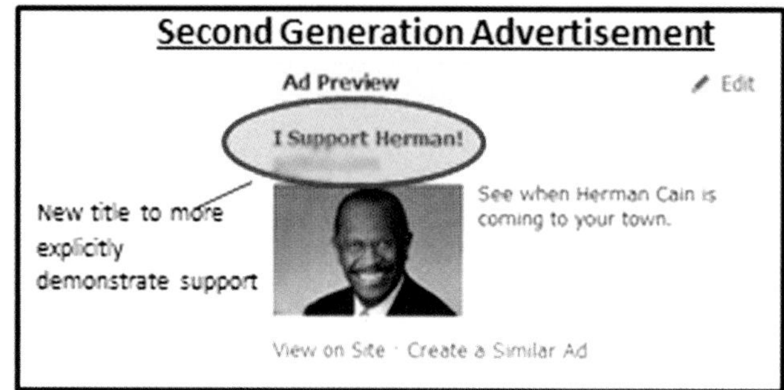

Figure 21.1 Second-generation advertisement for Herman Cain.

Figure 21.2 The Inspired coffee truck.

Assumption: People Will Be Inspired to Contribute to Chalkboards That Have Writing Prompts on Them

One student team came up with an idea that seemed illogical and lacked real innovation. The idea was to capitalize on the trends of food trucks and coffee drinking to start a coffee truck that would be in close proximity to college campuses where there are no "good" coffee shops near academic buildings.

The students called their trucks "Inspired" and believed that to attract a loyal following, they could cover the sides of the truck with chalkboards for people to write on (Figure 21.2). There would be prompts to encourage people to write, and the resulting messages would inspire all the customers. That, in combination with the high-quality coffee the truck would serve, would attract customers. So a key assumption that was fundamental to their business model (but not the only one) was that they could attract people and engage with potential customers by having them write on common blackboards regarding inspirational topics.

The team then set out to test this simple assumption, that people would write inspiring things on chalkboards voluntarily. They found a large blackboard wall in MIT's Stata Center in a heavily traveled corridor for students (similar to the environment where they would want to park a coffee truck) and wrote a prompt on it (see Figure 21.3).

As you can see, it says "________________ makes me Smile." The team then waited to see if students would, without any further prompting, fill in the other blanks. At noon (four hours later), the wall looked like the picture in Figure 21.4.

The entire wall had been filled; clearly students had gotten engaged with the process and enjoyed expressing themselves based on the entries which are not only very clever but also showed many contributors felt compelled to be creative, as well. Interestingly, one of the entries was "Coffee makes me smile," which further helped the student team's case.

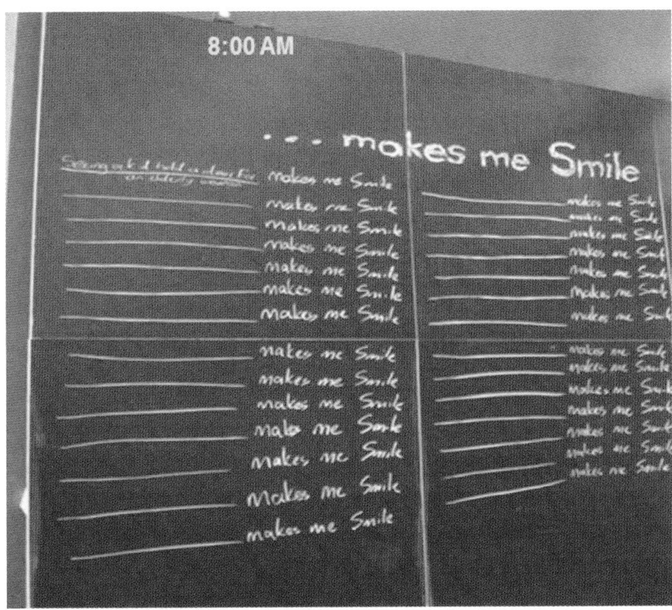

Figure 21.3 The blackboard with "Makes Me Smile" prompt at 8:00 A.M.

Figure 21.4 The blackboard with "Makes Me Smile" prompt at noon.

The team ran the experiment again on a different day, using a different phrase (Figure 21.5).

The quote was "Before I die, I want to ________________" and lo and behold, by noon the board was not only full, as you see in Figure 21.6, it was overflowing, with people adding additional comments in adjacent space.

Needless to say, the team had validated a key assumption in a much more compelling way than making a logic-based argument because they had real world data to back it up. I gave them an "A" for the assignment. Testing this assumption was also a lot more fun for the team than coming up with some abstract rationale—and it was more powerful.

Some of these assumptions should have been tested in the Persona stage while doing primary research; but I include this and the previous step so you can look back now with all of the collective wisdom you have gained to better assess the situation before you spring into full action. With this new wisdom, you should be able to identify the key assumptions you might have looked into or missed before, and now check to see that you are truly on the right path. You can never take all the risk out of

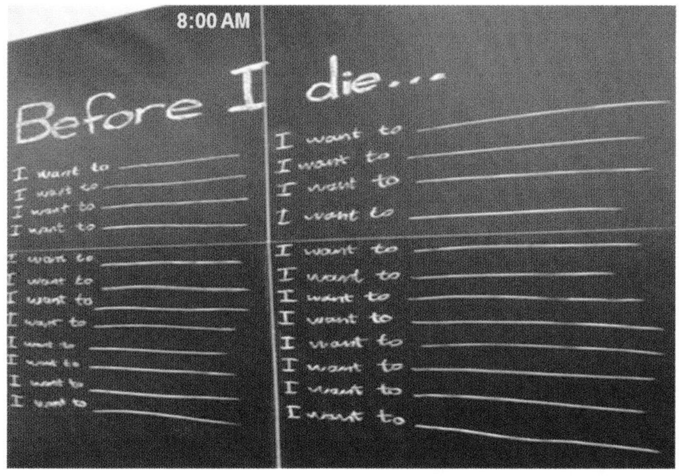

Figure 21.5 *The blackboard with "Before I Die" prompt at 8* A.M.

Figure 21.6 *The blackboard with "Before I Die" prompt at noon.*

a startup but you want to decrease it as much as possible while keeping the process moving quickly and efficiently.

SUMMARY

Testing key assumptions, particularly the most significant assumptions, such as cost targets and interest of lighthouse customers, prepares you well to sell your product because it complements the primary market research–based approach you have already taken. The convergence of your market research with empirical results from your experiments prepares you to put together a first-pass product and sell to customers.

STEP 22

Define the Minimum Viable Business Product (MVBP)

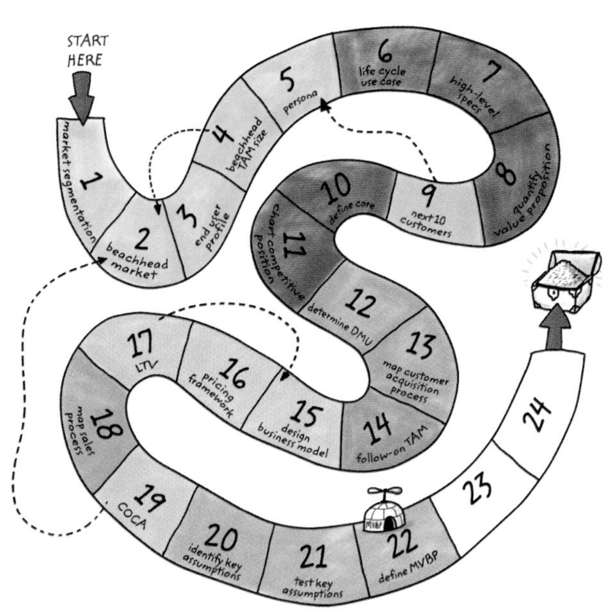

IN THIS STEP, YOU WILL:

- Integrate your assumptions into a systems test, consisting of the minimal product that a customer will still pay for.

Now we are feeling good about our product but we must show restraint; we will now cross the Rubicon and launch a minimally viable product that a customer will pay for, but keep the functionality as simple as possible so we can minimize risks and also continue to test the assumptions in a scientific manner.

The previous two steps have focused on testing individual assumptions. In this step and the next, we will develop and test what I am calling the Minimum Viable Business Product (MVBP). The MVBP combines your most important key individual assumptions into one integrated product that can be sold. The MVBP sets you up to test the most important overarching assumption that integrates the rest—that customers will pay for your product. As mentioned in the previous step, the Lean Startup definition of what a Minimum Viable Product is too limited and does not accurately describe a "product." The product you will build in this step will meet the three conditions of an MVBP.

THREE CONDITIONS OF A MINIMUM VIABLE BUSINESS PRODUCT

There are three core elements necessary to have a Minimum Viable Business Product. All three must be present for this step to be successfully completed. They are:

1. The customer gets value out of use of the product.
2. The customer pays for the product.
3. The product is sufficient to start the customer feedback loop, where the customer can help you iterate toward an increasingly better product.

As mentioned in Step 1 Market Segmentation, some business models rely on engagement from a primary customer who uses a product at below cost or no charge. A secondary customer pays for the product, typically by access to the customer or the customer's information. In such a case, you would design your MVBP so that the first and third conditions of a minimum viable product are met for your primary customer, and all three conditions are met for your secondary customer. One example of an MVBP for a primary/secondary customer business model is presented later in this step.

Your MVBP should balance simplicity with sufficiency. As Einstein said, "Everything should be made as simple as possible, but not simpler." Your odds of success are higher if you limit the number of variables in your initial product, getting something that works into the customer's hands quickly, even if it does not have all the functionality you would like to include.

The goal is straightforward—make a list of all of your key assumptions, narrow your assumptions to the most important, put it/them into a product the customer can use, and see if they will buy it.

EXAMPLES

Home Team Therapy

The student behind this idea, Tim Fu, had gone through physical therapy after ACL reconstructive surgery, and believed there was lots of room for improvement in how physical therapy during recovery was delivered. When the Microsoft Kinect system was released, he saw an opportunity to use it to provide patients with real-time automated feedback when they do their therapy exercises at home. Doctors could also see the home sessions and provide feedback of their own. The Kinect hardware and software system was built to allow users to interact with an Xbox videogame console using gestures, rather than a keyboard, voice, or touchscreen, and the Kinect could work on regular computers as well. While the original product was made for the gaming market, Tim envisioned it as a fundamental enabler for his application.

He found implementing his idea complicated, in part because as a startup, he had few resources. So he started to define his Minimum Viable Business Product based on whether doctors and patients would use and pay for his MVBP online system that assists them in physical therapy.

When Tim first started, he emotionally wanted to include the Kinect system in his product. The device was a real attention-grabber; so his first thoughts on a product (note that this is pre-MVBP) looked like what's shown in Figure 22.1.

Upon reflection, after asking himself serious questions about what was required to minimally launch to test his core assumptions and get into a feedback cycle with his customer, he simplified it to look more like what's shown in Figure 22.2.

If you notice, the elements of the old design that included the Kinect system are gone, which I found disconcerting at first because initially, it was the essence of Tim's vision. However, he was right that he could just use an online video for physical therapy and a very simple connection to the physical therapist in his MVBP. This eliminated the technological risk and many other risks such as how the patient would get the hardware, whether it would be compatible with a computer the patient already had, whether the user would be comfortable using the Kinect, and many other questions.

In this example, determining the Minimum Viable Business Product tested the most important assumptions possible to get the iterative learning feedback loop started:

1. Can we get patients to sign up?
2. Will they use the system?
3. Can we get doctors to sign up?
4. Can we get paid for this in general?

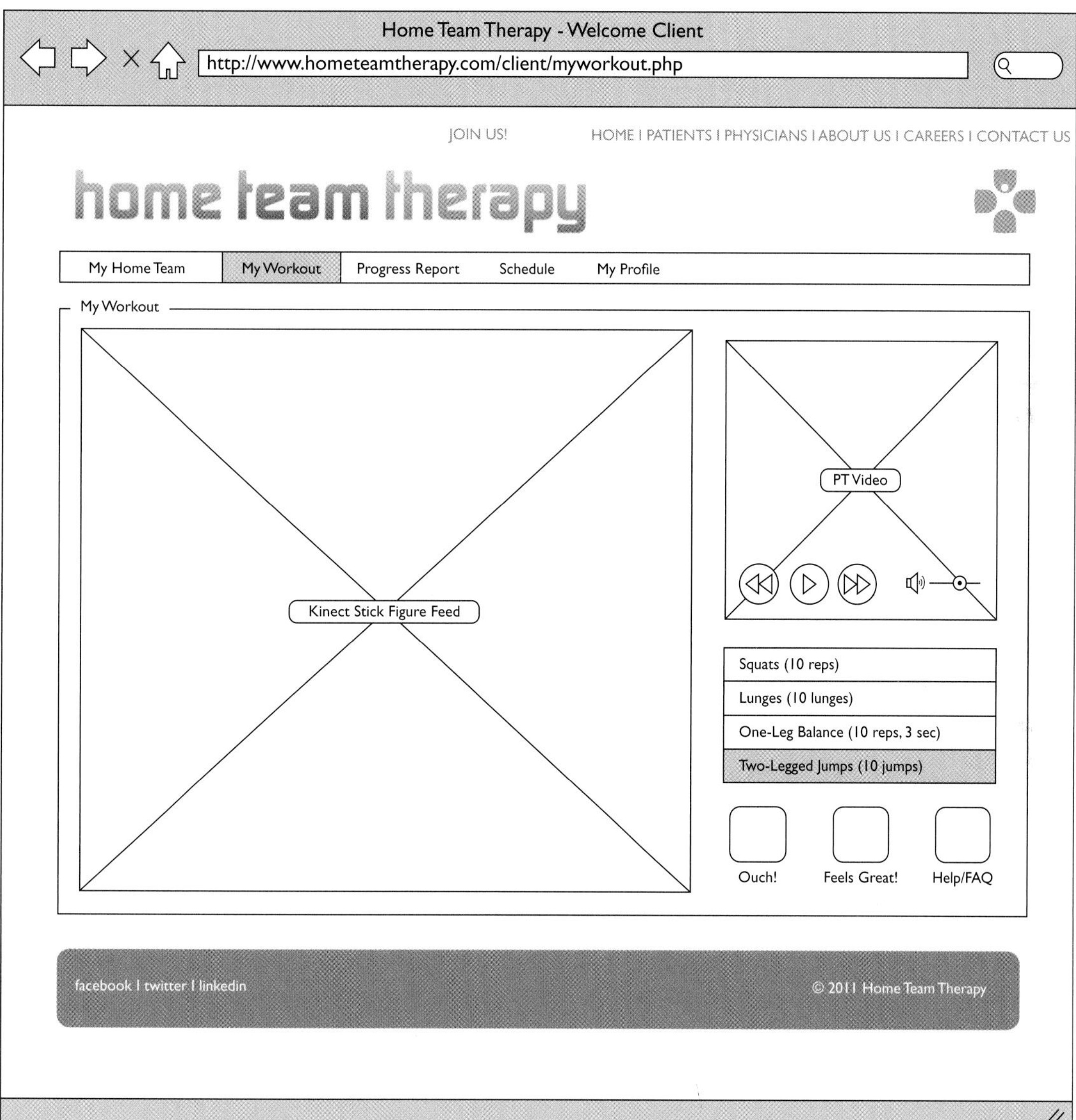

Figure 22.1 Home Team Therapy's stick figure wireframe.

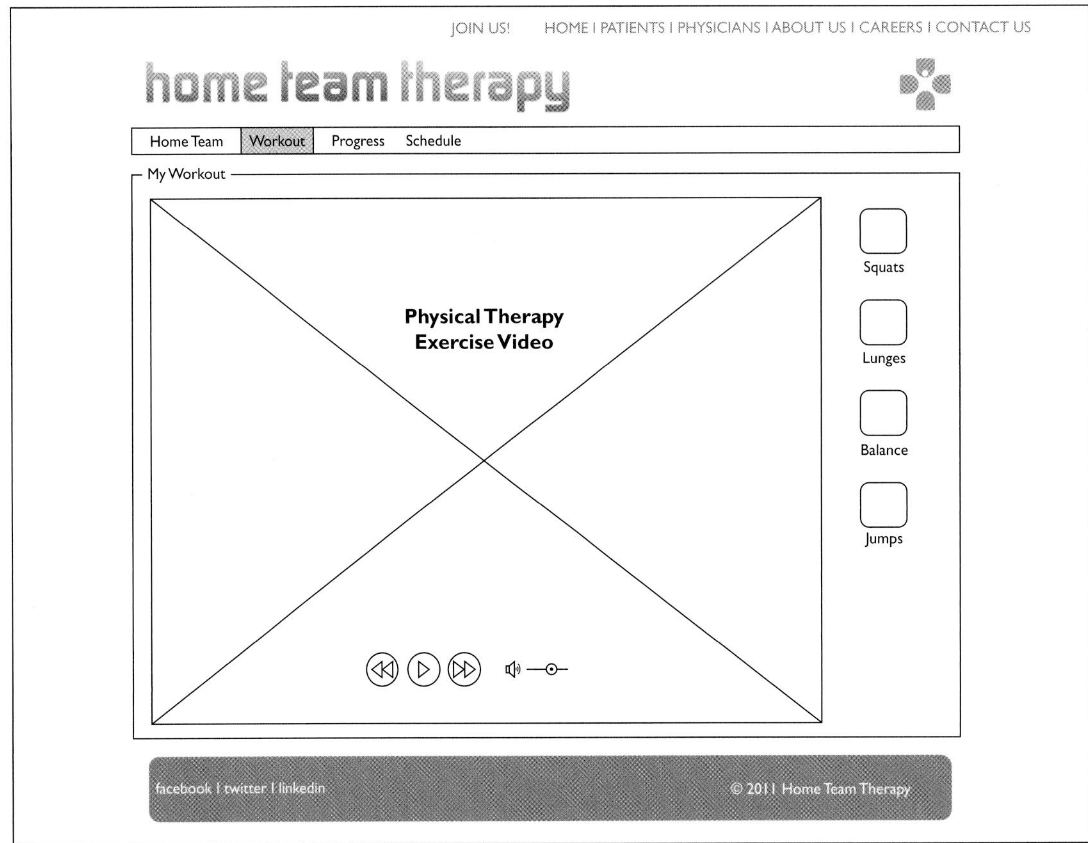

Figure 22.2 Home Team Therapy's therapy video wireframe.

5. We've done customer research, but how can we determine if these are the features that customers really want?
6. Are these the features that customers will pay for?
7. Are these the features that customers will always want, or does it appear that their preferences will change over time?

All the other sexy stuff such as the Kinect system could be added later; but for now, Tim had chosen his Minimum Viable Business Product wisely and was not distracted by the exciting vision and technology. He had simplified the definition of his MVBP and could now test his key assumptions in a product, beginning the iterative customer feedback loop that would make him successful.

Tim tested these assumptions with friends, family, and ultimately other physical therapy patients. It turned out that instructional videos were most useful to patients when they were still in the information-gathering phase, but they were really looking for other more valuable features in the long term. In developing your own MVBP, it's up to you to determine what those features are and how to design your product offering so you maximize value for your customers and your company.

StyleUp

One of my students, Kendall Herbst, had been a fashion editor at *Lucky* and *New York* magazine, and she had noticed the gap between traditional fashion advice channels and what actually helped a woman decide what to wear or to buy. She came to business school to refine her idea and in her first year got the idea to send women fashion advice that was tailored to each person's taste and to the local weather that day. She suspected women would love a dose of fashion inspiration when they need it most—when they are getting dressed—and that a condensed, personalized dose would be more effective than a cumbersome 600-page magazine. She tested this assumption by sending individual daily e-mails to a handful of female friends with an outfit each woman could re-create, as well as the weather forecast for that day. (See Figure 22.3.)

Women loved this idea. The initial group soon grew to almost 40 people. Many of these were Kendall's friends, and she could talk to them about what they liked and what she could improve. In this stage she learned some of the key products insights. For instance, some women preferred the inspiration the night before and others wanted to receive the e-mails first thing in the morning.

Figure 22.3 StyleUp e-mail.

She also learned that women wanted to shop these looks, if they did not own similar items already. Perhaps most importantly, Kendall also looped in women she did not know, and these women consistently opened the e-mails. This hinted the idea could scale, but clearly she needed some technical help.

Classmate Ryan Choi, who before graduate school was an early Salesforce.com engineer built a system for Kendall to categorize images and deliver them to many women at a time vs. one-to-one. Ryan also incorporated many of the early findings like customized time delivery and click-to-purchase links. In this business idea, the primary customer was the woman who received the free daily e-mail; the secondary customer would be a company related to fashion, such as a retailer, who would want access to the primary customer so they could convince the primary customer to buy their products. (See Figure 22.4.)

Together, Kendall and Ryan created the Minimum Viable Business Product:

- A backend system that could categorize images based on weather and style.
- An easy delivery mechanism to dispense these images every day.
- A database of beautiful images the targeted customer (busy, professional women) would be inspired to see, which included a source link (for copyright issues).
- Analytics to measure how deeply women were engaging with and sharing the service.

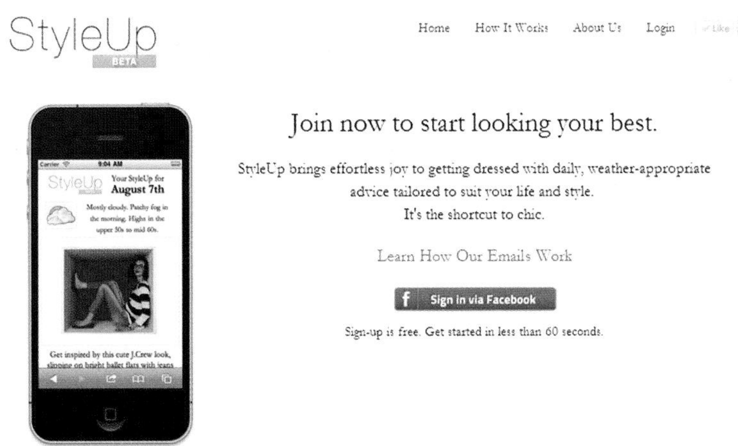

Figure 22.4 StyleUp sign-up page.

Without investing much money or going too far down a single path, Kendall and Ryan's goal was to show that women would like the value proposition enough to sign up, open the e-mails and tell their friends.

They were very confident they could add more features later; but they wanted to get more guidance after these original foundational features were implemented and used to know which ones to add and in what priority. They wanted to start the feedback loop with their target customers as soon as possible.

This MVBP also set them up well to test whether the secondary customer got value from the product and was willing to pay for access to the primary customer, since the MVBP has links that allow women to click to websites on which clothing items are sold.

ThriveHive

Two students, Max Faingezicht and Adam Blake, with different backgrounds (Max had worked at Intel and Amazon while Adam had worked in small companies) came together in my class and left determined to launch a new company that would provide new-age marketing tools and support to small companies that previously was not possible. Their vision was a platform that would bring together critical information for the brave new world of marketing in a cost-effective manner, including bringing together website analytics, e-mail, social media, and direct mail all under one roof. At the core of their system would be a leads report, which would show the business owner what was working and what wasn't. Every channel would be built through backend integrations to third-party providers, thus reducing the development costs. Customers would pay a monthly subscription for the use of the platform, starting from $99/month.

The first challenge they faced was figuring out how to make an MVBP when their value proposition hinged around bringing all the channels together in a simplified way. Early on they decided to build only the necessary integrations, those that required real-time response: Facebook and Twitter for social media. These were basic features without the bells and whistles. You could link your accounts and schedule a post, but you couldn't comment or even monitor your feeds. They decided also to develop an e-mail builder for customers to send e-mail campaigns. It used a basic e-mail editor, which provided limited editing functionality. Whenever the channels allowed for delays, they would just "fake it before you make it." A good example of this is the Postcard Builder. When a user hit the button to send a postcard, they would be able to upload a file and a list. They would see the additional cost right there and then they would hit "Send." Instead of building a system integration with a partner, in reality this sent an e-mail to the team with the details around the postcard. Someone would then go login to the third-party provider website and set the postcard to get printed, posted, and delivered on the date it was scheduled for. By faking it, they were able to see if people would use and be willing to pay for certain features before having to make the major investments to build them.

SUMMARY

You have previously tested individual elements of your business; however, the Minimum Viable Business Product (MVBP) represents a systems test of a product that actually provides value to the customer. The paying customer can use this to start a feedback loop that helps you iterate better versions of the product.

STEP 23

Show That "The Dogs Will Eat the Dog Food"

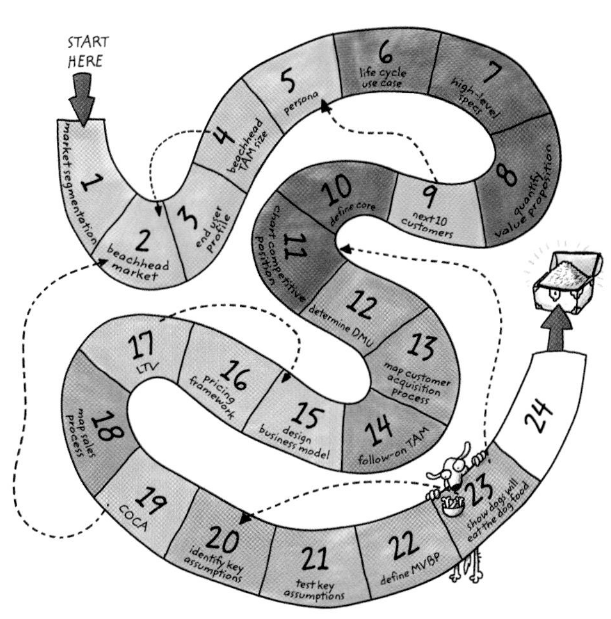

IN THIS STEP, YOU WILL:

- Demonstrate quantitatively that customers will pay for your Minimum Viable Business Product (MVBP).
- Develop metrics that indicate the level of word of mouth your MVBP is creating among customers.

Now that we have launched our product, show measurable proof that the customers are adopting the product; no rose-colored glasses—data is required.

In this step, you will take your Minimum Viable Business Product, put it in front of your target customer, and test whether this integrated system of assumptions will be accepted and paid for by your target customer, thus showing that your individual assumptions when assembled together actually work in the real world.

The following story is fictional, but has many parallels to very real companies:

> Once upon a time in a land called Ivory Tower, not so far away from here, there was a chemist who wanted to make better dog food. He studied to see what kind of food would improve the health, happiness, and financial and spiritual well-being of the dog.
>
> He came up with a breakthrough formula that was better for everyone and cost one-tenth the price of the cheapest dog food on the market. Dogs would sleep better at night, have a better demeanor, shed less hair, have whiter teeth, be friendlier to strangers, obey their owners more, and so on. They had tested in the lab from a chemical standpoint and were told that it would even taste better. Everything made logical sense. It was a business opportunity that was almost too good to be true.
>
> He sprang into action, raising a large sum of money and spending $3 million to build a plant to produce the dog food. He signed up distributors and kicked off a huge marketing campaign. To quote Jackie Gleason from *The Honeymooners*, "This thing is going to the moon, Alice!"
>
> The product shipped. Owners put the food in front of their dogs. And the dogs refused to eat the dog food. The company crashed and burned in a spectacular fashion.

"That's crazy! That wouldn't happen in real life," you may say. But it happens all the time.

When I worked at IBM during the 1980s and early 1990s, I saw that "electronic medical records" made all the logical sense in the world, so lots of smart people spent lots of time and money working on making it a reality. But guess what? For decades, even though the technology was sufficient and the logic compelling, the doctors simply wouldn't use electronic medical records—they wouldn't eat the dog food. It has finally changed, but for hundreds of startups for over two decades, they went out of business because the timing was not right.

Based on every detail you've uncovered about your product and your customer, it might make sense that your product would be viable; but ultimately a person is going to have to accept your new innovative product and humans are not always rational. Some behavioral economists have made a name for themselves in focusing their research on irrational human behavior—Professor Dan Ariely, the behavioral economist from Duke, probably being the most well-known. So after you have made your logical plans with individual experiments along the way, as in our great fable above, and before you invest large amounts of time and money, make sure the dogs will eat the dog food! And, oh yes, make sure the dog's owners (or friends, as the primary/secondary customer discussion from Step 22 explains) will *pay* for the dog food too.

With regard to testing to see if someone will pay for the dog food, the initial price of the product is not as important as showing that target customers will pay for the adoption of your product. It is good to "beta-test their wallet," as HubSpot co-founder Dharmesh Shah calls it.

Even if the dogs do not eat nearly as much dog food as you thought, you can now learn a tremendous amount because you have real data on the MVBP. You are now in an iterative learning feedback loop with your customer, which is where you will start to mine the gold that will make you rich—customer preferences. With today's tools, there are so many ways to measure if the dogs are eating the dog food, so entrepreneurs should take full advantage of these tools.

It is critical to first see if the target customer will buy and accept the product; but it is also important now to start to measure how much they will advocate to others in the TAM about the benefits of your product. What is the magnitude of the positive word of mouth your product is generating? This is often referred to as the virality coefficient. So in this step, measure if at all possible whether your customers tell others about your product, because this creates valuable word of mouth that will decrease your Cost of Customer Acquisition.

EXAMPLES

StyleUp

Once Kendall and Ryan released their MVBP, it was time to first measure the engagement and adoption of their target customer. They needed to see if women would respond to the service and encourage their friends to sign up. Consistent engagement and growth were the key metrics to value the progress and validate a business opportunity. Engagement included both whether women opened the e-mails and whether women clicked through to webpages where they could purchase the merchandise they saw in the e-mails, which was a potential way to monetize the product.

StyleUp's analytics showed that women were opening the e-mails every day, and some women were opening each e-mail an average of five times—which either means the recipient re-opened the message, or the recipient forwarded the message to her friends. The company's e-mail open rate is 70 percent, compared to an industry average of 14 percent. (See Figure 23.1.) The metrics showed that women were engaged and were looking forward to receiving the e-mails.

They also received key anecdotal support. Google's shopping editor Adelle McElveen wrote, "StyleUp inspires me to think about what I'm going to wear the next day, and how to not just dress for the weather, but to dress stylishly for the weather."

Beyond daily engagement, Kendall and Ryan could see that women were also telling their friends to sign up for StyleUp. It was easy to track this quantitatively via the referral link through which

Figure 23.1 NEW StyleUp e-mail open rates.

members signed up. Despite not spending money on marketing in the first few months, word spread to 1,500 people based on pure word-of-mouth traction and minimal press coverage. Even when they reached nearly 8,000 members, StyleUp had committed minimal capital and time to marketing and yet continued to see 20 percent month-over-month growth. The goal to create a product women love so much that they naturally share it was working and they had data to back it up.

Of course additional customer satisfaction metrics, like Net Promoter Score®, would be a valuable additional piece of data to gauge the long-term viability. This indicates the strength of the word of mouth for your product as well as their likelihood to be a repeat customer.

The second dimension that we mention above was to prove that the dogs, or someone associated or wanted to be associated with the dogs, would pay for the dog food. That is, clearly the women were taking to the product, but now the questions were "Can StyleUp can get paid for this customer engagement? Can StyleUp monetize the situation it has created?"

TechCrunch reported that StyleUp was using an affiliate model for monetization.[1] So to show that secondary customers—affiliates—would find value from StyleUp and be willing to pay to reach StyleUp's primary customers, three important metrics to measure would be click-through rates on the e-mails that were opened, the amount of money in sales that affiliates realized from the click-throughs, and the payments made to StyleUp for these sales. One might think that only the last of these three factors matters; but it is very valuable to know all three in order to provide a robust data set if the business model needs tweaking. In such a manner, they will be able to better understand the sustainable nature of the economics of the new venture.

[1] Leena Rao, "YC-Backed StyleUp Recommends Daily Personalized Outfits Tailored To Your Style And Location," *TechCrunch*, March 18, 2013, http://techcrunch.com/2013/03/18/yc-backed-styleup-recommends-daily-personalized-outfits-tailored-to-your-style-and-location.

With this combination of metrics, StyleUp will have developed a case that should be extremely compelling to themselves first, and then to any potential strategic partners (like investors). While it would not guarantee success, it would indicate that the odds of success are quite high.

ThriveHive

As introduced in Step 22, ThriveHive is a marketing platform for small but ambitious businesses. To test their MVBP, they signed up a small group of beta testers and offered the platform for free for a limited time in exchange for providing feedback sessions.

After a few months of private beta, they had gathered enough feedback to figure out which features people were using and which new features people were asking for. While great, the private beta had not yet proven if the dogs would eat and pay for the dog food; this was yet to come. All they had done was eat for free so far but the moment of truth was coming. As they ended the private beta, and gave each beta tester one full month to decide whether to start a paid subscription, they simultaneously began offering the product to the public with a 30-day free trial. The proof of whether the dogs would really eat the dog food and pay for it (because it created real value that exceeded the price) would be evident in their conversion rate to start with. This was the moment of truth.

Fortunately for Max and Adam, of the beta testers, 74 percent converted to a paid subscription, showing the team they had a successful MVBP—that customers got value from the product and would be willing to pay to continue using it. Another metric that would help the case would be signups from the public.

With the momentum of this success, Max and Adam continued to develop their product, and while the above testing is sufficient for the basic requirements of this step, their more-robust testing of whether the dogs would keep eating the dog food is valuable as well as you think beyond the 24 Steps into execution and scaling.

Specifically to make the business economically sustainable and scalable, Max and Adam focused on three key areas for further testing:

- Market Access: Can they generate leads in our target market using repeatable techniques?
- Sales Process: Can they sell to customers with unit economics that make sense?
- Deliver Value: Can they deliver more value than they capture?

Market Access ThriveHive decided to target very small businesses (<20 employees), so the question became: What are the most scalable and effective ways to reach that target? While some businesses like SCVNGR were using a direct sales approach to reach this market, ThriveHive decided instead to use only online methods in the beginning, due to the ability to start small and scale.

ThriveHive launched an organic content play to start building a presence in online search and social media, but that would take time to get off the ground. To start getting data fast, the team ramped up a Google AdWords campaign that could drive targeted traffic quickly.

All the work was done with the idea to generate enough leads to feed a single salesperson so the unit economics could be proven.

After about six months of work, the team had built a lead pipeline generating hundreds of qualified leads per month at a cost per lead that was in line with the unit economics model that was coming together on the sales side. More importantly, ThriveHive had shown the ability to scale the lead generation quickly as the company growth would demand.

Sales Process The sales process was a challenging model to prove out. Focusing again on the unit economics, ThriveHive brought on board a single inside sales rep to begin selling to the leads being generated. There were literally hundreds of variables at play, from the salesperson himself, to the process used to bring a customer on board, to pricing. The challenge was to figure out what was working and what wasn't, with almost no data. The sales process was slow and the numbers were so small that it was hard to know when the process needed to be tweaked when things were on track, or whether only more time was needed.

Similar to the market access, after about six months the unit economics started to work. Three major tweaks that helped everything come together were: to balance the give and the take during the sales and on-boarding process (there was a 30-day free trial), creating an account manager role to help ensure customer success during the free trial, and generating enough leads to feed a single salesperson.

Delivering Value ThriveHive decided to focus on delivering more value than it captured. While it might seem obvious, there are many successful companies built on exactly the opposite philosophy. Think about infomercials that sell you products you buy and never use; they can be great businesses, but ThriveHive felt that the only path to long-term success in this very small business market was to generate more value than it captured. The cost of acquiring the customers was going to be too high in order to survive if they left too quickly.

In order to measure progress on the value delivery front, ThriveHive tracked three critical metrics: monthly churn, customer referrals, and qualitative success metrics (what the customers were saying). On the churn front, ThriveHive decided to start without any contracts (even though the product is fundamentally one that delivers value over time). This left the company as exposed as possible to feedback.

By the time the market access and sales process had been vetted, ThriveHive was able to show results on all three value delivery fronts, which led the team to believe that they were successfully delivering more value than was being captured:

- Churn was already at the low end of industry comparables, even with a very immature product.
- More than 15 percent of the customer base was consistently being driven by existing customer referrals (without incentives).
- More than 50 percent of the businesses that had been with ThriveHive since the launch of the paid product were expanding their businesses due to marketing success that they attributed in large part to ThriveHive.

It was only when all three of the areas came together that ThriveHive felt that the dogs were genuinely and repeatedly eating the dog food in an economically and scalable manner.

SUMMARY

Take your Minimum Viable Business Product to the customers to see if they will actually use and pay for the product. Collect data to see if they are really using it and how engaged they are as users. Determine if they, or someone associated with them, will pay for it and also if they are advocating for your product with word of mouth. After you collect data over time, analyze it and especially look for trends and understand underlying drivers. Make sure you are intellectually honest and rely on real-world data and not abstract logic.

STEP 24

Develop a Product Plan

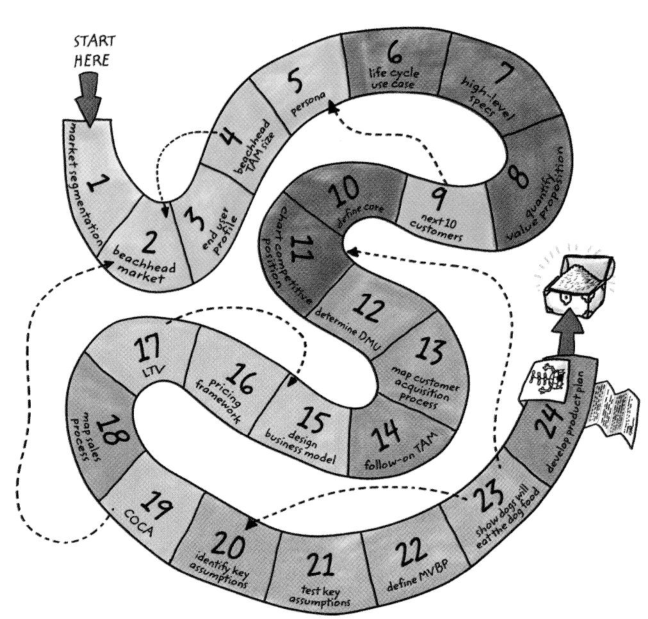

IN THIS STEP, YOU WILL:

- Go beyond the Minimum Viable Business Product (MVBP) to determine which features you will build out for the beachhead market.
- Determine which adjacent markets you will sell to after dominating the beachhead market, and how your product will have to change for each new market.

It is time to revisit your Follow-on Market TAM and develop a product plan so that your product is not just an island that leads nowhere.

Once you have shown that the dogs will eat the dog food, you must next map out the growth strategy for your product. The Product Plan you will develop in this step builds on the work you have done in the TAM for Follow-on Markets.

When you established your MVBP, you most likely took a number of features and put them on hold to concentrate on the bare minimum feature set required. In the Product Plan, you will select which of these features, based on your Persona's needs, to incorporate back into the product. There may be features that you thought the Persona would want up front; but as you further developed your ideas of the product and customer, you find they are much less important than other features you did not consider at first.

It is important to institute a protocol within the development of your product where you continuously ensure a high level of quality through process and mindset. When new features or functionality are released, even with the best of intentions, it usually takes a while in the marketplace to work the bugs out and refine the product. It is good to implement a process to validate the quality of the releases so that a focus on quality is built into the fabric and mentality of the company. If a company plans to drive growth by continually releasing new features quickly without ensuring and improving quality, a company is destined to have quality problems.

It is also important to think about when you should expand your market. Your Persona is for one specific market, your beachhead market, but once you achieve a strong position in that market—you become the de facto standard and achieve dominant market share for your solution (generally 20 percent and usually higher). You are cash-flow positive, so it's probably time to move to the next market. The beachhead is called "beachhead," after all, because it is merely a starting point for you.

That next market, or "pin" in the bowling alley metaphor, will have a different Persona but should still leverage your Core and be a logical next step for your business. The product for this next market might be a totally different product, significantly modified, the same product repackaged, or simply the same product depending on the new persona's needs and your growth strategy.

The Product Plan is subject to change as you move forward, so don't sweat the details and don't spend too much time on it. However you should have a general vision of where you see things going next so that you capture some of the broader TAM.

EXAMPLE

SensAble Technologies

Once we had become the standard in the toy and footwear industry, we planned to move to additional markets off the center of this bell curve (see Figure 24.1) like jewelry, animation, consumer products, electronics, and automotive.

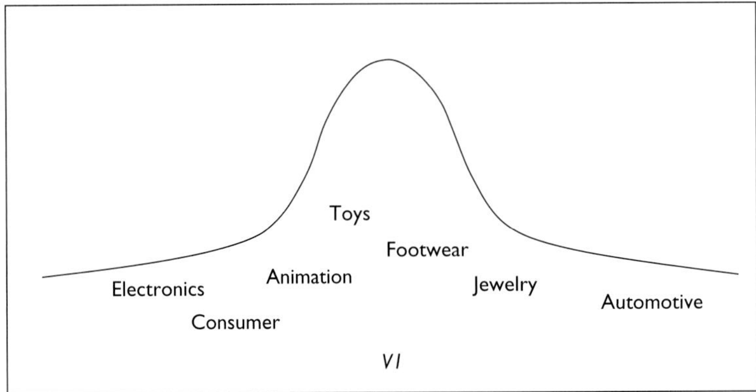

Figure 24.1 SensAble's version 1 product plan.

As we researched more closely these other industries we wanted to expand into, we realized that we were going to have to expand our functionality in two major areas. First we would need to do more than just sculpted forms. We would have to expand into other less organic or irregular forms that could be more easily represented mathematically, specifically geometric, or regular forms, and highly stylized forms. Second, to fit into the workflow of these new markets, we would need to support more file formats for our final digital output to their downstream systems. We would have to continue to support the standard rapid prototyping file formats (specifically the .stl file format), but we would have to add NURBS (Non-Uniform Rational B-Splines) support, which is the standard file format for CAD/CAM packages in all manufacturing industries, which more precisely represents the geometric shapes generated in the design process. In addition, as we continued to grow, we would have to add polygon support because this was the accepted file format for a number of the markets we were expanding into, most specifically the Digital Content Creation (DCC) market for 3D animation movies at places like Pixar.

Version 1 of our product focused on the beachhead market (Toy and Footwear); then we planned to branch out into the Jewelry market in version 2 (Figure 24.2).

Upon achieving success in these early markets, we planned to expand our markets to include jewelry and furniture by adding support for the creation of geometric or regular forms in the product and also support the export of our files in the NURBS for a broader group of industrial designers. To make it attractive to these new markets, we planned for version 3 of our product to be capable of creating both sculpted and regular forms, such as those used in jewelry and furniture. It would also be able to export to traditional CAD/CAM packages such as Pro/E, CATIA, SolidWorks, or

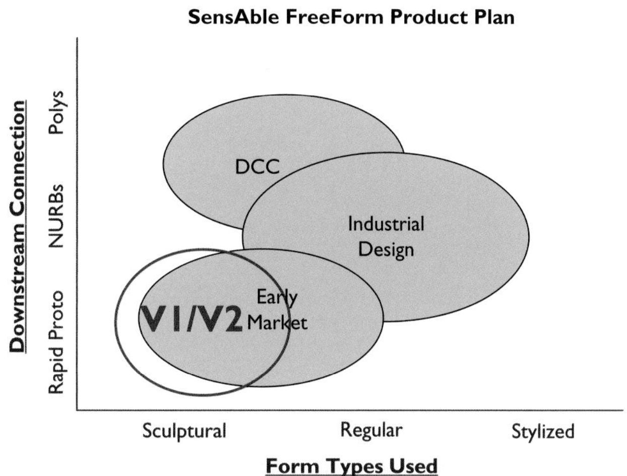

Figure 24.2 SensAble's version 2 product plan.

UniGraphics, which were crucial to our expanding business operations, especially as we expanded into industries with more sophisticated manufacturing operations. This version 3 of our FreeForm product is represented in Figure 24.3.

You can see the product increasing in its functionality. Because we were closely tying this to a target market, it would also be increasing the market opportunity in a very systematic way.

In the plan for FreeForm version 4, this trend continued and the market further increased with specific functional enhancements (Figure 24.4).

Finally, with FreeForm version 5, we were shooting for the stars but had a vision of how to get there. We were aiming to achieve a ubiquity in the industrial design marketplace and become a tool that all industrial designers had to have in their toolbox (Figure 24.5).

While this plan gave us a good starting point, allowing us to capture certain market requirements and group them into buckets within the plan, we knew from the start that our actual product progression would differ from the plan and that this would be okay.

As the famous general, president, and war hero Dwight D. Eisenhower once said, "Plans are nothing; planning is everything." By preparing a plan, you allow yourself to consider new possibilities, envision potential obstacles, and generally get your mind around what you are trying to accomplish. So the plan, while not unimportant, is simply a means to an end. It's a place to start, even if you know you will finish elsewhere.

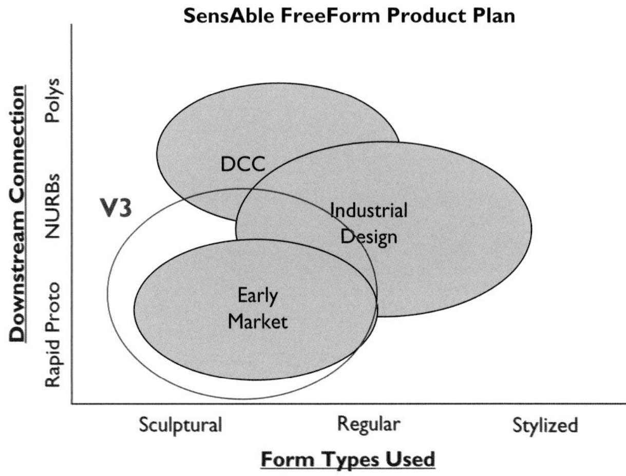

Figure 24.3 SensAble's version 3 product plan.

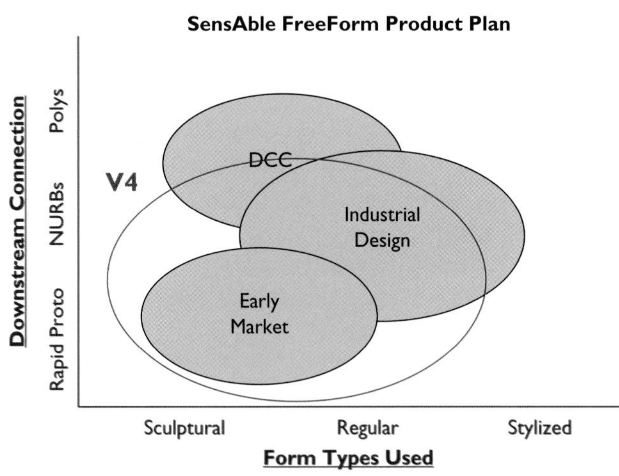

Figure 24.4 SensAble's version 4 product plan.

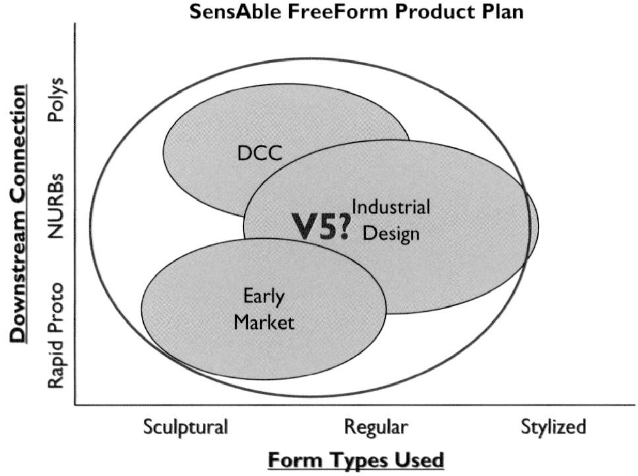

Figure 24.5 SensAble's version 5 product plan.

SUMMARY

Establishing a product plan is similar to the step to calculate the broader TAM. The idea is to get you thinking ahead so you raise your sightlines and don't get too bogged down in your beachhead market, which is only your first step as a business. You want to expand from the beachhead. It gives you a long-term vision that keeps you reaching and thinking ahead, especially in the design of your product and organization. Do not spend too much time here, though, because you still need to get the dogs to eat the dog food today, or else you will run out of money long before entering adjacent markets. Plans will change as you learn more from the beachhead, but to not have a plan is to put yourself in the hands of luck as opposed to your own methodical process.

POSTLUDE: A BUSINESS IS MORE THAN 24 STEPS

CONGRATULATIONS ON MAKING IT all the way through this handbook! The 24 Steps gives you a framework to get a rock-solid product–market fit at initial launch. But as your business expands beyond its MVBP, you will also need to learn about many other things including the following:

- Building a Company Culture
- Selecting a Founding Team
- Growing and Building the Team (HR Processes)
- Developing the Product
- Selling and Sales Execution
- Servicing the Customer and Building Customer Service Processes
- Building Your Financials and Managing Cash Flow
- Raising Money to Scale the Business
- Entrepreneurial Leadership and Scaling the Business
- Building and Utilizing Good Company Governance
- And much more

But all of that is for another time.

I hope that this book provides you with a framework to get started and to more intelligently and more effectively direct your actions to improve your odds of creating a new venture. But do not move away from a bias toward action, especially reaching out and doing primary market research and continually iterating toward a solution.

Entrepreneurship is not a spectator sport. It is action that gets entrepreneurs going—intelligent and adaptive action. We entrepreneurs want to constantly be moving and making progress, testing our ideas and products on real customers and spiraling toward success.

The solution to any of your business questions does not lie in this book but rather out there in the marketplace with a customer who has an unmet need. All this book does is help you to pull it out and think about how systemically you can produce a solution that will be economically sustainable from this information.

The world needs more and better entrepreneurs because our world's problems are becoming more dire, complex, and ubiquitous. Historically it has been the intrepid spirit and skill of the entrepreneur that has come up with the best solutions for the world's problems, and I have faith it will happen again and again and again. So hopefully this framework will make you more successful as you put it into action, as that has been the goal all along.

As for this book, please let us know what we can improve and we will take action. We love action. Visit us at www.disciplinedentrepreneurship.com.

GLOSSARY

adjacent market A new market that you can easily enter from the market you are currently in; requires its own persona.

beachhead market The first market your business sells in.

business A viable organization created to achieve a goal that does not depend on outside charitable contributions.

cash-flow positive When the cash received by the company exceeds the cash that is paid out in a particular month.

competitive position How well you meet your customer's top two priorities compared to any existing or likely competition, including the status quo for the customer.

Core The central element to your business that gives you a sustained advantage over your competitors.

follow-on market A market you enter after gaining significant market share in the market you are currently in, which for this book will be the beachhead market. Either an adjacent market buying the same application as the beachhead market, or an additional application for your current persona.

gross margin The difference between revenue and marginal costs for your product. Expressed as a percentage, so a 20 percent gross margin means your revenue from each unit of product is 20 percent higher than your cost of making a unit of a product.

innovation A new-to-the-world idea or invention that gets commercialized, either by an existing business or through starting a new business. It may be technology, process, business model, market positioning, or other. It can also be for each of these disruptive, incremental, or lateral.

innovation-based entrepreneurship Starting a new business based on a new-to-the-world idea or invention.

market A system in which the trade of goods and services takes place, characterized by three conditions: customers buy similar products, customers have similar sales cycles and value propositions, and there is word of mouth between customers.

marketing communications Getting word out to potential customers about your product with the primary purpose to increase exposure and to generate leads. Not to be confused with "product marketing."

primary market research Information gained by talking directly with, interacting directly with, and directly observing customers and potential customers.

product Physical goods, a service, or the delivery of information.

product–market fit When your product matches what customers in a specific market are interested in buying.

product marketing The process of finding product–market fit by finding out what the customer wants and mapping a product to it. Actual messaging to potential customers is called "marketing communications."

secondary market research Information obtained from market research reports and from indirect sources like the Internet or analyst reports.

target customer A group of customers in a market that you intend to sell the same product to. They share many characteristics and would all reasonably buy a particular product.

Total Addressable Market (TAM) The amount of annual revenue your business would earn if you achieved 100 percent market share in a market. Expressed in terms of dollars per year.

ABOUT THE AUTHOR

BILL AULET IS the managing director in the Martin Trust Center for MIT Entrepreneurship at MIT, as well as a senior lecturer at the MIT Sloan School of Management.

He teaches New Enterprises, Energy Ventures, and Applications of Advanced Entrepreneurial Techniques, in addition to running the Martin Trust Center, which supports student entrepreneurship education inside and outside the classroom, across all five schools at MIT. Since Bill became managing director in 2009, he has conceived, designed, and overseen the implementation of numerous innovative programs, from new courses (Linked Data Ventures, Entrepreneurial Product Marketing and Development, Energy Ventures, Applications of Advanced Entrepreneurial Techniques) and student initiatives (MIT Clean Energy Prize, MIT Entrepreneurship Review), to accelerators (Global Founders' Skills Accelerator, Beehive Cooperative) and thought leadership initiatives (Regional Entrepreneurship Acceleration Program or REAP). His work has won numerous awards; most recently, in April 2013, Bill was awarded the Adolf F. Monosson Prize for Entrepreneurial Mentoring at MIT.

Prior to joining MIT, Bill had a 25-year track record of success in business, having directly raised more than $100 million in funding for his companies and led the creation of hundreds of millions of dollars in market value in those companies. After working for 11 years at IBM, he was named an MIT Sloan Fellow, taking part in a one-year accelerated master's program in management. Upon graduation, he became a serial entrepreneur, running two MIT spinouts as the president/chief executive officer (Cambridge Decision Dynamics and SensAble Technologies). The latter became a two-time *Inc.* magazine 500 Fastest-Growing Private Company. With a presence in over 20 countries, SensAble has also won more than 24 awards and has been featured in *Fortune* magazine, *BusinessWeek*, the *Wall Street Journal*, and many other publications as a result of its innovative products and strong business foundation.

In 2003, Bill was recruited as chief financial officer to co-lead a turnaround of security technology company Viisage Technology. During his two-and-a-half-year tenure, and in a resource-constrained environment, Viisage developed a new strategy, overhauled its operations, made three major acquisitions, and executed two major fundraising rounds; as a result, its market value increased from $50 million to over $500 million.

His writings on entrepreneurship have been published by the *Boston Globe*, *The Huffington Post*, *Xconomy*, the Kauffman Foundation, MIT Sloan Experts, and the *MIT Entrepreneurship Review*. A former professional basketball player, Bill lives in Belmont, Massachusetts with his wife; they have four grown sons.

Bill holds a bachelor's in engineering from Harvard University and an SM from the MIT Sloan School of Management.

More information is available at www.disciplinedentrepreneurship.com.

INDEX